AF434694

PROBING FREEWILL

A Story of Autonomy & Inevitability

WALEED Mahmud

By the Author

<u>Undepressed</u>: A Comprehensive guide to Understanding, Managing, and Overcoming Depression

<u>This is NOT Education</u>: Rethinking the Education System

<u>Power & Ethics</u>: A Brief History of Western Moral and Political Philosophy

<u>Decrypting Globalization</u>: Understanding the Economic, Cultural, And Political afflictions of Nationalism, Migration and the Environmental Crisis

Follow on Medium: <u>medium.com/@waleedmtariq</u>

Follow on SubStack: <u>waleedmahmud.substack.com/</u>

Follow on Instagram: <u>instagram.com/waleedmtariq/</u>

Copyright © 2024 Waleed Mahmud Tariq

All rights reserved.

Dedicated to

My incredible family, whose unwavering support and love have been my anchor through the stormiest of times. Your belief in me has been a constant source of strength and inspiration.

To my beloved spouse, whose patience, understanding, and endless encouragement have made this journey possible. Your love has been my guiding light, illuminating the path even in the darkest moments.

Thank you for standing by my side, for your sacrifices, and for your unyielding faith in my dreams. This book is as much yours as it is mine.

Table of Contents

PREFACE

Free will is the foundation of our human experience. Our days and nights are filled with decisions, from the trivial, like choosing our outfits to the more serious, like choosing our careers. We've built our personal identities on the belief that these choices are ours and ours alone, defining our humanity. Our cultures and societies reinforce this notion into us from the moment we are born to the day that we pass away. The belief that we have the ability to make independent decisions forms the core of our moral, justice, and legal systems. The ability to distinguish between right and wrong is central to the belief that we are the authors of our own lives. As we understand it, free will underpins the essence of our existence.

But what if what we perceive to be free will is merely an illusion? What if the reality that we have been conditioned to believe, is not as unambiguous as depicted? What if freewill is nothing more than a persistent illusion? What if our understanding of freewill needs a complete overhaul? And if so, what does it mean for our sense of self and personal identity?

These questions form the heart and soul of this book. Here, we explore the science and philosophy of freewill, challenging conventional wisdom to its very core, and in the process, perhaps even finding our own selves. Through this expedition, we will stimulate our minds, grasp an eagle's eye view, and see the world with a fresh perspective. Our journey will be guided by factual knowledge, sound arguments, undeniable logic, and unfettered reason. As Dante so eloquently put it in his magnum opus,

"libero, dritto e sano è tuo arbitrio,
e fallo fora non fare a suo senno:
per ch'io te sovra te corono e mitrio"

Your will is free, straight, and whole,
And it would be wrong not to follow its discernment,
Wherefor, I crown, and mitter you, over yourself.

This book aims to contextualize the discourse on freewill and underscore its influence on our daily lives. The consequences of this conversation ripple throughout our lives. For a more structural and understandable dialogue, the book has been divided into 5 parts, each carrying an underlying theme, which is then tied back to the overarching theme of the book.

Fittingly, our journey begins by examining the roots of freewill in the first part of the book, "Tracing the Origins of Free Will," investigating the origins of concept and how it is imbued in our lives. We will do this by examining the evolutionary foundations of freewill, briefly learning about the brain, introduction to the concept of determinism, and critiquing freewill.

In the second part, we will dissect the science that questions the fundamentals of its existence. Here, we venture into the core of our decision-making - the brain, through the realms of biology and neuroscience. We will try to understand the inner workings of our decision-making capabilities by conceptualizing the interplay between different brain regions, the role of neurotransmitters and hormones, and the complex neural networks.

We will explore the biological underpinnings of freewill, or perhaps the lack of it. A wealth of scientific evidence from neurons to hormones and from our mind to our brain, questions the existence of freewill. How does our biology restrict or liberate us? How do our bodies and brains orchestrate our decisions and actions? By asking these questions, we hope to shed new light on the old debate around freewill, offering a fresh perspective that marries science with philosophy.

Apart from the brain, we will also learn about behavioral genetics, emergent systems, and other factors that pour into scientifically talking about the "Freedom of Choice.". By diving into this realm of science, we will reveal the inherent complexities that challenge the conventional idea of freewill.

The practical implications of comprehending these ideas will start reflecting in the third part of the book. Here, we engage the long-standing philosophical debates around the notion of freewill, comprehending classical and contemporary thinkers, examining their arguments, challenging their assertions, and driving forward with our knowledge and understanding. The aim here is not to provide a comprehensive historical account but to illuminate the complexities between freewill, determinism, and our sense of self.

PART III, "Morality, Responsibility, and the lack of freewill," continues this journey by encountering the delicate connections between freewill, responsibility, and morality. Our moral codes and our systems of reward and punishment are all predicated on the belief in freewill. If we challenge the existence of freewill, what does it mean for our understanding of good and evil and right and wrong? We will question the bedrock of our moral judgments and laws, imagining a world where freewill does not dictate our ethical and moral compass.

The idea of freewill is not restricted to the private corners of individual lives but rather dominates the very fabric of our societal structures. It dictates our understanding of justice, freedom, and morality, steering our social and cultural landscapes. We will closely examine these landscapes in our book while simultaneously considering a world where the concept of freewill does not rule our societies.

This book also recognizes and respects the myriad views that exist on the subject of freewill. Some of us ardently uphold the idea of freewill as a core tenet of human identity, while others view it as a comforting illusion. Regardless of where you stand in this debate, I hope this book can offer you a new lens through which to view the world and your place within it.

As you turn these pages, our discussion will be steered toward understanding a life without freewill. This will likely challenge your comfort zone, yet it is here where the most profound insights may emerge. We will look at how to make sense of our lives and how to find meaning, purpose, and happiness in a world without freewill. We will explore the potential liberation that comes from unshackling ourselves from the notion of freewill and the new paths to self-understanding this might open up.

In our multifaceted approach to understand freewill, we will navigate a vast array of topics, stretching from neuroscience to philosophy, society to morality, from legal systems to mental health and so much more. We will dive into the depths of our minds, grapple with the complexities of our behaviorisms, and navigate the complexities of our decisions and actions. It is undoubtedly going to be a profound but turbulent journey, one that is as vast and deep as the oceans, if not more.

Through this book, I intend to initiate a conversation about freewill and its place in our lives, and by the time you've finished reading it, we will have emerged with a more refined understanding of freewill, or perhaps the lack thereof, restructuring our assumptions about the freedom of choice.

I invite you to engage in a deep, introspective journey of self-discovery with me and hope that this exploration helps you consider your own life, your decisions, your relationships, and your place in the world in a new light. Ultimately, I hope that you find this exploration as enlightening, invigorating, and transformational as I have.

However, it is crucial that you approach this book with an open mind, ready to question and challenge your assumptions. The ideas shared in this book offer an unconventional perspective, stimulate thoughts, provoke deep reflections, and encourage meaningful conversations with others.

Let's delve into the exploration of freewill, its impacts, and its controversies, as we attempt to understand our actions, decisions, and the very essence of our being.

So, let's embark on this intellectual journey together, allowing ourselves the freedom to question, challenge, learn, and grow. There is something profound about investigating the underpinnings of our beliefs, thoughts, and actions. It shakes us, perhaps even disrupts us, but ultimately, it enables us to grow. Understanding the concept of freewill will lead us to confront some hard truths about ourselves, but it can also help us become more compassionate, more understanding, and more attuned to the human experience.

PART I: Tracing The Origins Of Freewill

The concept of free will is fundamental to the grand drama of life. The scenes of our existence are full of astounding complexity and variety because of freewill. The ability and the freedom to choose one path over another, cultivates a sense of self and independence in us, but reflecting upon the origins of choice reveals some profound and perplexing dilemmas.

Is our will truly free, or are we merely marionettes in the ballet of a deterministic universe?

In the first part of the book, we begin our descent into the historical epicenter of the free will debate. Our investigation ranges from the origin of life to the stringent mechanisms of the human mind, dissecting methodically what it means to have free will and the potential reality of existing without it.

Our investigation begins with the "Evolutionary Foundations of Free Will." From Africa's vast plains, where our ancestors first walked erect, to today's sprawling urban jungles, evolution tells a story of change, adaptation, and an innate survival instinct. This chapter investigates how these evolutionary dynamics may have spawned what we interpret as free will, investigating factors such as natural selection, genetic and environmental influences, and the emergence of freedom in diverse life forms.

Our journey through Chapter 2 dives into the hypnotic universe of cognitive neuroscience. This chapter examines the relationship between the mind and the brain, tangible "hardware" and the abstract mental domain, shedding light on the decision-making process and the frequently hazy line between conscious and unconscious thought. This chapter bridges the gap between the "hardware" and the "software" of our decision making capability.

As we progress through Chapter 3, the emphasis shifts from the freedom of will to its potential limitations. This chapter illustrates how our genetic coding and environmental contexts may be the unseen conductors guiding our decisions, in keeping with the deterministic view of a universe operating according to fixed or predictable patterns. Armed with persuasive evidence and test cases, we demonstrate how determinism may cast lengthy and frequently unnoticed shadows over our perception of free will.

In this section's fourth and final chapter, we challenge the very existence of free will. Is it an elaborate ruse, a cognitive delusion that provides a sense of comforting control? Or is it a perceptible, innate characteristic of our existence? To examine the validity of free will, we navigate through various experimental inquiries, everyday situations, and philosophical perspectives.

This introductory section aims to establish the seeds of thought, challenge the widely accepted narrative of free will, and dissect its extensive dynamics. Each chapter flows seamlessly into the next, guiding you through a thorough examination of the origins of free will. In conclusion, you may be questioning the very nature of decision-making and the extent of your independence.

However, keep in mind that this is only the beginning. This voyage will take us deeper into the neurobiology of choice, the ethical and legal repercussions of a world without free will, the historical and contemporary philosophical debates surrounding this topic, and finally the personal, societal, and cultural repercussions of our perceptions of freedom. Let's start tracing the origins of free will, understanding its core concepts, and possibly redefining our conception of freedom.

CHAPTER 1: EVOLUTIONARY FOUNDATIONS OF FREEWILL

We begin our journey by investigating the evolutionary roots of free will. This chapter takes us on a voyage through the history of human evolution, from the African plains to the modern cities we inhabit today. We will examine how the forces of natural selection, genetic and environmental influences, and the evolution of freedom in different life forms may have contributed to the emergence of what we perceive as free will. Let's explore the intriguing world of evolutionary dynamics and learn about the origins of our agency.

1.1 NATURAL SELECTION: THE ARCHITECT OF BEHAVIOR

Natural selection, a phenomenon introduced by Charles Darwin in 1859, is one of the most fundamental concepts of evolution. It is nature's magnum opus, responsible for the numerous behaviors exhibited by countless organisms across the globe, including humans. Over the previous countless generations, natural selection has meticulously sculpted the behaviors that have become so commonplace that we frequently overlook their remarkable origins.

Consider a simple example: a mother carefully nourishing her young. Although this behavior does not directly benefit the mother, it substantially improves the chances of survival for her offspring. In turn, increasing her chances of leaving more copies of her genes, through the ages. The emergence of this 'altruistic' behavior is a direct result of millions of years of evolutionary pressure exerted on the genetic composition of the mother that have increased its chances of survival through DNA replication. All life on Earth, including ourselves, bears the imprint of natural selection's continuous renovation.

Consider natural selection as a vast, dense forest of life, with each tree representing a species and each branch representing a different behavior. Some branches are robust and expansive while others are short and fragile, and others may have completely withered away. The branches which improve the trees survival rates are rewarded by nourishment, and therefore grow out extensively, the ones that make subtle contributions, grow subtly, and the ones that are detrimental to its survival rates, are malnourished, and in time, die out.

The perplexed architecture of the forest and the continuous reshaping of its branches vividly illustrates the vast diversity of behaviors that billions of years of evolution have carved.

Natural selection's influence is not limited to merely manufacturing behaviors. It also plays a crucial role in the interaction between the genetics and environment of an organism.

Consider the distinction between a static, predetermined computer program and a dynamic, adaptive learning algorithm. If behaviors were solely determined by genes — a concept known as genetic determinism — it would be analogous to a computer program that performed the same tasks regardless of the environment, leaving no room for adaptation. However, the behaviors we observe in nature demonstrate an exceptional degree of adaptability, resembling a learning algorithm that modifies itself in response to environmental stimuli.

The urban crow is an excellent illustration of this adaptability. While it is natural for crows to use instruments for foraging, their urban counterparts have demonstrated a remarkable ability to modify this behavior. Urban crows use garbage as tools, drop nuts on busy streets for passing vehicles to crack, and memorize garbage collection schedules in order to take advantage of new food resources. These adaptable behaviors demonstrate how natural selection has endowed species with the ability to modify their behavior in response to environmental changes, thereby augmenting their chances of survival in a world that is constantly changing.

This raises a question on how does natural selection explain behaviors that appear detrimental to an individual organism? The answer lies in the enthralling phenomenon of sexual selection, nature's own beauty contest, which favors characteristics that may not directly contribute to survival but increase an individual's attractiveness to potential mates, in turn, resulting in a higher chance of genetic replication.

Peacock plumage is one of the most spectacular examples of sexual selection in action. The peacock's brightly colored and voluminous tail is hardly practical, increasing its visibility to predators and hindering its flight capabilities. However, the peahen finds it irresistible, making it an evolutionary asset. This mate-choice-driven selection has produced an array of apparently absurd behaviors and traits throughout the animal kingdom, from the risky acrobatics of the bowerbird to the self-destructive mating habits of certain creatures, known semelparity or suicidal reproduction.

However, it is not always about flamboyant plumage or spectacular displays. Sexual selection influences subtle behaviors in a number of species, including humans. Consider the concept of gift-giving in human cultures as a courtship ritual. Considerable time and resources are devoted to what is essentially a symbolic gesture. This could be interpreted as a form of sexual selection, with the 'gift' functioning as an indicator of the giver's prowess in resource acquisition.

Furthermore, the influence of natural selection is arguably most conspicuous in the realm of social behavior. Humans are inherently social creatures whose lives are delicately interwoven with relationship networks. Our ability to collaborate in large groups, interpret complex social signals, and even our empathetic disposition can be traced back to the pressures of natural selection on our ancestors.

Consider a small group of primitive humans on the African savannah. Those who could effectively cooperate to hunt, gather sustenance, and fend off predators had greater chances of survival. These social skills were refined over generations, resulting in the sophisticated social intelligence that defines modern humans.

Natural selection does not necessarily result in cooperation and harmony. It can also promote competition and conflict among and within species. The 'selfish gene' theory posits that genes are in a constant conflict for survival, resulting in behaviors that frequently put individual interests ahead of group interests. Natural selection is, at its foundation, a balancing act between the benefits of cooperation and the ruthless imperatives of self-preservation.

A fascinating aspect of the influence of natural selection on behavior is its function in shaping our cognitive abilities. Whether it's our ability to solve complex problems or our artistic prowess, these are also the results of natural selection. The human brain, which is capable of reasoning, planning, and imagination, is arguably evolution's crowning achievement.

Our understanding of the influence of natural selection on behavior has far-reaching implications for numerous disciplines, ranging from psychology and neuroscience to sociology and economics. Recognizing that our behaviors are influenced not only by our culture and upbringing, but also by millions of years of evolutionary pressure, we can gain new insights into why we behave as we do and how our actions may change in the future.

At this juncture, it is essential to introduce gene-culture co-evolution, a theory proposing a feedback loop between genetics and culture. It implies that our genetic composition affects our cultural practices and vice versa.

This is exemplified by the evolution of lactose tolerance in certain human populations. Lactose, the 'sugar' in milk, is only digestible by most mammals, including early humans, during infancy and early childhood, when they are suckling. With the advent of dairy farming, however, those able to digest lactose throughout adulthood gained a nutritional advantage, resulting in the spread of lactose tolerance genes in populations that extensively consumed dairy.

This concept also applies to behaviors. Cultural practices can generate environments that select for particular behaviors, which can become imprinted in our genomes over generations. In societies where resources are limited and competition is fierce, for instance, traits like aggression and dominance may be favored. In contrast, in societies where cooperation and collective action are essential for survival, empathy and cooperation may be favored.

This has profound implications for comprehending human behavior. It suggests that not only our individual experiences but also countless generations of cultural evolution influence our actions. This also suggests that our behaviors can change over time due to the complex interaction between culture and genetics.

In addition, we must consider how natural selection has shaped our moral and ethical systems. At first glance, morality may appear to be a product of culture and intellect, unreachable by biology. However, evolutionary biologists contend that our moral sense has also been shaped by natural selection.

For instance, take reciprocal altruism, the notion that an individual will help others with the expectation of receiving assistance in the future. It has been observed in numerous animal species and is regarded as an evolutionary strategy to increase survival and reproduction chances.

This assumes the form of fairness and justice in humans. Those who treat others fairly and uphold social norms are more likely to receive assistance in times of need, thereby improving their chances of survival. These actions become ingrained as moral and ethical principles over time. The phrase, "Do unto others as you would have done to you," or the concept of "Karma" comes to mind.

The ongoing debate of nature and nurture is a persistent challenge in this discipline. How much of our behavior is determined by our genetic constitution (nature) versus our environment and experiences (nurture)? Although this dichotomy is somewhat simplistic — the scientific consensus is that both play a crucial role — it serves to showcase the complexity of behavior comprehension.

This issue is further complicated by the phenomenon of pleiotropy, in which a single gene influences multiple, apparently unrelated traits. A gene associated with aggressive behavior may also be implicated, for instance, in metabolism. Consequently, when natural selection acts on one attribute, it may also affect another. This can lead to unexpected correlations between different behaviors and attributes, complicating our efforts to identify the genetic basis for

14

particular behaviors. For example, the hormone, Testosterone, participates in both arousal and aggression, leading to complex interrelationships.

Then there is the issue of biological determinism, which is the belief that a person's behavior is solely determined by their DNA. This viewpoint has been criticized for oversimplifying the complex interaction between genetics and environment and for disregarding the capacity of humans to change and adapt. In addition, it can be abused to justify social inequalities and discriminatory practices by attributing them to inherent biological differences as opposed to societal structures.

Despite these obstacles, the discipline of behavioral evolution provides insightful explanations for why we behave as we do. It enables us to recognize that our actions are influenced not only by our present circumstances, but also by our evolutionary history. Understanding this allows us to become more conscious of our biases and intuition and to make better-informed decisions regarding our behavior.

Natural selection has a profound effect on human behavior, impacting everything from our daily actions to our moral principles. However, it is not the only factor that influences our behavior, and we must be careful not to oversimplify or exaggerate its significance. We acquire a deeper understanding of what it means to be human as we continue to uncover the complexities of this relationship.

1.2 GENETIC AND ENVIRONMENTAL FACTORS: THE TWIN FORCES

At this intersection we arrive where nature meets nurture. This juncture leads us towards a deeper understanding of why we behave the way we do. The DNA we inherit from our parents and the environment in which we grow up play a central role in carving our behaviors. They are the two faces of a coin, different yet inseparable.

Our genetic code, the biological software we are born with, has a significant say in our behavioral traits. From the simplest organisms like the single-celled amoeba to the most complex ones like humans, genes play an integral role in determining behaviors. These invisible strands of DNA, sitting in every cell, act like the unseen puppeteers pulling the strings of our behaviors.

Yet, our behaviors aren't merely the recital of our genetic script. They are a performance that unfolds on the stage set by our environment. The environment, in its broadest sense, encompasses everything external to our genes, ranging from the food we eat and the air we breathe, to our cultural practices and the socio-economic conditions we live in. In fact, even the mother's womb is a part of this environment.

To illustrate this, consider the development of language skills in children. A child is born with the genetic predisposition to learn a language, any language. However, the specific language that a child eventually speaks - be it English, Chinese, or Swahili - is determined by the linguistic environment that they are exposed to.

Next, let's explore the relationship of genes and environmental factors in shaping behaviors through groundbreaking studies that have reshaped our understanding of behavior and helped peel off the layers of complexity of who we are.

Here, we peek into the genetic code, encountering a fundamental component of our biological machinery that influences our behavior, the genes. These are sections of our DNA that code for proteins, the workhorses of the cell. Each gene acts like a unique set of instructions, guiding the production of a specific protein. These proteins, in turn, influence the physiological processes that underpin our behaviors.

A clear example of this influence is found in the genetics of taste. A variant of the gene TAS2R38 can make certain vegetables, like broccoli or cabbage, taste extremely bitter for some people. This genetic predisposition can significantly influence dietary choices and thus can affect an individual's behavior towards food.

However, the genetic influences on behavior are rarely as straightforward as the case of the TAS2R38 gene. Most behaviors are polygenic, meaning they are influenced by many genes, each contributing a small effect. This genetic orchestra plays a symphony that guides our behavior. But like any good symphony, the performance isn't solely reliant on the script; the venue plays a part too.

Enter "the environment," the grand stage where our genes express themselves. The environmental influences on behavior are as diverse as the environment itself. From the physical environment we live in to the social and cultural context of our upbringing, these external factors shape our behaviors in significant ways.

To illustrate, let's consider the classic example of height. While height is strongly influenced by genetic factors, it is also significantly affected by environmental factors like nutrition. A child with the genetic potential to be tall may not reach their full height potential if they don't receive adequate nutrition during their growing years.

While individual examples help highlight the roles of genes and the environment, the real magic lies in understanding how these two forces play out together, which takes us into the world of behavioral genetics.

Behavioral genetics is a field that uses genetic methods to investigate the nature and origins of individual differences in behavior. Here, we learn about some classic techniques used in behavioral genetics, such as twin and adoption studies, and illustrate how they've shed light on the gene-environment interaction.

Twin studies, especially those involving identical (monozygotic) twins, are a particularly powerful tool in behavioral genetics. Since identical twins share 100% of their genetic material, any differences in behavior between them can be attributed to environmental influences. A classic example is the Minnesota Twin Family Study, which found a strong genetic influence on traits such as IQ and personality, despite the twins being raised in different environments.

Likewise, adoption studies provide another window into the nature versus nurture debate. By comparing adopted children with their biological and adoptive parents, researchers can tease apart the influences of genetic and environmental factors. A seminal adoption study on antisocial behavior found that both genetic and environmental factors contribute to antisocial behaviors, but their effects vary with the quality of the postnatal environment.

While these studies underscore the importance of both genes and the environment in shaping behavior, they also highlight a more profound revelation - the concept of gene-environment interaction. This term refers to the situation where the effect of a gene on a behavior changes depending on the environment. For instance, the gene that influences how our body metabolizes alcohol may have a different effect on behavior in a society where alcohol consumption is commonplace versus a society where it is not.

Similarly, the environment can also influence how our genes are expressed – a burgeoning field of study known as epigenetics. This doesn't change the DNA sequence itself, but instead affects how cells *read* genes. For instance, chronic stress can lead to epigenetic changes that may make an individual more prone to anxiety and depression.

The genetic-environment interplay even extends to how we choose our environments, a concept known as gene-environment correlation. For instance, a person with a genetic predisposition towards thrill-seeking might choose to engage in activities like skydiving or rock climbing, further reinforcing this behavior. Similarly, a child with a genetic predisposition for extraversion is likely to seek out social situations, thereby shaping their own social environment. This in turn can further enhance their extraverted behavior, creating a cycle of reciprocal influence.

The elaborate mechanisms of gene-environment interaction and gene-environment correlation highlight the complexity and interdependency of these twin forces. They serve to remind us that even though our genes may lay the foundation, it is our environments and experiences that build upon it, ultimately crafting the mosaic of our behaviors.

A classic instance where genetic and environmental factors have been shown to coalesce is the development of social behavior in animals. Research has shown that Voles, a type of rodent, exhibit different social behaviors depending on their genetic makeup and environmental factors. Some species of voles are monogamous with strong pair-bonds, while others are polygamous, with males not engaging in parental care. Scientists discovered that the difference in these behaviors was linked to the distribution of a particular type of receptor in the brain - the vasopressin receptor. Furthermore, the distribution of these receptors, which was responsible for the different social behaviors, was found to be influenced by both genes and the environment.

Analogous to this, human behaviors are a product of similar processes of interaction between our genes and the environment. Take, for instance, the domain of human language. While there is no 'language gene' per se, certain genes such as FOXP2 have been implicated in language development. However, the development of language is not just dependent on our genetic makeup, but significantly on our environment - a child raised in a linguistically rich environment will develop language skills more effectively than one who isn't.

Even physical attributes, often thought to be determined purely by our genetic code, can be influenced by environmental factors. For instance, our height is known to be significantly influenced by our genes. However, it is also affected by environmental factors like nutrition and health during growth periods. Therefore, genes provide a potential for an attribute, but how this potential is realized is significantly influenced by the environment.

This delicate interplay between genes and environment forms a complex and dynamic narrative, one that underscores the beauty and sophistication of life. It is a narrative that challenges the oversimplified notion of determinism and champions the concept of interaction and adaptability. It is, in essence, the story of life's versatility, resilience, and ceaseless evolution.

A classic example of this relationship is the research surrounding the gene 5-HTTLPR, which is involved in serotonin transport, a mechanism implicated in mood regulation. Individuals with a certain variant of this gene were found to be more susceptible to depression, but only if they had also experienced stressful life events. Those with the same genetic variant who had not experienced significant stress did not show an increased risk for depression. This illustrates how a gene's influence on behavior can be contingent on environmental circumstances.

As we navigate further into this section, the field of molecular genetics comes into focus, offering insights into the fundamental processes that allow genes to influence behavior.

Every cell in our bodies houses a complete copy of our DNA, a molecule composed of two intertwined strands, each consisting of a string of chemical units called nucleotides. The sequence of these nucleotides carries the instructions for building and maintaining an organism. Within this sequence lie genes, specific segments of DNA that serve as blueprints for proteins.

But the link between our DNA sequence and behavior is not straightforward. Genes need to be 'turned on' or expressed to have an effect, a process that involves transcribing the gene's DNA sequence into RNA, and then translating that RNA into a protein. This gene expression is not fixed; instead, it can be influenced by various factors, including our environment. This interaction between our genetic blueprint and environmental influences is where the magic happens in terms of shaping behavior.

One example of this is the phenomenon of epigenetics, which are the changes in gene expression that occur without altering the underlying DNA sequence. These changes can come in several forms, such as the addition of a methyl group—a process called methylation—to the DNA molecule, which typically acts to suppress gene expression. Epigenetic modifications like these can be influenced by environmental factors and have been linked to a range of behaviors.

An example that underscores the power of epigenetics involves research on rats. Studies have shown that the amount of maternal care a rat pup receives in its early life—in the form of licking and grooming—can affect its stress response later in life. Rat pups that receive high levels of maternal care have been found to exhibit reduced stress responses as adults. This is not due to changes in their DNA sequence but rather to changes in the methylation of their DNA, specifically of a gene involved in the stress response.

However, as we continue to unravel the complexity of genetic influences on behavior, we must be cautious of a potential pitfall, that is, genetic determinism—the belief that genes determine behavior outright. This idea is misleading as it overlooks the crucial role of the environment and the dynamic nature of gene-environment interactions.

Let us now paint a comprehensive picture of the genetic influences on behavior, fully recognizing the gene-environment interaction by venturing further into behavioral genetics. This discipline revolves around the concept of heritability: the proportion of observed differences in a particular trait, in a particular population, that can be attributed to inherited genetic factors.

Consider this: you and a complete stranger have, on average, about 99.9% of your DNA in common. It's that remaining 0.1% that makes you unique. Some of that 0.1% contributes to the visible differences we see between people – height, hair color, and eye color, for example. But some of that 0.1% also contributes to differences in behavior. How much? That's where behavioral genetics comes into play.

By studying twins, particularly identical twins who share 100% of their DNA and fraternal twins who share, on average, 50% of their DNA, researchers can begin to tell apart the genetic and environmental contributions to behavior. The logic here is simple: if identical twins show a greater similarity in a particular trait than fraternal twins, it is likely that genetics plays a significant role in that trait.

This approach has been used to study a wide range of behaviors, from personality traits such as extraversion and neuroticism to mental health disorders like depression and schizophrenia. The findings have been intriguing, suggesting a significant genetic contribution to many aspects of our behavior. However, it's important to remember that genes are not destiny. Even when a trait is highly heritable, this does not mean it is not subject to environmental influences.

But behavioral genetics is not just about studying twins and calculating heritability estimates. It also involves understanding how we recognize those with whom we share our genetics, a crucial aspect of our behavior which has a profound effect on social interactions.

Research has shown that humans, like many other species, are capable of kin recognition, the ability to identify genetic relatives. This capability has a significant impact on our behavior, influencing everything from altruism to mate choice. For instance, studies have shown that we are more likely to engage in altruistic behaviors toward those who share more of our genes, a phenomenon known as kin selection.

From the meticulous mating dances of birds to the hive mentality of bees, animal behaviors provide a rich source of information for understanding the genetic influences on behavior. But amidst this exploration of genetics, we must not lose sight of the other half of the equation: the environment.

From the earliest moments of life, the environment begins to leave its everlasting imprint on us. It molds and refines our behavioral tendencies, complementing and interacting with our genetic inheritance. If genes are the blueprint, then the environment is the builder that interprets the plans. The environment can take many forms, from the broad influences of culture and society to the more immediate impacts of family, peers, and individual experiences. Each layer adds its own unique influence, shaping our behaviors in multifaceted ways.

Take, for instance, the influence of culture. Cultures, as shared systems of beliefs, values, customs, behaviors, and artifacts, provide the broad framework within which we operate. They instill in us certain norms and expectations about how we should behave, shaping everything from our dietary preferences to our attitudes towards work, family, and morality.

At a more immediate level, our family and peers play a critical role in shaping our behaviors. Parents, siblings, and extended family provide our earliest social environment, modeling behaviors and setting norms that we often adopt. Similarly, our peer groups become increasingly influential as we grow, shaping our attitudes, interests, and behaviors in countless ways.

But environmental influence extends beyond culture and social interactions. Our individual experiences and life events also play a significant role. Personal triumphs and traumas, successes and failures, all leave their mark on our behaviors. This influence is particularly evident in the context of learned behaviors. For example, if a child touches a hot stove and gets burned, they quickly learn to avoid repeating the behavior or someone with a genetic predisposition to anxiety may not display anxious behaviors unless triggered by a stressful environment.

In short, to understand the complexity of human behavior, one must appreciate the delicate balance and the closely knit relationship of our genetic inheritance and our environmental influences. They are two sides of the same coin, each contributing to every branch of our behaviors that define us as individuals.

The exploration of these twin forces of nature and nurture sets the stage for the following chapters, where we will delve deeper into the mechanisms of behavior, from the biochemical to the sociological, all with the aim of unraveling the fascinating complexity of human behavior and its implications for freewill.

1.3 FROM ANIMALS TO HUMANS: DEGREES OF FREEDOM

Natural selection, environmental influences, and genetic predispositions have crafted an elaborate selection of behaviors spanning all across the living world. We see the beautifully choreographed dance of nature and nurture all around us, whether we are observing a humpback whale breaching the ocean surface, or a cheetah sprinting towards its prey in the Serengeti. Similarly, us humans are also woven into this same fabric, with our behaviors molded by the same forces that govern our fellow creatures.

It's not hard to find evidence of this shared behavioral biology. Take fear, for example, a primal instinct shared by many species. From an antelope spotting a lion in the African plains to a human witnessing a car hurtling toward them at breakneck speed, the fear response is immediate and automatic. Both the antelope and the human experience a surge of adrenaline, a rapid heartbeat, a state of high alert, and so many other responses that we have yet to discover. In moments of fear, whether you're a human or an antelope, the biology of survival takes precedence.

But the story of our behaviors doesn't stop at our shared biology with other animals. Humans might as well be just another creature on the tree of life – but we have something that sets us apart, something that affords us a unique place in the world: our advanced cognitive abilities. These cognitive abilities create a greater degree of flexibility and complexity in our behaviors, providing us with an increased range of possible responses to situations - what we refer to as "degrees of freedom".

To put it into perspective, let's consider the behavioral responses to threat situations again. While the antelope's primary response to the threat of a predator is to flee, a human in a threatening situation has more options. They could choose to confront the threat, seek help, find a safe place to hide, or even use a tool or weapon to neutralize the threat. This ability to choose from multiple possible responses exemplifies our greater "degree of freedom" in behavior.

Our cognitive abilities don't just enhance our responses to threats. They affect every facet of our lives, from our social interactions to our problem-solving abilities. Consider language, one of the quintessential hallmarks of human cognition. Through language, we can communicate complex ideas, express emotions, give and receive directions, teach and learn from others, and even manipulate or deceive. In terms of "degrees of freedom," language opens up a nearly infinite array of possible sentences, allowing us to convey almost any conceivable thought.

Yet, while our advanced cognitive abilities provide us with a higher degree of freedom in our behaviors, they also introduce a greater complexity to our lives. We grapple with existential questions, moral dilemmas, and the quest for personal meaning; a multiverse of thought that seems absent in other animals. We have the ability to ponder the past and worry about the future, sometimes causing stress and anxiety. Here, we see the darker side of our advanced cognition, as these unique human experiences can lead to mental health issues like depression and anxiety disorders.

Let's now turn to the science behind these advanced cognitive abilities, and why humans have such a unique behavioral profile. Our hormones play a critical role in governing our behaviors, with effects ranging from the regulation of hunger and sleep to our response to stress. For instance, cortisol, often termed the 'stress hormone,' is released in response to stressful situations, preparing our body for a 'fight or flight' response.

However, chronic exposure to stressors can lead to prolonged elevated levels of cortisol, which is associated with a host of health problems, including anxiety and depression. Interestingly, stress and coping mechanisms vary greatly among individuals, owing to genetic variations and environmental influences, further highlighting the complexity of human behavior. Concurrently, remember that cortisol is not unique to humans, but is rather commonly found throughout the animal kingdom.

While this discussion of hormones and stress provides a snapshot of the complex biological machinery at play in our behavior, it is our brains that truly set us apart. Human brains are not simply larger versions of other animal brains. They are structurally and functionally unique, reflecting our advanced cognitive abilities and complex behaviors.

The prefrontal cortex, for instance, a part of the brain that has greatly expanded in humans, plays a crucial role in decision-making, social behavior, and personality expression. It is this part of our brain that allows us to exhibit self-control, think critically, plan for the future, and even question our existence - the very faculties that afford us our unique "degrees of freedom" in behavior.

We thus arrive at a critical juncture in our exploration of human behavior: the realization that our advanced cognitive abilities and the resulting "degrees of freedom" in our behaviors might provide the space where freewill potentially exists. This is where we step into the world of philosophy and ethics, questioning the boundaries of determinism and pondering the existence of freewill.

We, humans, with our complex brains and behaviors, seem to possess a level of freedom that other animals do not. Yet, this freedom is not absolute. It operates within the framework of our biology, deeply influenced by our genes and environment. However, it gives us the ability to choose, to express ourselves uniquely, and to shape our "so called" destiny. It is this fascinating space, where determinism meets freewill, where the familiar meets the unfamiliar. This is the space wherein this book resonates.

As we reach down into the nuances of our human cognition, it is essential to acknowledge another critical aspect of our "degrees of freedom": our capacity for cultural transmission and collective learning.

Unlike other animals, humans possess the unique ability to accumulate and build upon the knowledge of previous generations. This gives us a distinct advantage; while a chimpanzee or an elephant might learn from its immediate family or group, a human can learn from the accumulated wisdom of thousands of generations.

This ability, known as cultural transmission, allows us to pass down not only essential survival skills and knowledge but also our values, beliefs, and ways of understanding the world. Our societies, customs, arts, technologies, and languages are all products of this process. With each new generation, we add another layer to our collective knowledge, creating an ever-expanding array of behavioral choices and innovations.

An excellent example of this lies in our ability to manipulate and shape our environment to suit our needs. Where other animals adapt to their environment, we humans mold our environments to us. We construct houses, cultivate fields, build cities, and invent technologies, effectively changing the very landscapes of our existential planes.

But how does this relate to the concept of "degrees of freedom"? Essentially, the breadth and depth of human knowledge increase our potential behavioral responses to situations. The more knowledge we have at our disposal, the more choices we have. Consequently, the diverse and ever-changing cultural landscapes we inhabit significantly enhance our "degrees of freedom" in behavior.

This cultural aspect of our behavior is closely intertwined with our biology. Our brains are wired for learning and adaptability, enabling us to absorb vast amounts of information and acquire diverse skills throughout our lifetime. This plasticity of the human brain is a key evolutionary adaptation that underpins our advanced cognitive abilities and, by extension, our increased "degrees of freedom".

Yet, with these enhanced "degrees of freedom" comes a heightened responsibility. Our capacity to influence our world is immense, as is our potential to cause harm. From climate change to nuclear weapons, our advanced cognition and collective learning have given rise to existential threats that are now some of our biggest concerns as a species. This starkly illustrates the double-edged nature of our "degrees of freedom."

In essence, our advanced cognition, collective learning, and cultural transmission form the basis of our increased "degrees of freedom" in behavior. However, this doesn't imply an absolute freewill, as our choices and actions are still rooted in our biological makeup and shaped by our environment and experiences. Understanding this complex relationship of biology, environment, and culture is crucial in our quest to unravel the fabric of human behavior.

At this juncture, it is fitting to circle back to the central theme of this exploration: the question of freewill. While we may have greater "degrees of freedom" than other animals, is this equivalent to the conventional notion of freewill?

1.4 A New Understanding: Nature Via Nurture

In the history of human understanding, few debates have been as enduring, contentious, or impactful as the nature versus nurture controversy. This intellectual tug-of-war has long sought to answer one of humanity's most intriguing questions: Are we the products of our genes (nature), or are we molded by our environment (nurture)? Here, we dissect this argument, explore its complexities, and demonstrate its significance in shaping our perception of human behavior.

Diving into the historical progression of this debate, it is vital to acknowledge the key philosophers and scientists who contributed to this conversation. The nature argument traces its origins back to the likes of Plato and Descartes, who posited that certain knowledge and behaviors are innate. They argued that humans are born with specific natural abilities that are immutable and independent of environmental influences. Contrastingly, nurturists, led by philosophers such as John Locke, posited that the mind was a 'tabula rasa' or blank slate at birth, and all knowledge, skills, and behaviors are learned through experience and interaction with the environment.

Fast forward a few centuries, the advent of genetics reinvigorated the debate, tilting the scales in favor of nature. It became increasingly clear that our genetic blueprint carries instructions for everything from our physical traits to predispositions for certain behaviors. The discovery of DNA's structure by Watson and Crick in 1953 further cemented the idea that we are, in essence, slaves to our genes.

However, as we've expanded our knowledge in the realm of genetics, we've come to understand that the interplay between our genes and environment is far more complex than initially thought. It was in this context that the concept of epigenetics emerged, propelling us into a new era of the nature versus nurture debate. It posited that while our DNA sequence remains fixed throughout our lives, external environmental factors can influence how our genes function. These epigenetic modifications, which can even be passed on to subsequent generations, highlight that the 'nature versus nurture' debate is better framed as 'nature via nurture.'

A myriad of studies further underscore this interdependence between genes and environment. For instance, consider the behavior of the honeybee workers and queens. Despite having identical genetic material, their behaviors diverge drastically due to their different upbringings. While queens enjoy a rich diet of royal jelly, turning them into fertile, long-lived matriarchs, workers are destined for a short-lived existence, performing tasks like foraging and defense. This divergence in behavior, driven by different nurturing environments, underscores the powerful influence of nurture over nature.

Similarly, human behavioral patterns are a testament to this intertwined relationship between genes and environment. For instance, monozygotic or identical twins, despite sharing 100% of their genetic material, can exhibit significant differences in personality and behavior due to different life experiences. These findings are further confirmed by the famous Minnesota Twin studies, which found remarkable similarities in the behaviors of identical twins reared apart, underscoring the impact of genetics, and considerable differences due to disparate environments, highlighting the role of nurture.

Analogously, one can envision the nature-nurture dynamic as a music playlist on shuffle. While our genetic code lays out the list of songs (potential behaviors), the environmental influences determine the order of play, volume, tempo, and whether some songs get skipped or repeated.

The nature versus nurture debate's outcome has significant implications on the discourse around free will. If our actions were wholly dictated by our genes or environment, it would leave little room for free will. However, the emerging consensus that behavior is a complex interplay between genetic and environmental influences indicates that while our behavioral responses may be bounded, they are not predestined. We have, within those bounds, the ability to choose, to change, and to shape our behavior. This is the canvas on which the notion of free will is painted.

Let's remember that the nature versus nurture debate is not about taking sides. Instead, it's about understanding the association between genes and environment that crafts the unique spectacle of human behavior. In the chapters that follow, we will submerge into this complex spectacle, exploring how it impacts our ability to exercise free will, shape our identity, and determine our destiny.

In wrapping up this chapter, it is essential to chronologically reflect on the key themes we've covered and how they collectively enhance our understanding of the behavioral biology that underpins human action. We started our journey with the foundations of behavioral biology, dissecting how our actions are influenced by a host of factors that range from the biochemical level to our societal interactions.

Then we explored the genetic and environmental influences that shape our behavior, aptly described as the "twin forces." We recognized that while our genetic makeup provides a blueprint for our behavioral predispositions, our environments offer the landscape where these potentials manifest. Like sculptors chipping away at a block of marble, our genes and environments collectively shape us into the individuals we become.

This led us to the investigation of the varying degrees of freedom in behavioral responses, from animals to humans. We acknowledged that while we share an evolutionary history and basic behavioral principles with the rest of the animal kingdom, human behavior is marked by a unique complexity and adaptability. It is within this larger "degree of freedom" that the possibility of free will begins to emerge.

Finally, we compiled this into the enduring debate of nature versus nurture, coming to the understanding that it is not a binary choice but a closely knit link between the two. Like a playlist on shuffle, our genes offer a repertoire of potential behaviors, while our environment and experiences determine which song plays next, creating the symphony that is uniquely ours.

These multifaceted influences on human behavior pose intriguing questions about the existence and nature of free will. If our behaviors are largely shaped by factors beyond our immediate control, such as our genes and the environment, where does free will fit into the picture? Is there room for choice and agency amidst these deterministic influences?

The foundation laid in this chapter has set the stage for a deep dive into these questions. As we transition into the next chapter, we will explore how the cognitive processes in our brain might provide the machinery needed for free will to operate. We will investigate how our brains, the most complex structures in the known universe, might offer us the ability to choose, to change, and to shape our behavior within the confines set by our biology and environment.

As we embark on this exploration, let's remember that we are not merely observers of this journey but active participants. After all, it is our behaviors, our actions, our choices that we are dissecting – the very essence of what makes us uniquely human.

Chapter 2: The Cognitive Machinery of Free Will

As we move from the vast expanse of evolutionary forces to the fragile world within our cranium, we prepare ourselves to study the core machinery of cognition. This chapter represents the crucial intersection between what we have inherited from nature and what we build and perceive through our mental processes. The journey from genes and evolution to cognition might seem like a quantum leap, but in the grand continuum of understanding free will, it is an essential step.

In Chapter 1, we navigated through natural selection, genetics, and environmental influences, exploring how they lay the foundations for behavior and, potentially, free will. However, to understand the complete picture, we need to transition from the macroscopic level of evolution and genes to the microscopic universe of neurons and synapses. This is precisely the domain of cognitive neuroscience, the study of how our brain enables our mind.

It's within this cognitive machinery where elaborate decision-making occurs – a phenomenon that may or may not constitute free will. Each decision we make, conscious or unconscious, paints a stroke on the canvas of our lives. Unpacking how this mechanism unfolds within the confines of our neural architecture is paramount to understand free will.

This chapter sets out to explore how cognitive neuroscience has started to unravel the interface of the mind and brain, the neural underpinnings of decision-making, and the often-unsuspected role of unconscious processes. By looking at the cognitive and neural processes involved in our daily decisions, we will illuminate the invisible cognitive machinery and explore how this understanding redefines our notion of free will.

Understanding the cognitive machinery is not just a fascinating scientific journey; it's a critical part of our exploration of free will. This inquiry holds profound implications for our self-perception, moral responsibility, and societal structures. It's a testament to complexities of human nature, one that might help us reconcile our instinctive belief in free will with the deterministic undercurrents revealed by science.

2.1 COGNITIVE NEUROSCIENCE: THE INTERFACE OF MIND AND BRAIN

Before we begin, let's take a quick look at the brain and the mind. They are two distinct yet interrelated concepts, often used interchangeably but fundamentally different in terms of their attributes and functions.

The brain is a physical entity. It is a complex organ, the center of our nervous system, located within our skulls. The brain consists of roughly 100 billion nerve cells, or neurons, and is the control center for virtually all of the body's functions. It processes the information it receives from our senses, controls movement, creates thoughts, and houses our memories. The brain can be observed, studied, and even physically altered. Scientists can visualize the brain using tools such as magnetic resonance imaging (MRI) and computed tomography (CT) scans.

On the other hand, the mind is an abstract concept that refers to the cognitive processes that the brain executes. The mind encompasses our consciousness, thoughts, perceptions, emotions, memories, fantasies, and dreams. It's where we experience the world, through our senses and emotions, and it's how we interpret these experiences, through our thoughts, memories, and beliefs. The mind is subjective and personal; it's the part of us that feels, thinks, perceives, wills, reasons, and judges.

Put simply, the brain is the physical hardware, while the mind can be thought of as the software, or the conscious product of the brain's firing neurons. They are separate, yet deeply intertwined, each influencing the other in a myriad of ways. Despite the considerable strides made in neuroscience and psychology, the exact relationship between the mind and the brain remains one of the most compelling mysteries in science and philosophy. The mind-brain problem, sometimes known as the hard problem of consciousness, continues to intrigue researchers and provoke robust scholarly debate.

As we start learning about cognitive neuroscience, we essentially explore the junction where mind meets brain. This domain, an intersection of psychology and neuroscience, grants us insight into how our brain activity maps to cognitive processes such as perception, memory, and decision-making, integral to our discussion of free will.

The relevance of cognitive neuroscience to our inquiry is straightforward – if free will is seen as the capacity to make choices and decisions, then understanding the neurological underpinnings that facilitate these decisions becomes crucial. Furthermore, this knowledge serves as a key to unlock deeper discussions around conscious and unconscious processes, which will be the focus of the subsequent sections.

Cognitive neuroscience has its roots in cognitive psychology, a field that sought to study mental processes in a structured, scientific manner. However, the critical difference and indeed the leap that cognitive neuroscience made were in using advanced techniques to view the brain in action. Techniques such as electroencephalogram (EEG), functional Magnetic Resonance Imaging (fMRI), and Positron Emission Tomography (PET), among others, allow scientists to correlate brain activity with specific cognitive functions.

To better understand the cognitive processes, let's learn about a few key concepts of cognitive neuroscience.

Modularity of the Mind

One of the fundamental concepts in cognitive neuroscience is the idea of modularity - the proposition that specific areas in the brain are specialized for specific cognitive functions. In this perspective, the brain isn't a uniform, undifferentiated mass but a highly organized, modular system where different 'modules' or brain regions are responsible for different functions. This idea emerged from various observations and experiments, one of the most famous being the case of Phineas Gage, a railroad worker in the 19th century.

Following a severe brain injury where an iron rod pierced through his skull, damaging his frontal lobe, Gage's personality underwent a drastic change. His case was one of the first to hint at the localization of brain function, specifically suggesting that the frontal lobe played a crucial role in personality and social behavior.

Advancements in brain imaging techniques have since corroborated and refined these early observations, with different brain regions being associated with various cognitive functions. For example, the occipital lobe is largely responsible for visual processing, while Broca's area in the frontal lobe is crucial for speech production. This modular understanding of the brain provides an essential backdrop for our discussions on decision-making and free will.

But remember, while modularity does provide a framework, it's crucial not to fall into the trap of phrenology - the now-debunked theory that suggested that one could determine someone's personality traits by the bumps on their head. The brain's regions don't operate in isolation, and there's considerable communication and interaction between them.

Before proceeding further, it's worth noting that this understanding of brain functions' localization doesn't directly lead us to a comprehensive understanding of free will. The mechanisms of decision-making are distributed across the brain, involving a widespread network of regions rather than a single 'free will' center. Understanding this network, its functionality, and its influence on our actions will be crucial in uncovering the cognitive machinery of free will.

Neuroplasticity

The word 'plasticity' may evoke images of moldable substances like play-dough, and that's precisely what brain plasticity is all about. It describes the brain's extraordinary ability to modify its own structure and function in response to experience or damage. This trait is a testament to the brain's dynamic nature and represents a significant deviation from the previously held notion of the brain as a static organ.

Brain plasticity is a critical factor in cognitive neuroscience and our understanding of free will for several reasons. Firstly, it informs us that our brains are not merely slaves to our genes. While genetics lay the initial groundwork for our neural architecture, our experiences actively shape the brain's development and functioning. Thus, our choices and actions can, quite literally, shape our brains.

A vivid real-world example of this is seen in London taxi drivers, studied in 2006 by Eleanor Maguire and her team at the University College London. The drivers, who need to memorize the city's layout for their job, were found to have a larger posterior hippocampus, the brain area involved in spatial navigation, compared to the general population. Intriguingly, the size of this region correlated with the length of their driving experience. This example serves as a clear demonstration of our brain's plastic nature, which molds itself in response to our actions and experiences.

Secondly, brain plasticity also impacts our understanding of free will by suggesting that our choices and actions may change our future choices and actions. This is due to the brain's habit-forming nature, where repeated choices can 'strengthen' certain neural pathways, making them more likely to be activated in the future. This phenomenon is encapsulated in the adage 'neurons that fire together, wire together.'

Now, you might be wondering: if our past actions shape our future choices, where does that leave freewill? Well, this is where things get complicated, and these are precisely the questions we will grapple with in this chapter and the ones that follow.

The Role of Consciousness

The concept of consciousness is a central concern in cognitive neuroscience, and crucial for our understanding of free will. Most of us identify our conscious thoughts and feelings as the source of our free will. We feel that we are exercising free will when we make conscious decisions. However, cognitive neuroscience has revealed some surprising findings about the role of consciousness in decision-making.

Benjamin Libet's experiments in the 1980s posed the first significant challenge to this intuitive view. He found that before a person becomes aware of their decision to move their hand, there is already a buildup of brain activity related to the movement. This finding suggested that our decisions might originate from unconscious brain processes before reaching our conscious mind.

This doesn't necessarily imply that free will doesn't exist, but it complicates our understanding of it. It suggests that our conscious experience of making a decision may be the outcome of unconscious brain processes. This idea is sometimes called 'the illusion of conscious will,' which we'll explore in more detail later.

However, it's important not to jump to hasty conclusions from these findings. The field of cognitive neuroscience is still young, and our understanding of consciousness and its role in decision-making is far from complete. Furthermore, the leap from understanding brain processes to making claims about free will is a significant one, fraught with philosophical and scientific perplexities.

Communication and Interaction between Different Brain Regions

As we dive deeper into the complexity of the brain, we find that our actions are mostly the result of interactions between various brain regions. Cognitive neuroscience has shown that decision-making isn't the responsibility of a single brain area, but rather a complex cooperation between several regions. It's like an orchestra, where each section plays a unique role, but the final symphony is the product of their collective effort.

The prefrontal cortex (PFC), for instance, plays a crucial role in higher cognitive functions, including decision-making and planning. It can vaguely be thought of as "the human part of the brain,' overseeing and guiding other brain regions. Damage to this area can result in a syndrome called 'dysexecutive syndrome,' characterized by difficulties in decision-making and impulse control, even when basic cognitive functions like memory and attention remain intact.

Yet, the PFC does not work alone. It heavily interacts with the limbic system, the brain's emotional center. Our decisions often involve a close coordination between rational thought and emotion, mediated by the PFC and the limbic system, respectively. For example, the famous 'Iowa Gambling Task' studies by Antonio Damasio in 1994 revealed that individuals with damage to a part of the brain connecting these regions struggled with decision-making that required emotional input, emphasizing the necessity of their collaboration.

Moreover, cognitive neuroscience has shed light on the role of the basal ganglia, a group of structures involved in motor control and learning. It's implicated in the formation of habits, routines that we perform without conscious thought. This is significant because habits are a form of 'unfree' behavior - actions that we perform automatically, without conscious decision-making.

The Future of Cognitive Neuroscience and Free Will

Cognitive neuroscience has begun to sketch the outline of the complex neural networks that underpin our decisions and actions. Yet, much of it remains a mystery. As our technology and methodologies evolve, we may be able to tell apart these networks with greater precision, uncovering the neural correlates of free will in even greater detail.

However, it's important to note that the tools of cognitive neuroscience are only part of the picture. Our understanding of free will also hinges on philosophical and ethical considerations that go beyond the scope of empirical science. As we journey deeper into the brain's intricacies, we must strive to integrate these diverse perspectives, weaving them into a coherent, multi-faceted understanding of free will.

In this section, we've looked at how cognitive neuroscience provides insights into free will by examining the brain's structure, function, and the interplay between different regions. We've also touched upon the fascinating role of consciousness in our decision-making process and the brain's capacity for change. As we delve further into the following sections, we'll build upon these foundations, examining the neural underpinnings of decision-making and morality, further unraveling the concept of free will.

2.2 DECISION MAKING: THE NEURAL UNDERPINNINGS

Our every day is a series of choices and decisions, some seemingly insignificant - like choosing the type of cereal for breakfast, while others with profound implications - like choosing a career or a life partner. These choices, however minor or major they may be, are shaped by a vast network of neural activities in our brain. To grasp the concept of free will, it is crucial to comprehend how our brain, the command center of our body, facilitates the process of decision making.

Let us start by dissecting the neuroanatomy of decision making. At the heart of the matter lies our cerebral cortex, the brain's outer layer, often termed as the "thinking cap" of our body. This part of the brain is responsible for higher cognitive functions, including reasoning, problem-solving, and, indeed, decision-making. However, certain regions within the cerebral cortex play an exceptionally significant role when it comes to making choices.

The prefrontal cortex, nestled in the front of our brain, is akin to an orchestra conductor, ensuring every player or, in our case, every thought, emotion, memory, comes together harmoniously to create a well-rounded decision. Particularly, the dorsolateral prefrontal cortex aids in deliberating on choices by managing relevant information. When faced with a choice of job offers, for instance, it's your dorsolateral prefrontal cortex that helps you evaluate each option, analyzing the benefits and drawbacks of each.

Adjacent to the dorsolateral prefrontal cortex is the orbitofrontal cortex, the region primarily concerned with reward evaluation. This area lights up when we assess the rewards associated with our choices, be it the joy of indulging in a delectable dessert or the satisfaction of accomplishing a challenging task.

Next in our neuroanatomical journey is the anterior cingulate cortex, acting like a vigilant guardian, alerting us when a decision requires extra attention due to conflicting options or potential loss. Imagine deciding to invest in stocks; it's your anterior cingulate cortex that raises the alarm about the associated risks and urges you to tread carefully.

These regions do not operate in isolation. Rather, they communicate and collaborate, forming a coherent neural network that gives rise to our decisions. But how does this interaction take place? To answer this, we need to examine the neurobiology of decision making.

Every decision-making process starts with a stimulus, which triggers a cascade of neural activities. These stimuli can be internal (such as a thought or feeling) or external (such as a sight or sound). Once these stimuli are detected by our sensory organs, they're transformed into electrical signals, the primary language of our brain.

These electrical signals traverse through the brain's neural pathways, jumping from one neuron to another. At the crux of this neural communication is a tiny gap called the synapse. Picture the synapse as a bustling city intersection, where neurons are the drivers, and neurotransmitters are the vehicles carrying information from one neuron to another. This web of connections of electrical signals and neurotransmitters forms the essence of the neurobiology of decision making.

Among the myriad of neurotransmitters, dopamine and serotonin play pivotal roles in decision making. Dopamine, often termed the 'reward molecule', primarily influences how we perceive and pursue rewards. So, when you experience a burst of happiness after deciding to eat your favorite ice cream, it's essentially dopamine doing its magic.

On the other hand, serotonin, the 'mood stabilizer', significantly affects our emotional state, thereby swaying our decision-making process. Higher levels of serotonin *generally* promote positive emotions, thereby encouraging decisions that align with these positive feelings. For instance, you may be more inclined to opt for a challenging yet fulfilling task when your serotonin levels are high.

An exciting area of study in understanding the neural underpinnings of decision making is neuroimaging. Techniques such as fMRI and PET provide a peek into the active areas of the brain during the decision-making process. Through these techniques, we can see which brain areas light up when we're deliberating on choices or evaluating consequences, offering tangible evidence of the brain's activity while making decisions.

If the brain was a country, the prefrontal cortex would be the capital city. Located at the very front of the brain, it's this region that takes the reins during the decision-making process. It's where the evaluation of pros and cons happens, where future consequences are weighed, and where rational and logical choices are made.

Let's imagine that you're considering whether to go for a run or to stay in and watch a movie. Your prefrontal cortex will weigh the immediate gratification of watching a movie against the longer-term health benefits of going for a run. It's a tug of war between short-term pleasure and long-term gain, and the prefrontal cortex is the arbiter.

Underneath the prefrontal cortex lies the limbic system, home to our emotions. Composing several structures including the amygdala and hippocampus, the limbic system adds the emotional layer to our decision-making process. It's the reason why our choices aren't always rational and why we sometimes go with our "gut feelings." If the prefrontal cortex represents the mind, the limbic system represents the 'metaphorical heart' in our decision-making process.

Let's take a look at the amygdala, a small almond-shaped structure deep within the brain. The amygdala acts as the emotional thermostat of our brain. It triggers fear responses and alerts us to potential dangers, thus heavily influencing our decisions. Imagine walking on a secluded path late at night, and you hear a rustling sound from the bushes. It's the amygdala that triggers the fear response, urging you to leave the scene immediately.

Contrary to what we might think, not all decisions we make are conscious. A large chunk of our decision-making process happens below the threshold of our conscious awareness, in the unconscious territory. This isn't necessarily a bad thing. If we had to consciously deliberate on every tiny decision, we would suffer from decision fatigue. Instead, our brain smartly delegates some decisions to the unconscious mind, enabling us to focus on more critical matters.

The unconscious decision-making process is largely driven by our past experiences, learned patterns, and ingrained habits. Let's say you're driving home from work. You don't need to consciously decide when to turn the steering wheel or when to press the brake. Your unconscious mind takes care of these decisions, based on your past experiences of driving.

All these neural and cognitive mechanisms come together like a well-orchestrated symphony, enabling us to make decisions, big and small, every single day. And although our decisions might sometimes seem arbitrary or irrational, they're the result of incredibly complex neural activities and cognitive processes happening within the confinements of our brain.

It's also crucial to consider the influence of the neurotransmitters on decision making. While the subsequent chapters in this book will delve deeper into this aspect, it is important to highlight the roles of the two previously mentioned neurotransmitters, dopamine and serotonin, that significantly impact our decisions.

Dopamine, the "reward" neurotransmitter, is closely associated with pleasure and reward-seeking behaviors. Dopamine plays a pivotal role in making decisions that we perceive will bring us immediate gratification. For instance, choosing to eat a chocolate cake instead of a salad for lunch might be influenced by the dopamine pathways in our brain. The prospect of the delicious, satisfying taste of the cake triggers a release of dopamine, leading us to make the decision.

On the other hand, serotonin is associated with mood regulation, impulse control, and long-term planning. It is hypothesized that higher serotonin levels help facilitate more thoughtful, long-term beneficial decisions. For example, choosing to invest money in a retirement fund, even though it means less cash in hand now, could be influenced by serotonin-mediated pathways in the brain.

The constant push-and-pull between dopamine and serotonin pathways forms the neurobiological basis of many of our everyday decisions. The balance between these two neurotransmitters is critical in making decisions that are both satisfying in the short term and beneficial in the long run.

Even the act of making simple decisions is not as simple as it seems. It requires complex processing within the brain that involves multiple regions. Our decision-making process is highly susceptible to errors, biases, and irrationality, adding to the delicacies of free will. The cognitive biases that are often present in our decision-making process are another area of interest in neuroscience. These biases are systematic errors in thinking that affect the decisions and judgments that we make.

Consider the classic cognitive bias known as the "anchoring effect." This is a cognitive bias where individuals rely too heavily on an initial piece of information, known as the "anchor," when making decisions. For example, when shopping, the first price you see for a type of product acts as an anchor and influences whether you see other prices as reasonable.

How does this play out in the brain? Studies have shown that anchoring effects can be linked to the brain's tendency to create shortcuts in order to make the processing of information easier. This is the brain favoring the most energy-efficient decision-making process. However, this tendency can lead to flawed decisions as the initial piece of information may not be the most reliable.

Biases are just one example of how our decision-making is not always entirely logical or rational, and this only adds to the complexity when discussing free will. We're not only dealing with a brain that is influenced by a variety of factors (both internal and external), but we're also dealing with a brain that doesn't always operate on pure logic.

The study of the neural underpinnings of decision making is like a window into the functioning of free will. It allows us to witness how decisions are not simply a product of rational thought, but are also influenced by various complex processes in the brain. The findings in this field serve as a stepping stone in understanding the complexity of human free will, which we will continue to explore throughout this book.

In the following sections, we will explore further the idea of conscious versus unconscious decision making and the daily decisions that construct the cognitive basis of free will.

2.3 CONSCIOUS VS. UNCONSCIOUS: THE SILENT DRIVERS

Picture a time when you arrived at home after a long drive, only to realize you have no recollection of the route you took, or even changing the gears during your journey. While your conscious mind may have been lost in thought or focused on the music, your unconscious mind navigated the vehicle. This autopilot is the unconscious mind, always at work, silently driving a significant portion of our actions and decisions. On the other hand, your conscious mind commands your active attention, involving you directly in the process. Both are continuously at work, shaping our reality and our perceptions.

Conscious processes are tasks we actively focus on. This level of consciousness involves the awareness of ourselves and our environment. Imagine trying a new recipe, calculating your expenses, or learning to play a musical instrument. You're conscious of every step, every note, and every calculation. This focused state of mind is your conscious process at work, demanding your undivided attention.

In the framework of decision making and free will, conscious processes come into play when we make deliberate choices. If you are consciously deciding to save money for an upcoming trip, or choosing to react calmly in a heated argument, these are instances of conscious decision-making. Every conscious process, due to its direct link to our awareness, also contributes to the sense of agency, a key aspect of our perception of free will. It gives us the impression that we are in control, steering our life's vehicle.

Let's pivot to unconscious processes, the backstage operators of our mind. As a concept first proposed by Sigmund Freud in 1915, the unconscious mind is a reservoir of feelings, thoughts, urges, and memories that are outside of our conscious awareness. Most of the operations of the mind remain out of conscious awareness, yet they significantly influence our behaviors, decisions, and feelings.

For instance, an unconscious bias towards a certain food may stem from a negative experience in childhood, subtly influencing our dietary choices in adulthood. Our innate fear of heights may deter us from choosing a career as a pilot, without us consciously recognizing this influence.

In terms of free will, unconscious processes add another layer of complexity. They direct a significant portion of our decisions and actions, usually without our conscious realization. This becomes even more intriguing when we recognize that many unconscious processes were once conscious. Remember the driving example? Over time, what started as a very conscious process of learning to drive has, through habituation, become largely unconscious.

As we go deeper into understanding how our conscious and unconscious minds work, we see that the different aspects of our cognitive functioning are continuously interacting. It's an intriguing dynamic, akin to an iceberg, where the conscious

50

mind is the visible tip above the water, while the vast unconscious mind lurks beneath the surface.

Think about it in the context of daily routines. You don't consciously process each step while brushing your teeth or tying your shoelaces, but you do when learning to play a new musical instrument. Here, the unconscious processes automate routine tasks, freeing up our conscious mind for more complex ones. This division of labor between the two systems is essential for our efficient functioning.

The interplay of conscious and unconscious processes also comes to light when we consider the more subtle aspects of our behavior, such as our decision-making process. Suppose you have consciously decided to adopt a healthier lifestyle. While this decision seems purely conscious, your unconscious mind might be subtly influencing this decision. It might be drawing on past experiences, memories, or associations that link fitness with positive concepts such as attractiveness, longevity, or social acceptance.

In other words, while your conscious mind is the 'director' making the conscious decision, your unconscious mind is the 'scriptwriter' drafting the narrative based on prior experiences, learned behaviors, and deeply ingrained biases. The end result is an ongoing dialogue between these two entities, guiding our decisions in a manner that we often don't fully understand.

This brings us to the central question of how these processes interact with the concept of free will. The sense of agency we derive from making conscious decisions can be likened to the captain of a ship navigating through the ocean. It feeds our belief in free will, making us feel like we are in control, steering our life in a direction of our choice.

However, what if the tide, currents, or the winds (unconscious influences) subtly or sometimes drastically change the ship's course without the captain's (conscious mind) knowledge? This scenario accurately illustrates our life's decision-making process, where we believe we are consciously making independent decisions, while they are continuously influenced and sometimes even overridden by our unconscious mind.

This unconscious influence on our conscious decisions can lead to an illusion of free will. We might perceive ourselves to be freely deciding our course of action based on rational thought, but in reality, these decisions could be influenced by unconscious biases, emotions, or ingrained beliefs.

This back-and-forth between conscious and unconscious processes, in turn, creates a complex, dynamic model of free will. It reveals that our free will is not an absolute or independent entity. Instead, it's a product of our cognitive processes, subtly and continuously being shaped and molded by both our conscious deliberations and unconscious influences.

It's clear that both conscious and unconscious processes significantly contribute to our actions, decisions, and the perceived sense of free will. These processes act as the silent drivers, steering our life journey, often in ways we may not immediately recognize or understand.

The more we comprehend these processes, the better equipped we are to appreciate the nuanced nature of free will. Instead of viewing it as an absolute entity, we begin to understand free will as a dynamic product of our complex cognitive machinery. In the following sections, we will continue to unravel this concept, further exploring the cognitive underpinnings of our everyday decisions.

2.4 Daily Decisions: The Invisible Cognitive Dance

Every day, we navigate through a maze of choices, decisions, and judgments. These range from mundane choices, like deciding what to wear for work, to profound ones, such as choosing a professional field of study. While these decisions may appear significantly different in their depth and gravity, they are all an intrinsic part of the diverse tableau of free will. These decisions, choices, and judgments provide a reflection of our desires, ambitions, fears, biases, and even the constraints that we operate within, creating a mirror-like image of the interplay between conscious and unconscious cognitive processes. But the question that propels us forward is: How does this complex machinery of choice operate beneath the everyday mundaneness of our lives?

Our day begins with a chain reaction of decisions. The moment the alarm clock rings, we find ourselves standing on the precipice of a myriad of choices. The immediate and seemingly inconsequential decision to snooze or not to snooze propels us into the day. Then comes the decision of which side of the bed to roll off, followed by more significant choices, like selecting an outfit, deciding the day's meals, or plotting the route to work.

These decisions, as trivial as they may seem in isolation, collectively lay the groundwork for our day. They shape our mood, determine our productivity, and orchestrate the symphony of experiences that each day unfurls before us. Let's explore the underlying cognitive processes that drive these mundane decisions, often flying under the radar of our conscious awareness.

For instance, consider the seemingly simple task of choosing an outfit for the day. On the surface, it appears to be an automatic decision, one that we make without dedicating much conscious thought. However, a closer inspection reveals that behind the scenes of this 'simple' decision, our brain is devising a complex cognitive plan, delicately balancing various factors and considerations.

As you stand in front of your wardrobe, your brain kicks into high gear. It considers practical variables, such as the day's weather and the activities on your schedule. It factors in the comfort and appropriateness of different clothing items. Moreover, it even takes into account intangible factors, like your emotional state and societal norms and expectations.

The act of choosing an outfit may appear mundane, but it provides an illuminating glimpse into the hidden complexities of everyday decisions. While we may not actively deliberate over these choices, they aren't haphazard or random. Instead, they reflect the dynamic interplay of conscious and unconscious factors, underscoring the role of free will in shaping our everyday experiences.

This facet of our daily life illustrates the often-underappreciated complexity of what we might consider 'autopilot' decisions. Even in the seemingly automatic, mundane choices we make, free will is at play, deftly navigating the vast sea of conscious and unconscious considerations. The cognitive processes involved in these decisions are as dynamic and fluid as the concept of free will itself.

Moving on to more engaging decisions of the day, the choices we make consciously, we realize they are like the visible tip of an iceberg, belying the depth and complexity of the processes that occur beneath the surface. Take, for instance, the decision of choosing a meal. You might consciously decide to opt for a healthy salad over a tempting pizza slice.

On the surface, it appears to be a conscious, reasoned decision, a victory of rational judgment over indulgent desire. But what happens behind the scenes? Your conscious decision is informed by past experiences, nutritional knowledge, health goals, emotional state, societal expectations, and even unconscious biases against certain food types.

In making this conscious choice, you're unconsciously integrating a wide array of information, highlighting the complex choreography of cognitive processes that shape our everyday decisions. The decision-making process may appear linear and straightforward, like a well-trodden path. However, it's more akin to navigating a labyrinth, complete with twists, turns, and unexpected diversions, symbolizing the interplay between free will and the deterministic influences in our lives.

This idea echoes the concept of 'bounded rationality,' proposed by Nobel laureate Herbert Simon in 1957 through his book, 'Models of Man.' Simon suggested that our decision-making capacity isn't purely rational, as traditional economic theories propose. Instead, it's constrained or 'bounded' by the information we have, the cognitive limitations of our minds, and the finite amount of time we have to make a decision.

In the context of our daily decisions, this means that we're often making the best choice from a limited set of options, within the confines of our understanding and the constraints of our circumstances. Hence, even when we believe we're making conscious, rational decisions, they're inevitably shaped by unconscious factors and environmental constraints, subtly directing the 'choices' within decision-making frameworks.

Examining closely, the ballet of decision making begins with a cue – a stimulus that triggers the need for a decision. In response to this cue, our brains gather and process relevant information, drawing on both conscious knowledge and unconscious memories and associations. Our brains then evaluate the possible options, weighing their potential outcomes based on our goals, values, and priorities.

Again, I would like you to remember that this evaluation process is influenced by cognitive biases – systematic errors in thinking that affect our decisions and judgments. For example, the 'status quo bias' might make us gravitate towards familiar choices, while the 'confirmation bias' might cause us to favor information that aligns with our existing beliefs.

Once the evaluation is complete, we make a decision and take action. However, the ballet doesn't end here. The outcomes of our decisions feed back into our mental database, influencing our future decisions and subtly shaping our behavioral patterns. This feedback loop illustrates the dynamic, evolving nature of our decision-making processes, underscoring the role of experience and learning in shaping our free will.

To understand this dynamic better, let's consider some everyday scenarios. Suppose you're deciding where to go on your next vacation. The conscious decision-making process might involve factors like cost, distance, weather, and personal preferences. You might do some research, read reviews, ask for recommendations, and then finally decide based on your findings and calculations.

However, beneath this conscious process lies a sea of unconscious influences. Your preference for a beach vacation over a city break might be informed by positive associations with the sea from your childhood. Your decision to avoid certain destinations might be based on subconscious biases. Your choice might also be influenced by societal factors - for instance, choosing an 'Instagram-worthy' location because of the subtle societal pressure to share impressive travel pictures.

Another example could be the decision to buy a new car. You might think that you've made a logical, conscious decision based on factors like fuel efficiency, price, and safety ratings. However, the unconscious mind has its say as well. You might be drawn to a specific brand because of its perceived status or positive experiences with the brand in the past. You might favor a particular model because it's similar to the one your parents drove or avoid another because it's associated with a negative incident.

These observations demonstrate that our daily decisions, even those that appear to be entirely conscious, are influenced by a mix of rational thinking, unconscious biases, and learned associations. They highlight the complexly intertwined correlation between conscious and unconscious processes in our decision-making, a correlation that shapes the trajectory of our lives.

Let's take a brief look at cognitive biases. These cognitive blind spots play a significant role in our decision-making processes. They act as mental shortcuts or 'heuristics,' helping us make decisions quickly in a complex and uncertain world. However, they can also lead us astray, causing us to make irrational decisions or develop skewed perceptions. Think of them as 'efficiency over accuracy' rules.

For instance, the 'availability heuristic' might cause us to overestimate the likelihood of events that come easily to mind. This could lead us to fear flying more than driving, even though statistically, flying is safer. Similarly, the 'confirmation bias' can make us more likely to seek out and believe information that confirms our pre-existing beliefs, fueling polarization and misinformation, while making us prone to indoctrination and dogmatic inclinations.

Recognizing and understanding these biases can help us navigate the decision-making process more effectively. It can make us more aware of the unseen influences on our decisions, giving us a greater sense of control and enabling us to make better, more rational choices.

This invisible cognitive symphony we partake in every day raises intriguing questions about the nature of free will. If our decisions, even the seemingly conscious ones, are significantly influenced by unconscious processes, to what extent are we truly free?

This question becomes even more entangling when we consider the deterministic nature of the brain. Our brains are physical entities, bound by the laws of physics. Every thought, emotion, and decision we make is the result of neuronal activity, which is determined by a complicated interaction of genetic and environmental factors. In this light, can we truly claim to have free will, or is our perception of free will merely an illusion born of our inability to perceive the underlying deterministic processes?

On the one hand, this perspective can feel unsettling. The idea that our choices might not be entirely our own challenges deeply held beliefs about self-determination and personal responsibility. It contradicts our subjective experience of making conscious, deliberate decisions.

On the other hand, understanding this cognitive reality can also be empowering. Recognizing the unconscious influences on our behavior can make us more self-aware and help us understand why we do the things we do. It can make us more empathetic and aid us to understand why others might act the way they do. It can also guide us towards making better decisions, by making us aware of our cognitive biases and encouraging us to question our automatic responses.

This elaborate phenomenon, in which conscious and unconscious processes intertwine inside our minds, forms the crux of our journey into the enigma of free will. It sets the stage for our exploration into the shadows of determinism, the illusion of free will, and the neurobiology of choice - journeys that will take us deeper into the heart of what it means to be human.

The journey so far into the cognitive machinery of free will has led us through fascinating landscapes. We have traversed the terrain of cognitive neuroscience, examining the interface of mind and brain. We've explored the neural underpinnings of decision-making, discovering the critical role of brain regions like the prefrontal cortex and limbic system.

We have witnessed the tango between conscious and unconscious processes that underlies our daily decisions, a dance invisibly choreographed by a multitude of factors, from past experiences and learned associations to cognitive biases and societal influences. Through these journeys, we have begun to glimpse the integral machinery that underlies our perception of free will.

Chapter 3: Deterministic Shadows on Free Will

Freedom, choice, and autonomy – these are the ideals that we, as human beings, often cherish and champion. They construct our perception of ourselves as conscious agents, navigating through the labyrinth of life with a compass powered by free will. Yet, as we explored in the preceding chapters, this compass is not entirely self-directed. It is influenced, shaped, and in many ways, dictated by forces beyond our immediate control. Here, in Chapter 3, we venture further into the deterministic forces that cast long, pervasive shadows on our concept of free will.

The term 'determinism' traces its roots back to philosophy and has been tightly bound into the fabric of various scientific disciplines. In essence, it argues that every event or state of affairs is the inevitable output of previous states of affairs. If determinism holds, then the future is a sealed book and free will, an illusion.

Yet, is our future fixed in the deterministic universe, or are there just predictable patterns that give an illusion of a predestined existence? This chapter begins by exploring this dichotomy, opening the floor to an engaging conversation between free will and determinism.

As we embark on this exploration, I invite you to keep an open mind. The goal here is not to diminish the concept of freewill but to paint a holistic picture of all the forces that contribute to our decisions. By the end of this chapter, I hope to provide you with a broader understanding of the correlation between freewill and determinism.

3.1 The World of Determinism: Fixed Future or Predictable Patterns?

In our journey of understanding the underpinnings of free will, we inevitably stumble upon the formidable concept of "determinism" that has sparked philosophical, scientific, and moral debates throughout human history. The world of determinism can be both intimidating and enlightening; it challenges the most profound beliefs about our autonomy, yet it provides a scientific and philosophical framework to comprehend the complex machine of nature and, more specifically, human nature.

Determinism, in its broadest sense, is the philosophical proposition that every event or state of affairs, including every human decision and action, is the inevitable and necessary consequence of antecedent states of affairs. In essence, determinism holds that nothing happens by chance. In the deterministic worldview, the future is not an open horizon but rather a closed book already written – the ink of causality has already drafted our stories, and we are but actors performing our pre-ordained roles.

The deterministic perspective, however, is not monolithic. One can distinguish between what can be termed as 'hard determinism' and 'soft determinism'. 'Hard determinism' subscribes to the belief in a fixed future, where every event, choice, or action is predetermined and unalterable, much like the path of a stone thrown with a known force and direction is predetermined by the laws of physics. Imagine a perfectly precise supercomputer that knows the location, velocity, and properties of every atom in the universe. According to hard determinism, such a machine could accurately calculate and predict the state of the universe at any future moment.

On the other hand, 'soft determinism' proposes the existence of predictable patterns rather than a fixed future. It contends that while the future is not already written page by page, there are certain recurring patterns, probabilistic principles, and natural laws that make the world less random and more structured. It's like predicting the weather – while meteorologists can't predict the exact movement of every air molecule, they can predict general patterns and trends, providing a reasonably accurate forecast.

In the context of human behavior, soft determinism suggests that while our decisions are not predestined, they are not random either. They tend to follow certain patterns influenced by our biology, experiences, and environmental factors. Understanding these patterns may not allow us to predict a person's every decision, but it can provide a statistically reliable forecast of their likely behavior in given circumstances.

The two versions of determinism appear starkly different at first glance. However, they share the underlying principle of causality – the notion that every event has an antecedent cause or a set of causes. Nothing happens in a vacuum, devoid of antecedent conditions. This principle extends to human actions and choices as well. From a deterministic viewpoint, when you decide to pick up this book and read it, you're not truly making a spontaneous decision. Instead, this action is a consequence of various preceding factors, including your curiosity about the subject, the accessibility of the book, the spare time at your disposal, and countless other variables.

Now, let's examine the role of determinism in our understanding of free will. Determinism seems to directly challenge the idea of free will. After all, if our actions and decisions are a result of causes that we have not chosen, how can we claim that we are making free choices? If a supercomputer could, hypothetically, predict our every decision based on the complete knowledge of our brain's state and environmental factors, where does that leave free will?

Such profound questions lead us to the apparent contradiction between determinism and free will – a philosophical problem referred to as the paradox of free will. It is a debate that has engaged the minds of scholars, scientists, and thinkers for centuries, and it is far from settled.

At this point, it's worth noting that accepting determinism doesn't necessarily deny the experience of making choices. Even in a deterministic universe, we still go through the process of decision-making. We weigh pros and cons, deliberate, and finally choose one option over the others. The key argument of determinism is that this process, and its ultimate outcome, is shaped and influenced by factors beyond our conscious control.

Determinism also doesn't entail that human behavior is perfectly predictable. Even if our choices are influenced by antecedent factors, the sheer complexity and number of these factors make it practically impossible to predict human behavior with perfect accuracy. We're not like a simple physical system with a handful of variables. We're immensely complicated biological machines existing in a web of interconnections and influences that range from our genetic makeup to the culture we're born into.

By exploring determinism, we're not trying to strip away our humanity or reduce us to mere automata. Instead, we're attempting to understand the forces that shape our decisions and actions – to uncover the threads in the fabric of our behavior. It's an investigation into why we do what we do, why we choose what we choose. It is, in a sense, a journey to understand ourselves better.

This understanding of determinism carries significant implications for the concept of free will. If the future is predictable and our actions are determined, it could mean that free will is nothing more than an illusion – a compelling one, granted, but an illusion nonetheless. Even if we feel that we are making independent decisions, we might just be playing out a script written by the laws of nature and our past experiences.

This deterministic perspective finds resonance in the words of the famed psychologist B.F. Skinner. Skinner, a staunch advocate of behaviorism, argued that human behavior, including our perceived choices, is the result of environmental influences and conditioning. Skinner's work exemplified the idea of predictability, demonstrating through various experiments that organisms (including humans) adjust their behavior in response to environmental stimuli. His experiments showed that, given enough information about an organism's environment and its history of interactions with that environment, we could accurately predict the organism's future behavior.

Skinner's views, while controversial, highlight the deterministic lens through which we can view human behavior and decision-making. Even as we believe ourselves to be making free and autonomous decisions, we are influenced by factors outside our control – factors that shape our responses and steer our choices in ways we may not be consciously aware of.

Understanding the deterministic nature of our actions and decisions can be unsettling. It challenges our fundamental perception of ourselves as autonomous agents. If our choices are not truly our own but are influenced by factors beyond our control, do we have free will?

This is the question that we must grapple with as we delve deeper into the subject. However, before we do so, let's consider another aspect of determinism: its role in science and particularly in the science of the brain. Neuroscience, with its in-depth explorations of the human brain and its functions, provides intriguing insights into the deterministic nature of human behavior.

The science of the brain, particularly the field of cognitive neuroscience, has made remarkable strides in illuminating the complexities of human thought, emotion, and behavior. Through methods like fMRI and EEG, neuroscientists have been able to peer into the workings of the brain and unravel the biological underpinnings of our cognitive processes.

In this context, the deterministic perspective has found new grounds in the form of biological determinism, which suggests that our actions and choices are shaped by our biological makeup   particularly the structure and functioning of our brain. Biological determinism asserts that our behaviors, including the choices we make, are governed by the neural circuits in our brain and the biochemistry of our neurotransmitters.

Notable experiments in neuroscience have lent credence to this view. Earlier, we learned about the famous Libet experiment where Benjamin Libet revealed the intriguing phenomenon that a specific electrical change, known as the 'readiness potential,' occurred in the brains of his subjects before they consciously decided to perform a voluntary action.

This finding suggested that the decision to act was initiated in the brain before the person was consciously aware of it. Libet's experiments were controversial and have been subject to much debate, but they certainly pointed towards a deterministic understanding of human action – a view where our choices may be initiated by our brain even before we consciously make them.

More recent studies have furthered our understanding of this phenomenon. A study by Soon et al. in 2008 expanded on Libet's work, showing that brain activity related to a decision could be detected up to 10 seconds before the subject reported being consciously aware of making the decision. This research further supported the idea that our brain might be 'deciding' for us before we are consciously aware of the decision.

This again, however, does not necessarily negate the existence of free will. Some argue that this preliminary brain activity might just be the brain preparing for action, providing us with the readiness to act when we consciously decide to. In this view, free will may still play a crucial role in shaping our final decision, even if the initial stages of the decision-making process are determined by our brain activity.

There are several other areas where determinism has made its mark, casting a deterministic shadow over the concept of free will. Genetic determinism is one such area. It posits that our behaviors and choices are significantly influenced, if not determined, by our genes. Researchers have identified specific genes that seem to play a role in a wide range of behaviors, from risk-taking and aggression to empathy and altruism. For instance, variations in the dopamine D4 receptor gene (DRD4) have been associated with novelty-seeking behaviors, suggesting that our propensity to seek out new and exciting experiences may be written into our genetic code.

Yet, genetics alone do not determine our destiny. The gene-environment interaction also adds another layer to the determinism vs. free will debate. Research has shown that the same genetic variant can lead to different outcomes depending on the person's environment. For example, a person with a specific variant of the serotonin transporter gene, which has been linked to increased risk of depression, may never experience depression if they grow up in a nurturing and supportive environment. This interaction between our genes and our environment further complicates the deterministic perspective.

However, even within this complex dynamic, there seems to be a degree of predictability that lends itself to a deterministic interpretation. Certain genes, when combined with specific environmental factors, can significantly increase the likelihood of particular outcomes. But does this equate to a fixed future, as strict determinism would suggest? Or does it merely provide us with predictable patterns, giving us a sense of probability rather than certainty? These are the questions that continue to intrigue and challenge researchers in this field.

Determinism also finds echoes in the field of psychology, particularly in the form of environmental determinism. This perspective suggests that our actions and choices are influenced, if not determined, by our environment – the physical, social, and cultural circumstances that we find ourselves in. From this viewpoint, our upbringing, our socioeconomic status, our cultural norms, and even our physical surroundings can significantly shape the choices we make.

A compelling example of environmental determinism can be found in the Stanford Prison Experiment, conducted by psychologist Philip Zimbardo in 1971. In this study, participants were randomly assigned to play the role of either a prison guard or a prisoner in a mock prison set up in the basement of Stanford's psychology building.

Despite knowing that it was an experiment, the participants quickly adopted the behaviors and attitudes that corresponded to their assigned roles. The 'guards' became increasingly sadistic, while the 'prisoners' became passive and compliant. The experiment had to be cut short due to the alarming escalation of abusive behavior. This study dramatically illustrated how our environment can shape our behavior, often in ways that we would not predict or consciously choose.

However circling back to our question, does environmental determinism, like genetic determinism, equate to a fixed future? Or does it merely point to predictable patterns? The Stanford Prison Experiment certainly demonstrated a powerful pattern: individuals placed in a certain environment (in this case, a mock prison) tended to behave in a certain way (as aggressive guards or passive prisoners). However, it is essential to remember that not all participants responded in the same way. Some 'guards' resisted the urge to abuse their power, and some 'prisoners' attempted to rebel against their oppression. This variance highlights a potential limitation of deterministic views: they can predict tendencies, but they cannot account for every individual's response.

Determinism also extends its shadow into neurobiology. Some researchers argue that our decisions and actions are ultimately the result of neural processes that we have no conscious control over. These processes are influenced by our genes and our environment, yes, but they also have their dynamics.

For instance, our brain is continually receiving and processing information, making predictions about the future, and updating its predictions based on new data. This ongoing process of prediction and updating, known as predictive processing, plays a significant role in our decision-making. But, much like genetic and environmental determinism, this neurobiological perspective raises questions about
68

predictability and certainty. Can we predict someone's decisions based on their brain activity? To what extent are our choices predetermined by our neural processes?

At this juncture, let's dive deeper into a pivotal concept that broadens our understanding of determinism; chaos theory. Chaos theory is a field of study in mathematics that studies complex systems whose behavior is highly sensitive to slight changes in conditions. It is often summarized with the phrase coined by Edward Lorenz, "Does the flap of a butterfly's wings in Brazil set off a tornado in Texas?" In essence, chaos theory suggests that within the apparent randomness of chaotic complex systems, there are underlying patterns, interconnectedness, repetition, and feedback loops.

In the context of human behavior, chaos theory presents an interesting dichotomy. On one hand, it emphasizes the deterministic nature of these systems. Small changes in initial conditions (such as slight differences in a person's genetic makeup or environment) can lead to dramatically different outcomes in their behavior. This sensitivity to initial conditions is known as the butterfly effect.

On the other hand, chaos theory also underlines the inherent unpredictability of these systems. Even with perfect knowledge of a person's genes and environment, it would be practically impossible to predict their behavior with absolute certainty. The complexity and interconnectedness of the variables at play make accurate long-term prediction a challenging feat, at best.

Consequently, chaos theory provides a fascinating lens through which to view the deterministic factors influencing our behavior. It helps us understand how deterministic processes can lead to patterns that are predictable in the short term, while also yielding outcomes that are highly variable and unpredictable in the long term.

In retrospect, it becomes evident that the deterministic world does not necessarily mean a fixed, unavoidable future. It's a world of predictable patterns, yet shrouded in complexities and uncertainties. The confluence of genetics, environment, and neurobiology spins the complex web of determinism. Yet, amidst this deterministic shadow, individual variance and the chaos theory remind us of the vast realm of unpredictability. It's a balancing act between nature's law and the randomness within it that shapes the universe and the beings within it.

3.2 Genetics and Neurobiology: The Unseen Puppeteers

Genes and neurons, the fundamental units of heredity and cognition, respectively, are instrumental in constructing the architecture of our behavior and decision-making processes. They are the silent puppeteers manipulating our actions, often unbeknownst to us, casting a shadow on our perception of free will.

The science of genetics opens a window into our understanding of how traits, including behavioral tendencies, are passed down generations. The Human Genome Project and the subsequent advancements have enabled us to decode genetic blueprints and identify specific genes associated with particular behavioral traits.

For instance, the heritability of intelligence, a topic of intense debate, has been quantified through twin and adoption studies. The consensus among researchers suggests that about 50% of the variance in intelligence can be attributed to genetic factors. Similarly, genes associated with personality traits, such as extraversion and neuroticism, have been identified, suggesting a genetic predisposition towards certain behavioral patterns.

These discoveries do not imply a deterministic view of behavior. Instead, they suggest that our actions and choices might be influenced by our genetic make-up to some extent. It is the gene-environment interaction that shapes our behavior and underpins human nature.

We have previously discussed epigenetics, but let us take a closer look at it in the current context. The term "epigenetics" refers to modifications in gene expression without changes in the underlying DNA sequence. These alterations, which can be influenced by environmental factors, can dramatically affect our behavior. For instance, stress, exposure to toxins, and even maternal care have been shown to cause epigenetic changes influencing behavior and health outcomes.

The previously mentioned study of rat pups who received a high level of licking and grooming, and thus showing lower stress responses as adults, demonstrated the effect of epigenetic changes brought about by maternal care. Such findings highlight the profound effect of the environment on our genetic make-up and, consequently, our behavior. The dance between our genes and our environment is a complex tango, making our behaviors, decisions, and perceived free will a lot more defined than it appears.

Similarly. revisiting Neurobiology, the study of the nervous system and its functioning, gives us incredible insights into the biological basis of our behaviors. Our brain's structure and function, influenced by both our genes and our environment, can significantly sway our behaviors. For instance, the frontal lobe, particularly the prefrontal cortex, is crucial for decision-making and impulse control. Damage to or abnormal functioning of this area can lead to impaired judgment and risky behavior, as exemplified by the famous case of Phineas Gage, a railway worker who survived a severe brain injury.

While the roles of genetics and neurobiology in our behaviors are well-documented, the interconnectedness between the two subjects adds another layer of complexity to our understanding. Our genetic make-up shapes our brain's architecture, which in turn influences our behavior. Conversely, our experiences and behaviors can bring about changes in our brain's structure and function, demonstrating the dynamic interaction between genetics, neurobiology, and behavior.

To elaborate, consider neuroplasticity, the ability of the brain to change and adapt in response to experiences. Neuroplasticity underpins our capacity to learn and adapt. It is through changes in neural connections and pathways, prompted by experiences and learning, that we acquire new skills or modify our behaviors.

This dynamic changeability of the brain, directed by both our genes and our environment, leads us to the phenomenon of 'experience-dependent gene expression.' This means that certain genes become activated or deactivated based on our experiences, thus influencing our behavior and decision-making processes.

Having revisited genetics and neurobiology under the shadows of determinism, we must now re-question what it means for our perception of free will. If our genes and our brain can significantly sway our actions in a deterministic fashion, to what extent are we truly free in choosing our decision?

The deterministic perspective would argue that we are but puppets on the strings of our biology and environment, with our perceived autonomy being a mere illusion. This view, however, undermines the complexity of human behavior and the vast scope of individual variability. After all, if our behaviors were solely determined by our genes and brain, how could we account for the myriad of behaviors exhibited by individuals with similar genetic and neurobiological profiles?

The indeterministic or libertarian perspective, on the other hand, posits that our free will is not just an illusion; we do have genuine freedom to make choices, regardless of our genetic and neurobiological influences. However, this perspective also has its limitations, as it disregards the substantial evidence pointing to the biological influences on our behavior.

Perhaps the most reasonable stance lies somewhere in the middle, recognizing both the role of biological factors and the capacity for free choice. Our genes and our brain undoubtedly play a significant role in our behaviors and decisions. Yet, we are not mere puppets of our biology. Instead, our biology serves as a backdrop upon which we paint the unique picture of our behaviors and choices, exercising our free will within the boundaries set by our biological framework.

3.3 THE ENVIRONMENTAL IMPRINT: INVISIBLE CONSTRAINTS ON CHOICES

We have repeatedly underscored that human beings, in all their complexity, are an intriguing blend of biological and environmental influences. While we've dissected the impact of our genetic material on our choices, behaviors, and identity, the focus of this section lies on the equally significant influence our environment exerts on us. After exploring 'nature' – the genetic influence – we now turn our gaze towards 'nurture' – the environmental impact.

We often assume that our lives commence with birth – the moment we exit the womb and take our first breath. Yet, our existence starts much earlier, cocooned within the womb, a world within a world, where the rhythm of our mother's heartbeat is our first symphony, and her emotions our initial language.

The womb is our first environment, and it subtly shapes us. The placenta, once considered a perfect barrier, is now understood to be more of a semi-permeable membrane. It allows some substances - hormones, nutrients, drugs, and toxins - to cross its boundary, thereby offering the external environment a direct line to the developing fetus.

Pioneers in prenatal psychology have unveiled how these early experiences within the womb can influence our behaviors long after birth. Take, for example, the phenomenon of 'fetal programming.' This term refers to the idea that experiences in the womb can 'program' the development of the fetus in ways that have lasting effects on health and behavior.

For instance, consider maternal stress during pregnancy. When an expecting mother experiences significant stress, her body responds by releasing an abundance of stress hormones, notably cortisol. These hormones can cross the placental barrier, reaching the developing fetus. Even though the fetus isn't directly experiencing the stressful situation, it's still affected by the hormonal response it incites.

One study in this domain found a link between prenatal exposure to maternal stress and increased risk for attention deficit hyperactivity disorder (ADHD) in the child. Similarly, another research found a connection between prenatal stress exposure and heightened risk of developing anxiety or mood disorders in adolescence and adulthood. Similarly, stress hormones can also affect physical health, increasing the likelihood of cardiovascular disease in adulthood.

The influence of the womb as our first environment is a vivid demonstration of how the environment shapes us even before we are born. Moving beyond the womb, our environment continues to impact our behaviors, attitudes, and perceptions in ways we might not realize. In the words of Robert Sapolsky, our world is an "arena of layered influences." Environmental stimuli may dictate our behavioral responses without us recognizing these invisible constraints.

For instance, let's take the environmental context of poverty. A child growing up in a socio-economically disadvantaged neighborhood will likely be exposed to stressors such as violence, lack of educational resources, food insecurity, and more. These conditions shape the child's brain, leading to increased susceptibility to health issues, lower academic achievement, and potentially harmful behavior patterns.

Researchers call this the "neighborhood effect," illustrating how our environment shapes us. It's not just about personal choices or individual responsibility but also about societal structures and systemic issues that restrict opportunities and choices.

Another aspect is cultural conditioning, where societal norms and expectations dictate behaviors. Culture acts as an invisible puppeteer, guiding our actions, attitudes, and even the expression of our emotions. For instance, consider the cultural expectation for men to suppress their emotions. This cultural norm can lead to harmful consequences, such as increased aggression and decreased emotional literacy among men.

Through these examples, we see the profound and multifaceted impact of our environment on our behavior. While we like to believe in our autonomy, our choices and behaviors are often influenced, sometimes significantly, by the environmental constraints around us.

Apart from socio-cultural environments, another invisible environmental constraint shaping our behavior and health includes exposure to environmental toxins. Pollution, lead, and other harmful substances can have dramatic effects on our cognitive abilities, behaviors, and overall health.

Let's examine the infamous case of lead exposure. Lead is a neurotoxin that can cause severe cognitive impairments, behavioral issues, and physical health problems. Unfortunately, children living in older, poorly maintained homes or areas with high pollution are often at greater risk of lead exposure.

Lead pipes used in the water supply of older residential areas or lead-based paints, which can peel off and be ingested, are common sources of lead exposure in children. Even low levels of lead exposure can significantly affect IQ levels, attention span, and increase behavioral issues such as aggression.

This is not a choice these children or their parents have made, but rather a harmful constraint imposed by their environment. The impact can last a lifetime, affecting not just their health but also their ability to learn, succeed in school, and participate in society.

On a broader scale, pollution and climate change can also impact human behavior. Research is beginning to link increased pollution levels with mental health issues, cognitive decline, and increased aggression. Meanwhile, the stress and trauma of more frequent and severe weather events due to climate change can also have profound effects on mental health and community behaviors.

The invisible constraints of our environment, therefore, have significant implications on our health, behavior, and society at large. It underscores the necessity of considering these constraints in discussions about choice and human behavior.

Our behaviors are also molded by the built environment around us. This involves the physical layout of cities, neighborhoods, and buildings we occupy. A well-designed city can promote healthy behaviors such as walking or cycling, leading to better physical health, while a poorly planned city might lead to higher levels of stress, obesity, and related health problems.

Take, for instance, the city planning approach of some European cities like Copenhagen and Amsterdam. These cities are famed for their extensive and well-utilized cycling infrastructure. The design of these cities makes cycling a convenient, safe, and appealing option for transportation. As a result, many residents choose cycling over driving for daily commuting, which significantly contributes to higher levels of physical activity and lower rates of obesity.

In contrast, many urban areas, particularly in the U.S., are designed around the use of cars. Wide roads, spread-out amenities, and a lack of safe and convenient walking or cycling routes make it challenging for residents to opt for active transportation methods. Consequently, this can contribute to sedentary lifestyles, leading to higher rates of obesity and associated health issues.

These examples illustrate that our choices are often molded by the invisible constraints of our environment. We are more likely to engage in behaviors that our environment makes easy and less likely to engage in behaviors that our environment makes difficult.

This insight has important implications for how we think about promoting healthy behaviors. It's not just about individual willpower or motivation, but also about structuring environments in a way that makes healthy behaviors the default option.

3.4 The Evidence: Case Studies and Statistical Proof

Let us dive right into a peculiar study by Seymour Benzer and Ronald Konopka, stepping into the world of fruit flies. These two researchers set the stage for understanding the rhythmic behaviors in animals with their groundbreaking work on Drosophila melanogaster, commonly known as the fruit fly. This research, pioneering at the time, led to the discovery of the first "clock" gene.

This gene, named 'period', exhibited a controlling influence over the fly's circadian rhythm—a biological process that displays an endogenous, entrainable oscillation of about 24 hours. The fruit flies with a mutation in the 'period' gene had disrupted sleep-wake cycles, showcasing the profound effect of genetic determinants on behavior. Through the lens of behavioral genetics, this study offers an astounding glimpse into the genetic foundation of behavior and its dynamic mechanics even in relatively simpler organisms.

However, how does genetic influence translate to more complex organisms, such as humans? For this, we turn to the case of Phenylketonuria (PKU). This inherited disorder, characterized by an inability to metabolize phenylalanine, a common amino acid, has had a profound impact on our understanding of the coalition between genetics and behavior. If left untreated, PKU can lead to intellectual disability, seizures, behavioral problems, and mental disorders.

The discovery of the PKU condition sparked a revolution in newborn screening programs globally, leading to early dietary interventions that effectively mitigated the drastic behavioral and cognitive impacts of the condition. This is a classic example of genetic determinism buffered by environmental intervention, demonstrating the power of genetic insight for beneficial action.

For a more interactive case, consider the Mouse Party project from the Genetic Science Learning Center. This project vividly brings the perplexities of genetic and environmental influences in drug addiction to light.

In a typical Mouse Party scenario, different mice, genetically predisposed to various levels of drug susceptibility, are exposed to the same drug environment. The varied reactions underscore the role of genetic differences in addiction susceptibility, painting a picture of the complex genetic landscape that underlies individual responses to drugs. The Mouse Party project provides an easily understandable, yet profound, illustration of the role of genetics in compounded behaviors such as drug addiction.

Another case that illuminates the web of genetics, environment, and behavior is the Dunedin Multidisciplinary Health and Development Study. Conducted in New Zealand. This longitudinal research followed the lives of 1,037 individuals born between 1972-1973, right up until their mid-40s.

In one of the most significant findings, the researchers discovered a genetic variant of the MAOA gene, a gene involved in the breakdown of certain neurotransmitters. This variant was associated with a higher risk of developing antisocial behavior; but only if the individual had also experienced maltreatment during childhood. In this manner, the Dunedin Study served as a striking reminder of the interactive nature of genetics and environment in shaping behavior.

We also find a plethora of statistical evidence underlying the role of genetics and environment in behavior. For instance, twin studies have been a cornerstone in our understanding of the genetic basis of behavior. By comparing the similarity in behavior between identical (monozygotic) twins, who share 100% of their genes, and fraternal (dizygotic) twins, who share only about 50% of their segregating genes, researchers have been able to estimate the degree of genetic influence on a wide range of behaviors, including intelligence, personality traits, and various mental health conditions.

Moreover, adoption studies provide further evidence for genetic influences on behavior. By comparing adopted children with their biological and adoptive parents, researchers can disentangle the effects of genetics and environment. For example, if adopted children are more similar in behavior to their biological parents (who contribute their genes) than their adoptive parents (who provide their environment), this would suggest a strong genetic influence. This has indeed been the case for a range of behaviors, including IQ, reading disability, and rates of criminal convictions.

Simultaneously, these studies also highlight the role of the environment. For example, the increased risk of substance abuse in adopted individuals whose biological parents had substance use disorders was amplified if they were also raised in an environment with high familial stress.

The Colorado Adoption Project (CAP) lends itself as an invaluable resource. Conducted over a span of 20 years, this study collected a wealth of information on adopted children and their adoptive and biological parents. Interestingly, while the study found that, like previous adoption studies, adopted children resemble their biological parents more than their adoptive parents in IQ, it also highlighted the influence of the adoptive environment. For instance, the adoptive parents' socioeconomic status was found to significantly predict the adopted children's IQ scores in early childhood.

80

The CAP also demonstrated the dynamic nature of genetic and environmental influences over time. While the influence of the adoptive environment on IQ declined over time, the influence of genetics increased, a phenomenon known as the "Wilson Effect." This finding underscores that the relative influences of genetics and environment are not fixed but can change throughout an individual's life course.

Exploring specific behaviors, the Swedish Twin Registry, one of the largest twin registries in the world, has provided a trove of insights into the genetic and environmental underpinnings of alcohol use disorders. The researchers found substantial genetic influences on alcohol use disorders, but they also found that the individual's environment played a significant role. For instance, they found that individuals who were exposed to an environment that encouraged alcohol use were more likely to develop an alcohol use disorder, even if they had a lower genetic risk.

In the context of personality, the landmark Minnesota Study of Twins Reared Apart (MISTRA) presented astonishing findings that underscore the role of genetics. This study, which examined identical twins reared apart from early life, found a high degree of similarity in personality traits between the twins, suggesting a strong genetic influence. However, they also found that shared environmental factors played a significant role in shaping personality, once again demonstrating the strong ties between genetics and environment.

However, it's important to interpret these findings in light of the debate on free will. While these studies highlight the considerable influence of genetics and environment on our behaviors, they still do not negate the role of free will. Each of us is a unique combination of our genetic makeup and our life experiences, and this unique combination influences our propensity for certain behaviors. But propensity is not predestination. We are not simply puppets of our genes or our environment; instead, we actively interact with and shape our environment, and this process of interaction and shaping provides a space for free will.

Furthermore, our understanding of the nature of free will itself is evolving. We now understand that free will does not necessarily mean the freedom to act in any way imaginable but rather refers to the ability to act in line with our character and values, which are themselves shaped by our genetics and environment.

Consequently, while it's clear that our behaviors are deeply influenced by our genetics and environment, this does not exclude the possibility of free will. It merely compels us to reimagine what free will means in the context of these influential dynamics.

CHAPTER 4: THE ILLUSION OF FREE WILL: A HARSH REALITY?

Are we the authors of our own life, or are we merely living out a prewritten script? This question has teased the human mind for centuries, perhaps millennia, and now sits atop this book. The notion of free will, the idea that we are all free to make our own decisions independent of any external or internal influence, is deeply ingrained in our psyche. It fuels our perception of self, our moral and ethical judgments, and our sense of accountability. But is this freedom of choice real, or is it merely an illusion?

What if the choices we make, the decisions we think we consciously control, are not truly our own but are subtly guided by forces beyond our conscious awareness?

The concept of 'Fixed Action Patterns' (FAPs) in ethology provides a compelling argument against the notion of free will. Ethologists define FAPs as innate, stereotyped behavioral sequences that are triggered by very specific stimuli, known as sign stimuli or releasing stimuli. FAPs are exhibited by all individuals within a species, suggesting a genetic basis for these behaviors. They are invariant and follow through to completion, even if the original stimulus is removed.

One of the most striking examples of FAPs is the egg-retrieval behavior exhibited by the greylag goose, as studied by the

Austrian zoologist Konrad Lorenz. When a greylag goose notices that an egg has rolled out of her nest, she extends her neck toward the egg, uses the underside of her bill to pull it back into the nest, and then uses her body to roll the egg back under her. Remarkably, this behavior proceeds even when the egg is removed mid-retrieval.

Similarly, another study was conducted by Kinji Imanishi in 1952, where he observed cultural behavioral patterns in Japanese macaques. The FAP studied by Imanishi was potato washing, a behavior learned and subsequently passed down among generations of macaques.

Imanishi transported a group of macaques to Koshima Island and provided them with sweet potatoes that were covered in sand. One young female macaque, named Imo, discovered that she could wash the sand off the potatoes in a nearby stream before eating them. This action was significantly more efficient and enjoyable compared to the consumption of sandy potatoes.

What was particularly interesting about Imo's potato washing was that it qualified as a FAP because it entailed a series of unchangeable, coordinated behavioral actions that are triggered by a specific stimulus (in this case, the sandy potatoes). Once initiated, FAPs are usually carried through to completion, just like the greylag goose's egg-retrieval behavior.

Over time, other young macaques observed Imo's behavior and began to imitate it. Eventually, this behavior was adopted by older macaques too. Notably, the potato-washing behavior did not spread randomly across the macaque population. Instead, it was passed down socially, primarily from mother to offspring or between peers. This sequence of events suggests that the potato washing was a culturally transmitted behavior, a tradition within the macaque troop.

Imanishi's study is an excellent example of how FAPs can emerge and evolve within primate populations. While the initial behavior might arise as a creative solution to a problem, it can quickly become a standardized response within the community. This form of learning and transmission of behaviors demonstrates the fascinating layers of primate social structures and their capabilities for cultural transmission.

This inherent drive to complete the action, even in the absence of the initial trigger, challenges the notion of conscious decision-making. If a goose has no control over its instinct to retrieve an egg, or a macaque has no control over its 'potato-washing,' what about us? Could our behaviors also be similarly pre-programmed, guided by unseen strings?

If this is indeed the case, then looking back at Libet's experiment and his 'preconscious processing' in this context means that what we perceive as a conscious choice is essentially an illusion – a retroactive narrative we concoct to make sense of our actions.

These findings point to a more layered understanding, one that integrates both unconscious and conscious processes. As some have suggested, we may have the ability to veto our initial, unconscious decisions in a period before they are implemented – a concept referred to as 'free won't.' This view provides a potential reconciliation of our intuition of freedom with the deterministic nature of our brains.

Moreover, it is crucial to keep in mind that the existence of predetermined patterns of behavior and unconscious decision-making processes doesn't necessarily equate to fatalism, the belief that all events are predetermined and therefore inevitable. While our genetic makeup and environmental influences shape our preferences, biases, and tendencies, the outcome isn't necessarily fixed. We can think of ourselves as boats floating down a river. While the current (our genetic and environmental makeup) guides our direction, we still have the ability to steer the boat and influence our course within certain limits.

That being said, it is also essential to recognize the power of conscious thought in this grand scheme of things. Even though a considerable portion of our choices might be determined by unconscious processes, it does not imply that conscious thought is pointless or irrelevant. On the contrary, it plays a vital role in our lives. Conscious thought allows us to reflect on our actions, learn from our past experiences, plan for the future, and adapt to changing circumstances. This, in turn, can shape our unconscious biases, preferences, and tendencies.

One could argue that understanding the deterministic factors that influence our behavior could allow us to use our conscious thought to counteract these influences better. For instance, knowing that we have a genetic predisposition for certain unhealthy behaviors could lead us to make a conscious effort to avoid such behaviors.

Learning about this intersection between deterministic factors and free will makes it apparent that we can learn, adapt, and influence our own choices to a significant extent, carving our unique path in life, despite the deterministic shadows.

While Libet's experiment and its successors have significantly contributed to our understanding of the human mind, they are not without their share of criticisms. The primary concern revolves around the extent to which these laboratory-based tasks reflect real-world decision-making processes. Critics argue that the decisions made in these experiments are too simplistic and detached from our day-to-day experiences to meaningfully represent free will.

Another point of criticism is the interpretation of the readiness potential itself. Some researchers suggest that it might not signify a decision-making process, but instead, a buildup of brain activity that increases the likelihood of a particular action being taken. According to this view, the conscious decision to move happens independently, and the readiness potential simply reflects the brain's preparation for possible actions.

Furthermore, there are philosophical and ethical implications to consider. The consequences of a deterministic view of free will are profound and far-reaching, affecting everything from our personal sense of agency to our legal systems. To offer a balanced perspective, let's now explore everyday scenarios and how they might be influenced by both deterministic factors and free will.

Even considering the routine task of getting ready for our day in the morning shows us how mundane activities are filled with hundreds of little choices that we don't give a second thought to; from the moment we decide to get out of bed to our choice of clothes and breakfast and the route and means of transport we take to work. We've started to learn now that even though these appear to be conscious decisions guided by our free will on the surface, these decisions are influenced by a variety of deterministic factors.

The decision to get out of bed is largely dictated by our internal biological clock or circadian rhythm, which regulates sleep-wake cycles. The choice of what to wear might be influenced by the weather, the activities planned for the day, or societal expectations and norms. The food we eat for breakfast could be determined by our dietary habits, health concerns, and the availability of food items at home. The route and means of transport we take to work might be influenced by traffic conditions, roadworks, or our familiarity with the path.

All of these deterministic factors subtly guide our decisions without us consciously realizing it, illustrating how the invisible chains of determinism are woven into the fabric of our daily lives. Yet, within these constraints, we still exercise our agency. We decide when to rise within a range of acceptable times, choose our attire from the clothes available to us, select our breakfast from a set of dietary options, and choose our route within the available paths. This coalition between determinism and free will is a show that we partake in every day, one so seamless that we often overlook its existence.

Even when we think we are defying patterns, such as when we deliberately take a different route to work or choose a different breakfast, we are still operating within a deterministic framework. For instance, the decision to change our route could be sparked by a desire for novelty, which is itself a trait influenced by genetic and environmental factors. Similarly, the choice to have a different breakfast could be a reaction to a health report, a friend's suggestion, or a change in the availability of our regular food choice, all factors beyond our individual control.

On a broader scale, determinism can be seen in societal trends and behaviors. For example, economic factors like income levels and education significantly determine a person's lifestyle choices, including diet, exercise, and healthcare. This is not to say that individuals from lower-income households cannot make healthier choices, but that the available choices are significantly constrained by economic factors.

Moving away from the everyday, let's consider significant life decisions such as our career choices. These are also influenced by a combination of genetic predispositions, upbringing, educational opportunities, societal norms, and the prevailing economic conditions during our formative years. For example, a person born into a family of musicians is more likely to pursue music, not only because of potential genetic predispositions but also because of exposure to music from an early age and the availability of resources and opportunities to learn and practice music.

As we progress through our investigation of free will, it's vital to broaden our gaze and take into account some intriguing additional perspectives. The scientific community is an ever-evolving one, characterized by continuous questioning, investigation, and discovery. New findings can shift our understanding, introduce us to novel concepts, or even cast doubt on previously accepted ideas.

More recently, advances in neuroimaging techniques have allowed scientists to predict a person's decisions even before they are aware of them. For instance, a study published in 2008 by researchers at the Max Planck Institute for Human Cognitive and Brain Sciences showed that the outcome of a simple decision - whether to press a button with the left or right hand - could be predicted from brain activity up to ten seconds before the subject was aware of their decision. These and other studies indicate that what we perceive as a conscious, deliberate choice is often the end product of a series of unconscious brain processes, as originally depicted by the Libet experiment.

In 1994, the renowned British scientist Francis Crick, co-discoverer of the DNA molecule's structure, published 'The Astonishing Hypothesis.' The book boldly claimed that our joys, sorrows, memories, ambitions, and even our fragile sense of personal identity and free will are no more than the collective behavior of nerve cells and associated molecules. Crick's hypothesis attracted both admiration and outrage, paving the way for an unflinching exploration of free will's basis in the brain.

Shifting gears a bit, it's fascinating to revisit the case of Phineas Gage, a case that provides an interesting perspective on the brain's role in shaping our behavior and decisions. Gage, a 19th-century railroad worker, survived a severe brain injury when an iron rod accidentally impaled his skull. Miraculously, Gage was able to walk and talk immediately after the accident, but his personality underwent a dramatic transformation.

The formerly responsible and well-liked Gage turned into an impulsive and unreliable individual. The injury had damaged Gage's frontal lobes, specifically the prefrontal cortex, a brain area we now know is crucial for decision-making, impulse control, and social behavior. Gage's dramatic personality change post-injury provides a powerful reminder of our biology's potential to shape our choices and behaviors.

Further diving into the neuroscientific landscape, the split-brain experiments by Roger Sperry and Michael Gazzaniga have yielded some of the most startling insights into the nature of consciousness and free will. In patients with severe epilepsy, surgeons sometimes sever the corpus callosum, the band of nerve fibers connecting the two cerebral hemispheres, to prevent seizures from spreading across the brain. Studying such 'split-brain' patients, Sperry and Gazzaniga found that when the hemispheres can't communicate, they may develop separate conscious experiences. The patient's left hand (controlled by the right hemisphere) could perform a task the patient would claim ignorance of, suggesting that our unified sense of self, which seems to make choices freely, might be an illusion crafted by our brain.

Everything we've learned so far, reiterates and reinforces our initial question: If so much of our behavior is determined by factors beyond our control, where does that leave free will? Is there any room for genuine autonomy, or are we merely 'puppets' on the strings of our genes and environment?

Interestingly, even as we grapple with understanding the neuroscience of free will, psychology, the discipline that typically deals with concepts like will and decision-making, has been wrestling with a crisis of its own. The so-called 'reproducibility crisis' has cast a long shadow over many of psychology's most famous findings. In this crisis, researchers have found that many psychological studies' results, when repeated, do not produce the same findings.

A study attempting to replicate 100 psychological experiments found that over 60% did not yield the same results. This crisis extends to studies on free will. Some of the most critical experiments in the field, such as Libet's experiments, have been challenged on replicability grounds. These challenges to replicability remind us that science is a continual work in progress and that our understanding of free will remains provisional and subject to revision.

So, it's a difficult question, and one that has no easy answers. However, pursuing this question in itself could lead to a more nuanced understanding of freedom. One that recognizes the constraints imposed by our biology and environment but also appreciates the space within these constraints for choice and agency.

The fact that our behaviors are influenced by deterministic factors does not mean that we are merely passive observers in the theater of life. Even within the framework of determinism, there is room for agency - for actively shaping our destinies based on the options available to us. This view of free will may not align with the traditional concept of complete autonomy, but it reflects the complexity of human behavior and the multifaceted influences on our decisions and actions.

The concept of free will, then, may not be an illusion after all - but its nature is likely much more complex than we initially imagined.

CONCLUDING PART I

To get some context on the first part of our journey, let's look at Lily's life. Lily's evolutionarily hardwired instincts, such as her aversion to danger and drive to nourish herself, exemplify the guiding hand of natural selection. Her upbringing in a remote countryside and the genetic legacy passed down from her parents highlight the web of environmental factors and genetics in shaping her behavior. Her capacity for complex thought, which allows her to navigate the rigors of modern life with relative ease, exemplifies the degree of freedom that human cognition affords over other species.

The cognitive machinery of free will is visible every day in Lily's life. The interface of mind and brain is displayed in her decision-making processes, whether she's choosing what to wear, what to eat, or how to respond to a stressful situation at work. Both her conscious deliberations and unconscious impulses work in tandem to drive these decisions. Often, she's not even aware of these cognitive functions occurring beneath the surface of her conscious awareness.

However, the deterministic shadows on free will also loom over Lily. Her life is a testament to the predictability of deterministic patterns. Her genetics, predisposing her to a love for music and an aversion to mathematics, act as unseen puppeteers, orchestrating her choices from behind the scenes. The small rural town she grew up in has also left an imprint, influencing her preferences and behaviors in ways she's not always conscious of, such as the love for her local music.

Lastly, Lily's life invites us to confront the grand illusion of free will. From the outside, it appears that she enjoys absolute freedom of choice. Yet, when we dissect her decisions, we find them influenced by a multitude of factors, from her biology to her upbringing, forming the invisible chains of determinism. Lily, like all of us, is left at the confluence of these myriad forces, shaping her life and the decisions she makes.

Thus, by examining Lily's life through the lens of our exploration in Part I, we observe the concepts of evolution, cognition, determinism, and the illusion of free will come to life, shedding light on the forces that govern our perceived free will. Through her, we can see that we all embody the same trials and tribulations, freedoms and constraints, and rewards and punishments as of Lily. Every fragment of knowledge and understanding applicable on Lily is equally applicable on us.

PART II: THE NEUROBIOLOGY OF CHOICE

As we pivot from the philosophical and theoretical quandaries of free will, determinism, and choice in Part I, we delve into a more grounded and empirical territory in Part II. This section lifts the curtain on the fascinating world of neurobiology and its influence on the choices we make. This exploration underscores the interplay between our brains and the myriad of decisions we confront daily.

Within the realms of neuroscience, we unravel the mystery behind the complicated structures and processes that guide our decision-making. The knowledge acquired from this journey forms the foundation of our understanding of the brain as the command center of our bodies. While these biological phenomena seem distant from our immediate experiences, they carry the profound essence of our existence.

This part of the book seeks to elucidate how the labyrinth of neurons, neurotransmitters, and hormones govern our decisions, often subtly steering our choices without us realizing it. Through this lens, we shall discover that the concept of choice, as a biological phenomenon, isn't as simple as it seems.

CHAPTER 5: THE COMMAND CENTRE OF DECISION MAKING

Embedded within the confines of our skull, the brain, a three-pound universe of cells, holds sway over the decisions we make, the actions we perform, and ultimately, the lives we lead. Acting as the command center, it influences our choices more profoundly than we often realize.

This chapter peels back the layers of the human brain, revealing it not as a monolithic entity but a symphony of specialized regions and networks. From the silent communication between synapses to the interactions between emotions and reason, we shed light on the unseen forces shaping our decisions.

In the following sections, we will dive into the hotspots of decision-making within the brain, the silken web of neural networks that underpin our choices, the complex tango between emotions and decision-making, and the striking insights gleaned from imaging studies. This chapter seeks to impart a new appreciation for the biological marvel that is the brain and its central role in our decision-making process.

5.1 BRAIN REGIONS: THE DECISION MAKING HOTSPOTS

The brain is a fascinating universe of neurons, forming an intricate and unimaginably complex network. Each nook and cranny of this vast universe carries out unique functions, contributing to the many aspects of human consciousness, identity, behavior, and, most importantly, the decision-making process.

Overview of the Brain's Structure

Our brain, made up of two hemispheres, is laterally specialized. This lateralization of brain function means each hemisphere has skills the other does not. The left hemisphere, for example, typically specializes in language and logic, while the right hemisphere specializes in spatial tasks and visual imagery. The corpus callosum, a bundle of nerve fibers, bridges the two halves, allowing them to communicate and coordinate. This fundamental structure plays a crucial role in how we perceive the world and make decisions. We'll delve into this in detail later.

Prefrontal Cortex: The 'CEO' of the Brain

The prefrontal cortex, an extensive part of the brain located at the very front, is often referred to as the 'CEO' of the brain due to its critical role in complex cognitive behavior, decision-making, and social behavior. This is where our conscious decisions are made, our thoughts are organized, and our social behavior is regulated.

In the famous case of Phineas Gage, a railroad worker in the 19th century, an accident led to a metal rod passing through his skull, damaging his prefrontal cortex. Miraculously, Gage survived, but his personality underwent a dramatic shift. Once a responsible and capable foreman, Gage became impulsive, irresponsible, and socially inappropriate after the accident. His inability to make good decisions and stick to plans – a condition called dysexecutive syndrome – is often associated with damage to the prefrontal cortex, underlining the crucial role this region plays in decision-making.

Anterior Cingulate Cortex (ACC): The 'Error Detector'

The anterior cingulate cortex, located at the front of the corpus callosum, is heavily involved in the process of decision-making. One of the ACC's key functions is detecting when something is amiss, essentially serving as an 'error detector.' This capability plays a significant role in decision-making, particularly in situations that require conflict resolution.

A common method of observing the ACC's function is through a cognitive test known as the Stroop test. In this test, participants are asked to say the color of a word rather than reading the word itself (e.g., the word 'red' printed in blue ink). The ACC is crucial in helping resolve the cognitive conflict created by the discrepancy between the color and the word. Studies using functional magnetic resonance imaging (fMRI) have shown increased ACC activity in participants during the Stroop test, emphasizing its importance in conflict resolution.

Insula: Gut Feelings and Risky Decisions

The insula, a region of the cortex located deep within the brain, has a wide range of functions, but one of its most intriguing roles is in processing 'gut feelings' and guiding risky decisions. The insula integrates interoceptive signals, feelings originating within the body, into conscious feelings and into decision-making processes.

Research has shown that individuals with damage to the insula lose the ability to feel certain bodily sensations and are more likely to make risky decisions. For example, in a study led by Professor Antonio Damasio, patients with insular damage showed a marked increase in risky behavior in gambling tasks. This provides a fascinating insight into how our 'gut feelings' can play a fundamental role in guiding our decisions.

Temporoparietal Junction (TPJ): Empathy and Moral Judgments

The temporoparietal junction, located where the temporal and parietal lobes meet, is a critical region for social cognition and decision-making. The TPJ is thought to contribute to our ability to take on others' perspectives and to understand their mental states – a fundamental aspect of empathy.

Research involving moral dilemmas such as the famous 'Trolley Problem' has shown that the TPJ becomes particularly active when we're making moral decisions. The Trolley Problem is a hypothetical scenario where a runaway trolley is headed towards five people tied on the tracks. There's a lever that could divert the trolley onto another track where only one person is tied. The moral dilemma is whether it's right to intervene and cause one person's death but save five. fMRI studies have shown that the TPJ is involved in evaluating the beliefs and intentions of others in such scenarios, thus influencing the decisions we make.

Basal Ganglia: The Seat of Habit and Reward

Deep within the brain lie the basal ganglia, clusters of neurons primarily involved in reward-based learning, habit formation, and the initiation of voluntary movement. The basal ganglia have a significant influence on decision-making, particularly decisions related to seeking pleasure or reward.

Studies involving dopamine, a neurotransmitter heavily involved in the brain's reward system, have revealed that it's predominantly released in the basal ganglia. This process occurs whenever we experience something pleasurable or rewarding. Over time, as certain behaviors are consistently rewarded, they can become habitual - a testament to the role of the basal ganglia in decision-making. A clear example can be seen in addiction studies, where repeated rewarding experiences (like the pleasure from consuming drugs) lead to habit formation and compulsive behavior.

Amygdala: The Emotional Decision-Maker

The almond-shaped structure in our brains, known as the amygdala, is integral to emotional processing. It plays a significant role in generating and regulating emotions, especially those related to fear and aggression. Furthermore, it's involved in the formation and retrieval of emotional memories, which considerably influence our decisions.

One famous example is the case of S.M., a woman with Urbach-Wiethe disease leading to the calcification of her amygdala. As a result, she became unable to experience fear, even in situations that would typically be perceived as threatening. This rare case underscores the critical role the amygdala plays in our emotional responses and, subsequently, our decision-making processes.

Hippocampus: The Memory Keeper

The hippocampus, a small, seahorse-shaped structure deep within the brain, is critical for memory formation and spatial navigation. The memories it helps form - particularly episodic memories - significantly influence our decision-making processes.

This region's importance was highlighted in the case of patient H.M., who had parts of his hippocampus removed to control severe epilepsy. The surgery was successful in reducing his seizures but left him unable to form new episodic memories, severely impairing his ability to make decisions based on recent experiences.

Ventral Striatum: The Reward Evaluator

Part of the basal ganglia, the ventral striatum (including the nucleus accumbens) plays a critical role in reward evaluation, a key aspect of decision-making. It's primarily involved in the anticipation of reward, using this anticipation to guide behavior and decision-making.

A wealth of research has shown that the ventral striatum becomes particularly active when individuals expect a reward. Interestingly, this activity seems to reflect not only the magnitude of the expected reward but also the uncertainty surrounding it, suggesting that this area might also be involved in decision-making under conditions of uncertainty.

In sum, the brain's decision-making hotspots form a network of complex interactions, each contributing uniquely to the choices we make. Our brain, indeed, is the command center of decision making.

5.2 Neural Networks: The Intricate Web of Choices

The human brain, a maze of approximately 86 billion neurons, interconnected by trillions of synapses, is the command center that orchestrates all our decisions. As we delve deeper into understanding the brain's structure, it becomes evident that it's not just the discrete regions, but also the complex networks of neurons, that hold the key to our decision-making processes.

A neural network is a series of interconnected neurons that create a communication pathway for information to flow. It's much like a busy highway system where messages travel from one part of the brain to another, forming the basis of our thoughts, emotions, behaviors, and crucially, our choices.

One such influential neural network resides within the prefrontal cortex, an area involved in planning complex cognitive behavior, personality expression, decision-making, and moderating social behavior. The basic activity of this brain region is considered to be the orchestration of thoughts and actions in accordance with internal goals. When you're deciding whether to have an apple or a doughnut for breakfast, it's your prefrontal cortex that weighs the health benefits of the apple against the sugary allure of the doughnut.

Next, we journey into the brain's emotional powerhouse: the limbic system. This network, comprising structures such as the amygdala, hippocampus, and cingulate gyrus, is where our emotions and memories lie. The limbic system plays a critical role in emotional decision-making, triggering responses such as happiness, fear, or anger that can dramatically influence our choices.

The brain's reward system, driven by dopaminergic pathways—specifically, the mesolimbic and mesocortical pathways—is another key player in decision-making. These pathways are activated when we engage in activities that promote survival (like eating) or during rewarding experiences (such as social interaction), hence heavily influencing our decisions related to these activities.

Lastly, the default mode network, including regions like the medial prefrontal cortex and posterior cingulate cortex, is essential in decision-making. This network is active when the brain is at wakeful rest, not focusing on the outside world, and is involved in self-referential thinking—a form of introspective analysis that greatly influences our choices.

One of the hallmarks of neural networks is their plasticity: the ability to change and adapt in response to new experiences, including our decisions. Just as a river can carve a canyon over time, our decisions—our repeated thoughts and actions—can shape our neural networks. For instance, continually choosing to learn a new instrument can strengthen the neural connections associated with musical skill.

Inversely, maladaptive changes in these networks can influence our choices and behavior, often leading to neuropsychiatric conditions. Depression, anxiety, addiction—these are all examples of what can happen when these intricate networks are disrupted, leading to an impaired ability to make healthful decisions.

The future of decision-making research lies in further untangling these complex neural networks. Cutting-edge technologies like functional magnetic resonance imaging (fMRI) and transcranial magnetic stimulation (TMS) are providing novel insights into these networks and how they influence our choices.

Research has played a significant role in our understanding of these networks. A study using neuroimaging techniques found that during a decision-making task, both the prefrontal cortex and limbic system were activated, demonstrating their role in decision-making processes.

Additionally, therapeutic interventions like deep brain stimulation (DBS), which targets specific neural networks, have provided unique insights into the role of these networks in decision-making. For example, DBS of the subthalamic nucleus—a part of the brain's reward system—has been found to influence decision-making in patients with Parkinson's disease.

Our understanding of decision-making is incomplete without considering the vast, interconnected highways of the brain's neural networks. As we map these narrow pathways, we edge closer to understanding how we make the choices that define our lives. This understanding holds promise not only for illuminating the mystery of decision-making but also for refining treatments for neuropsychiatric conditions that impact the capacity to make choices.

The journey into the realm of neural networks is an exciting venture. And as we continue to chart the course of these neural highways, we remain hopeful of uncovering even more intricate details about how our brain makes decisions.

5.3 EMOTIONS AND DECISION MAKING: A COMPLEX TANGO

The human brain, a complex and elaborate network of neurons, is often likened to an orchestra. If so, emotions are the symphony it performs, a stirring harmony that influences every decision we make. Every crescendo and diminuendo, every grandioso and pianissimo, is a reflection of the brain's emotional state influencing our choices and, ultimately, the notion of free will.

Before we delve into the depths of this intriguing saga, it's crucial to understand the driver of this serene performance - the limbic system. The limbic system, a collection of brain structures located on both sides of the thalamus, right under the cerebrum, is considered the emotional processing hub of the brain. It's a complex system of networks and nerves that controls basic emotions (fear, pleasure, anger) and drives (hunger, sex, dominance, care of offspring).

Each structure in the limbic system plays a unique role in managing our emotions. The amygdala, for instance, triggers the emotional responses associated with memory, such as the heart-pounding fear remembered from a near-miss accident. The hippocampus, on the other hand, is associated with forming these emotion-laden memories. Meanwhile, the hypothalamus is crucial in activating the 'fight or flight' response, a clear testament to how deeply our survival instincts are wired into our emotional responses.

Delving deeper, we encounter the cingulate gyrus that regulates aggressive behavior and the septal nuclei, often referred to as the brain's 'pleasure center', that influences our choices by creating feelings of pleasure and reward. If these structures get damaged, as observed in many neurological disorders, it severely impacts emotional processing and, by extension, our ability to make independent, rational decisions.

Let's consider a real-world example. Imagine walking down a lonely road late at night. Suddenly, a dark silhouette emerges from the shadows, and your heart rate quickens, your palms get sweaty – classic signs of fear. This emotional response isn't a conscious choice but an instinctual survival mechanism, a performance choreographed by your limbic system.

This example also introduces an interesting aspect - the influence of past experiences on our emotional responses. If you've been mugged before, your reaction might be more extreme than someone who hasn't had such a traumatic experience. Such fear and trauma-based responses demonstrate that even our emotions, seemingly impulsive, are subjected to the influence of past experiences and learned behaviors.

The discussion brings us to a vital point - while we may believe ourselves to be rational beings, making conscious decisions, our choices are often a complex tango between our emotional brain and our cognitive brain. Now we dive into the role of specific emotions, from happiness to fear, sadness to surprise and aggression, and how they steer our decisions, often without us even realizing it.

We start with aggression, a potent and primordial emotion, which plays a compelling role in the human decision-making process. Aggression is not just a primitive instinct but also a complex behavior pattern influenced by a myriad of factors within our brain.

The amygdala, a part of the limbic system mentioned earlier, plays a critical role in triggering aggressive responses. Animal studies have shown that when the amygdala is artificially stimulated, it can elicit aggressive behavior. In contrast, lesions or damage to the amygdala can lead to reduced aggression, illustrating the amygdala's crucial role in modulating aggressive behaviors.

Consider a scenario where someone cuts in front of you in a queue. Your immediate reaction might be to voice your anger aggressively. This is your amygdala in action, prompting you with an emotional response. However, the choice you make next, to confront the person or let it go, is a back and forth between your amygdala and your prefrontal cortex, the rational decision-making part of your brain.

The prefrontal cortex acts as a modulator of our emotional responses. It is the conductor of our brain's symphony, regulating and restraining the emotional outbursts from the amygdala. Damage to the prefrontal cortex, as seen in the famous case of Phineas Gage, can lead to an inability to control aggressive impulses, resulting in socially inappropriate behavior.

However, the relationship between aggression, emotion, and decision-making is not a one-way street. Higher cognitive processes, including conscious decision-making, can also influence our emotional state and aggressive responses. In essence, our free will and conscious choices can also affect our emotional responses and, by extension, our aggression levels.

While the neurobiology of aggression is still a rapidly evolving field, what we do understand is that aggression is not merely a base instinct but a complex interplay of various brain regions, neurotransmitters, hormones, and our past experiences. And this intricate dance has profound implications on our understanding of free will.

The correspondence of emotions and decision-making goes beyond just aggression. Other emotions, such as fear, happiness, sadness, and surprise, also play crucial roles in shaping our choices. Each emotion carries a distinct signature in the neural activity, contributing uniquely to our decision-making processes.

Let's take fear as an example. Fear is another emotion that is closely tied to the amygdala. When we encounter a threatening situation, our amygdala springs into action, releasing a flood of stress hormones that prepare our body for a "fight or flight" response. This emotional reaction can influence our decisions, often making us choose safety and risk aversion.

However, just like with aggression, our prefrontal cortex can step in and modulate our fear response. It can evaluate the actual risk involved, and if it deems the threat to be less significant than our initial fear response suggested, it can suppress the amygdala's output, calming our fear and enabling us to make a more rational decision.

Similarly, happiness and sadness can also sway our decisions. Several studies have shown that our emotional state at the time of decision-making can bias our choices. For example, when we are happy, we are more likely to make optimistic choices, underestimating risks. On the other hand, when we are sad, we tend to be more cautious and risk-averse.

Further into this dance, we come across surprise - an emotion that instantly draws our attention and can significantly influence our decisions. The anterior cingulate cortex (ACC) and the orbitofrontal cortex (OFC) are key players in the processing of surprise or unexpected events. If an event deviates from our predictions, these brain regions kick in, indicating a need to update our understanding and adjust our decision-making strategy accordingly.

For example, suppose you decide to take a particular route to work based on your previous experiences of it being the fastest. One day, you encounter an unexpected traffic jam on this route that makes you late. The surprise you experience due to this unexpected event would activate your ACC and OFC, signaling a need to reconsider your decision next time.

Another area where emotions intermingle with decision-making is in moral judgments and decisions. Neuroimaging studies have shown that when we make moral decisions, there is an interplay between our emotional responses, governed by the amygdala, and cognitive processing in areas such as the dorsolateral prefrontal cortex. For example, when faced with a moral dilemma, such as whether to lie to protect a friend, our emotional reaction towards lying may clash with our rational calculation of the potential benefits of protecting the friend. The decision we ultimately make depends on the complex interaction between these emotional and cognitive processes.

In essence, our emotions don't just color our world with feelings; they play a fundamental role in shaping our choices and guiding our actions. They interact with our cognitive processes, with the result of this interaction steering the wheel of our decision-making. However, we must remember that we are not merely puppets to our emotions and the influence of emotions on our choices is not a sign of our decisions being 'unfree' or determined. Instead, it reflects the complexity of our decision-making processes, where various factors, including our emotions, cognitive processes, and environmental factors, interweave to guide our choices.

Yes, our emotional state can influence our decisions, but it's not the sole driver of our choices. Our consciousness, our reasoning abilities, our values, and beliefs all interact with our emotions to guide our decisions. So while our emotions are an important piece of the puzzle, they are just that - one piece in the delicate balance of human decision-making.

In the next section, we will delve deeper into the underlying neural activity and explore how neuroimaging studies have offered insights into this world of decision-making. It's fascinating to realize that our decisions, which we often believe are the products of our conscious, rational thinking, are subtly and continuously influenced by our emotional states. It raises a compelling question - how much of our choices are truly "free," and how much are they swayed by the tides of our emotions?

5.4 THE NEURAL ACTIVITY: INSIGHTS FROM IMAGING STUDIES

Welcome to the world of neuroscience, where the electrified pathways of the brain are no longer a mystery, thanks to the advancements in neuroimaging techniques. Neuroimaging, as the term suggests, enables us to image or visualize the structure and functionality of our brains in a non-invasive manner. These techniques are much like the periscope of a submarine, giving neuroscientists a peek into the unfathomable depths of our neural circuits. But why is it important for us to understand the technology behind neuroimaging? Simply put, it's the lens that has brought us face-to-face with the otherwise invisible cognitive processes that determine our decisions and, in extension, our sense of free will.

As we embark on this exploration of neuroimaging's role in decision-making research, it's crucial to remember that we're dealing with an observable phenomenon, not mere theoretical conjecture. It is a testament to the fact that neuroscience is as grounded in reality as any other empirical science. Now, let's take a look at how neuroimaging helps us decode the decision-making process.

Functional Magnetic Resonance Imaging (fMRI)

This technique provides a dynamic view of the brain at work by measuring changes in blood flow to different regions. A landmark study by Soon et al. (2008) utilized fMRI to predict a subject's decision before they were consciously aware of making it. By observing the prefrontal and parietal cortex, researchers could determine up to 10 seconds in advance whether a subject would press a button with their left or right hand. This not only contributes to the debate around free will, but it also demonstrates the efficacy of neuroimaging in capturing the decision-making process in action.

Positron Emission Tomography (PET)

PET scans measure metabolic activity in different brain regions by detecting the radiation emitted by a small amount of radioactive material injected into the body. They provide valuable insights into the biochemical processes associated with decision-making.

Electroencephalography (EEG)

EEG measures electrical activity in the brain, offering a high temporal resolution which is essential to understand the rapid processes involved in decision-making. Studies using EEG have shown that neural markers, such as the readiness potential, can predict decisions even before individuals report being aware of making them. It played a central role in the Libet study.

Magnetoencephalography (MEG)

MEG measures the magnetic fields produced by neuronal electrical currents, offering insights into the fast-paced dynamics of neural networks. Researchers using MEG have also studied the timing of decision-making processes and the regions involved, contributing to our growing understanding of the complex interplay between brain regions during decision making.

Diffusion Tensor Imaging (DTI)

This technique visualizes white matter tracts – the brain's communication highways that connect different regions. DTI studies have shed light on how the efficiency of these connections can impact decision-making abilities, such as the speed and accuracy of decisions.

Relevance of Neuroimaging Studies to Our Understanding of Free Will

Beyond the empirical data these tools provide, their real value lies in the larger context of our quest to understand free will. Each study serves as a tangible checkpoint in the journey, further unraveling the interplay of factors involved in decision-making. The implications of these studies are profound. They not only challenge our traditional understanding of free will but also encourage us to redefine it in light of new scientific evidence.

Moreover, understanding the technology and methodology behind these studies promotes informed skepticism. It's easy to be swayed by the authoritative voice of "science says," but having an appreciation for how these conclusions are reached fosters critical thinking. We are, after all, not just passive consumers of knowledge but active participants in the process of understanding ourselves.

While we can observe activity and patterns, deciphering what these activations mean in terms of our subjective experience, consciousness, or the concept of free will requires careful interpretation. The brain is not a simple input-output machine, and while we can observe activity and patterns, the interpretation of this data requires caution. Neuroimaging provides us a map of the active areas of the brain, but it doesn't give us a definitive answer on what these activations mean in terms of our subjective experience, consciousness, or the concept of free will.

Moreover, the question of free will is not just a scientific or philosophical conundrum; it's deeply personal and shapes our understanding of ourselves and our interactions with the world. The results of these neuroimaging studies, while fascinating, should not detract from our lived experiences. Instead, they should serve as tools for inquiry, challenging us to question, understand, and perhaps even redefine our notion of free will.

And so, despite the profound insights garnered from these neuroimaging techniques, we stand at the edge of a vast expanse of the unknown. What we have learned is a mere ripple in the ocean of the brain's complexities. The brain is not a simple input-output machine. It's a dynamic, self-organizing system where the whole is far greater than the sum of its parts. This complexity presents significant challenges in our quest to fully understand decision-making and the nature of free will.

The understanding of free will through the lens of neuroscience is an exciting frontier, teetering on the border between philosophy and empirical science. Every new study, every data point, every image of the active brain, adds another piece to the complex puzzle of human decision-making. Yet, much of the picture remains concealed, awaiting discovery. As our neuroimaging techniques become more refined and our analyses more nuanced, we look forward to illuminating more of this hidden landscape and, in the process, deepening our understanding of ourselves.

While we revel in the advancements of neuroimaging techniques, it's crucial to tread with informed skepticism. After all, in science, as in life, it's not just the destination but the journey that matters. In the pursuit of understanding free will, we are not merely passengers but active participants, charting the course through the intriguing maze of the human mind.

Chapter 6: Neurotransmitters and Hormones

As we delve deeper into the unseen mechanics of choice and decision-making, we encounter a world teeming with complex biological interactions. These interactions, happening within the confines of our nervous system, set the stage for our perceptions, emotions, thoughts, and ultimately, our actions. Among these myriad interactions, a special role is played by the chemical messengers of our body: the neurotransmitters and hormones.

Each choice we make, each decision we ponder upon, and each thought that forms in our mind, is the end result of a series of precise chemical interactions. Like skilled linguists translating thoughts into actions, neurotransmitters relay messages between neurons, turning electrical signals into chemical ones, shaping the language of the brain.

Meanwhile, hormones, the silent influencers, maintain a steady undercurrent, shaping our decisions subtly yet significantly. Originating from various glands in our bodies, these hormones have profound effects on our mood, energy levels, and risk-taking tendencies, all of which feed into the choices we make.

In this chapter, we will dive deeper into these essential biological messengers and their indispensable roles in our decision-making processes. Through this exploration, we hope to illuminate the vast connections that link our biology to our behavior, our chemicals to our choices.

6.1 NEUROTRANSMITTERS: THE MIND'S LINGUISTS

Every day, billions of neurons in our brain are in a non-stop chatter, transmitting and receiving signals that govern our every thought, emotion, and behavior. At the heart of this communication network are chemicals known as neurotransmitters, the brain's linguistic maestros.

Imagine being at a busy airport, where a multitude of languages fill the air. Some travelers are rushing to catch a flight, while others wait patiently, huddled in their seats. The loudspeaker announces arrivals and departures, each call setting people into motion. Now, replace the travelers with neurons, and the announcements with neurotransmitters, and you have a simplified snapshot of the workings of our brain.

Just like the distinct languages spoken at an airport convey different messages, different neurotransmitters have their unique effects on the neurons they interact with. They can instruct a neuron to fire a signal, prevent it from doing so, or change its overall excitability. They do so by fitting into special proteins on the neuron's surface, known as receptors, like a key fitting into a lock. This is the fundamental process that underpins everything our brain does, from the most mundane task to the most profound thought.

Our brains have many neurotransmitters, but let's focus on the major players: Dopamine, Serotonin, GABA, Glutamate, and Norepinephrine. Each of these has a distinct influence on our mood, cognition, and decision-making processes.

Dopamine: The Reward Seeker

Dopamine is often labeled as the "pleasure chemical," but that's a bit of a misnomer. Dopamine is more about seeking rewards rather than enjoying them. Picture dopamine as the excitable friend who loves the thrill of a treasure hunt, more than the treasure itself. This neurotransmitter motivates us to pursue actions that might yield rewards, driving behaviors such as learning, exploration, and making choices.

Serotonin: The Mood Regulato

Serotonin, in contrast, is like the soothing voice of reason. It influences our mood, helping to keep negative feelings at bay, and impacts impulse control and social behavior. Its role in moderating our emotional states underpins its influence on our decision-making processes, especially under conditions of stress or uncertainty.

GABA and Glutamate: The Balancers

GABA (gamma-aminobutyric acid) and Glutamate maintain a delicate balance within the brain. Think of them as the conductor of an orchestra, ensuring each instrument plays in harmony. GABA is the primary inhibitory neurotransmitter, acting like a brake to prevent neurons from firing too much. Glutamate, on the other hand, is the primary excitatory neurotransmitter, pushing neurons to fire. This delicate balance orchestrates the symphony of our thoughts and decisions.

Norepinephrine: The Alertness Enhancer

Norepinephrine is the brain's sentinel, governing arousal, alertness, and our fight-or-flight response. It is like an alarm system, preparing the body to react to perceived threats or opportunities.

The Dance of Neurotransmitters: Interactions, Influence and Free Will

The fascinating world of neurotransmitters weaves an intricate tapestry of neurochemical interactions that influence our behavior and decision-making processes. They don't operate in isolation but instead perform a delicate tango, each one influencing and being influenced by others, in a complex system that shapes our thoughts, emotions, and decisions.

For instance, let's take the experience of deciding to have a coffee in the morning. It appears to be a simple, conscious decision – you like coffee, and you choose to have one. However, beneath this straightforward decision is a sophisticated neurochemical ballet.

The desire for the reward of the coffee's taste and the energy boost it provides stimulates dopamine production, pushing you towards that decision. Dopamine could be likened to an enthusiastic friend nudging you towards the coffee shop, exciting you about the impending reward.

The role of norepinephrine, the alertness enhancer, in this situation is twofold. First, it may be that you didn't sleep well last night. The lower alertness signals your brain to release more norepinephrine to compensate. Second, the anticipation of caffeine, which you know will increase alertness, further stimulates the production of norepinephrine.

Simultaneously, serotonin, the mood regulator, is at work. A decrease in serotonin levels could leave you feeling somewhat down, making that cup of coffee, with its rewarding properties, seem even more appealing.

Finally, GABA and Glutamate, the balancers of the brain, are maintaining a delicate equilibrium. Glutamate is increasing activity in the neurons associated with decision-making and reward anticipation, while GABA is moderating the activity to prevent overexcitation.

So, the simple decision to grab a coffee is, in fact, the culmination of a complex interplay between neurotransmitters, each nudging you towards that choice in its unique way.

This interplay between neurotransmitters casts our understanding of free will in a new light. The seemingly straightforward decisions we make each day are the result of these chemical charades. So, while we may feel we're exerting conscious control over our decisions, our neurotransmitters have a significant influence.

This doesn't negate the concept of free will, but rather broadens our understanding of it. It shows that our decisions are not solely the product of conscious thought, but also the result of complex neurochemical processes. It's a humbling reminder that our conscious selves are only a part of the decision-making story.

6.2 HORMONES: SILENT INFLUENCERS OF DECISIONS

Hormones: they're like the subtle background music in a movie, guiding the narrative without ever becoming the main focus. Just as a movie's score manipulates our emotions, setting the scene for joy, sadness, fear, or anticipation, hormones quietly dictate the state of our bodies and, consequently, our minds.

Neurotransmitters might take center stage when it comes to communication within the brain, but the hormones, secreted by various glands throughout our body, exert their influence more quietly and subtly. Transported through the bloodstream, they reach every nook and cranny of our bodies, bringing about changes that can profoundly influence our decisions. Let's acquaint ourselves with the key characters of this hormonal narrative:

Cortisol

Often termed the "stress hormone," cortisol acts like an alarm system in your body. It is released in response to stress and low blood-glucose concentration. While we usually think of stress as something negative, cortisol plays an important role in helping us respond to danger. But just like an alarm that won't turn off, chronic stress (and consequently, persistent high levels of cortisol) can be damaging.

Oxytocin

Known as the "love hormone" or "cuddle hormone," oxytocin plays a crucial role in bonding, social interaction, and childbirth. Its levels increase during hugging and orgasms, reinforcing relationships and generating feelings of contentment.

Testosterone

Testosterone is often associated with aggression and competition. Although it is considered a male hormone, it exists in both genders, affecting our mood, sexual desire, and physical health. In the context of decision-making, it's been linked with risk-taking behaviors.

Estrogen

This group of hormones, which includes estradiol, plays a vital role in mood regulation. Apart from their central role in sexual and reproductive development, particularly in women, estrogen levels also have a significant impact on the brain and can influence mood and cognition.

Hormones and Decision-Making

While the influence of hormones on physical processes is relatively well-known, their impact on our mental states and decision-making is less understood. The reach of hormones extends far beyond the regulation of metabolism, immune response, or even sex. They subtly tweak our moods and attitudes, modulate our perceptions and biases, and shape our decisions, often without us having any awareness of their influence.

The impact of hormones on our decisions operates on several levels. For example, cortisol, the stress hormone, can make us more risk-averse when it comes to financial decisions. A study found that participants with higher cortisol levels were less willing to take risks in a game that simulated financial decisions.

Testosterone, on the other hand, has been associated with increased risk-taking, assertiveness, and competitiveness – characteristics that can profoundly influence the decisions one makes, particularly in social and competitive contexts. A study involving a single-dose administration of testosterone to women found that they were more likely to take risks in a computer simulation designed to mimic real-life decision-making.

Oxytocin, the bonding hormone, can make us more trusting and generous in our decisions, particularly in social contexts. Researchers have found that when participants are given a dose of oxytocin, they're more likely to display trust in a game where they have to decide how much money to give to a stranger.

Similarly, estrogen's impact on cognition can influence decisions in various ways. For instance, fluctuating levels of estrogen across the menstrual cycle in women have been associated with changes in certain cognitive abilities, such as verbal memory and executive function, that could influence decision-making.

Let's dig deeper into these hormonal influences. Consider a business meeting or negotiation setting. A male executive, under the influence of heightened testosterone levels, might make assertive, competitive decisions to establish dominance and secure a deal. In contrast, an executive under the influence of elevated cortisol levels due to stress might play it safe, preferring to avoid risky proposals. Meanwhile, a negotiator with increased oxytocin levels might be more likely to foster collaboration, build trust, and seek mutually beneficial agreements.

The implications of these hormonal influences can also be seen in everyday scenarios. For instance, a student under stress during exams, with high cortisol levels, might prefer to stick to safer, well-studied topics rather than take a risk on a question that might yield more marks but is less familiar. Or, a person who just finished a workout and has an endorphin rush might make more optimistic decisions, such as deciding to take on a challenging project or making a big investment.

Estrogen and progesterone, two hormones that fluctuate across the menstrual cycle in women, can also influence decisions. Research has shown that during the high-estrogen phase of the cycle, women might be more inclined to make social decisions, like spending time with friends or attending social events. In contrast, during the high-progesterone phase, when the body prepares for a potential pregnancy, decisions might lean more towards personal safety and resource conservation.

Moreover, hormonal influences on decision-making can have long-term impacts on our lives. The decisions we make under the influence of these hormonal states can lead to the formation of habits, which can, in turn, shape our future behavior and decision-making tendencies. Hence, these silent influencers are silently steering the ship of our decisions in directions that we might not always consciously comprehend.

6.3 FROM CHEMICALS TO CHOICES: CONNECTING THE DOTS

In this journey of exploring the complex world of decision making, we have delved into various areas of neuroscience and psychology, unveiling the nuanced characteristics of neural activity, hormones, and neurotransmitters. These biochemical entities weave together to form the tapestry of our decisions, beliefs, and ultimately, our perception of free will. In this section, we aim to illustrate this interplay by piecing together the knowledge we have gathered so far, highlighting how these elements interact to shape our choices.

Dopamine, serotonin, cortisol, and oxytocin are some of the key players in this complex drama. Dopamine, often touted as the "reward" neurotransmitter, plays a crucial role in our decision-making processes. It motivates us to seek pleasure and avoid pain, creating a reinforcing loop of reward-seeking behavior. It's the driving force behind our cravings, from the benign desire for a chocolate chip cookie to the destructive pull of addictive substances.

On the other hand, serotonin serves as the mood stabilizer, helping us maintain a balanced emotional state. Low levels of this neurotransmitter have been linked to impulsive behavior and aggressive tendencies. Serotonin helps us regulate our emotional responses, ensuring that our decisions aren't entirely hijacked by transient emotional states.

Cortisol, the "stress" hormone, sets off alarm bells in our bodies, priming us for action. It sharpens our focus, boosts our energy, and heightens our vigilance – all beneficial effects in a life-threatening situation. However, when this alarm system is chronically activated, it can cloud our judgment and skew our decision-making processes.

Then, there's oxytocin, often called the "love" hormone. Oxytocin helps us bond with others, fostering trust and promoting social cooperation. This hormone nudges us to make decisions that strengthen social connections, even when it may not be in our immediate self-interest.

While each of these actors has its unique role, they don't operate in isolation. They're engaged in complex mechanisms, influencing, and being influenced by each other. This interplay happens not only within an individual but also across individuals within a social group. For instance, the release of oxytocin in one person can trigger a similar response in others, promoting a shared emotional experience and coordinated behavior.

To illustrate this interplay, let's consider the case of John, a middle-aged software engineer. We'll follow John through a typical day, highlighting the different situations he encounters and the decisions he makes. We'll map these scenarios onto the neurochemical landscape we've discussed, connecting the dots between the balance of neurotransmitters and hormones and the choices he makes.

John wakes up to the sound of his alarm clock. His heart rate increases and his body floods with cortisol, shifting him from the calm state of sleep to the alertness required for the day ahead. As he groggily moves out of bed and towards the kitchen, his brain begins to anticipate the hit of caffeine that his daily cup of coffee provides. This anticipation causes the release of dopamine, the neurotransmitter responsible for motivation and reward.

His first decision of the day arrives: should he have a healthy breakfast of fruits and oatmeal, or should he give in to his craving for a sugary donut? His prefrontal cortex, the rational part of his brain, nudges him towards the healthier choice, recognizing its long-term benefits. However, the dopamine-driven reward system, craving the immediate pleasure of the donut, creates a conflict.

The interplay of these two systems – the short-term reward system and the long-term decision-making system – reflects the dual-process theory of decision-making we discussed in Chapter 4. John manages to resist the temptation of the donut, a decision made possible by a well-functioning prefrontal cortex and stable serotonin levels that help regulate his mood and suppress impulsive behavior.

As John begins his workday, he faces a multitude of decisions. Each one – whether it's solving a coding problem, responding to an email, or planning a project timeline – involves a wide berth of neurochemical activity. For instance, when faced with a particularly challenging problem, his body might release cortisol, heightening his focus. As he successfully resolves the issue, his brain rewards him with a hit of dopamine, reinforcing his problem-solving behavior.

Midway through his day, John experiences a moment of frustration when a coworker fails to meet a project deadline. His initial reaction is one of anger – an emotional response driven by a surge in the hormone testosterone and a rapid-fire release of the neurotransmitter glutamate. However, before he reacts harshly, he takes a deep breath, allowing his serotonin levels to calm his immediate emotional response.

His empathy for his coworker, understanding the pressure they might be under, is influenced by the release of oxytocin. This promotes bonding and trust, reminding John of the importance of maintaining strong, positive relationships in his workplace. His final decision, to handle the situation calmly and constructively, reflects a careful balance of these hormones and neurotransmitters.

As John wraps up his day, he faces one last significant decision: Should he stay late to finish a task or go home and spend time with his family? The stress of the workload triggers a release of cortisol, pushing him to stay and complete the work. However, the desire for social bonding, driven by oxytocin, pulls him in the opposite direction. The tug-of-war between these biochemical forces shapes John's final choice.

In this single day, John has made countless decisions, each influenced by a complex web of neural and hormonal activity. From the moment he woke up, to his decisions about food, work, social interactions, and finally, his decision to end his workday, John's choices have been shaped by the subtle force of neurotransmitters and hormones. These biochemical messengers, while silent and unseen, play a profound role in our decision-making processes.

Through understanding this interplay, we gain insights into the biological basis of our decisions and behaviors, ultimately leading us to a deeper understanding of the concept of free will. Our choices are not just abstract concepts; they are grounded in the very real and tangible world of biochemistry.

This understanding does not diminish the concept of free will but rather enriches it. Recognizing the biochemical influences on our decisions allows us to better comprehend why we make the choices we do. It invites us to consider not just the 'what' but the 'how' and 'why' of our behaviorisms. For a better grasp, let's take a look at John again.

Let's reconsider the same scenario with a vital piece of additional information: John has a significant family history of depression. Despite leading a seemingly healthy lifestyle, John battles with a mood disorder that shapes his day-to-day experiences and decisions, often beyond his conscious control.

John wakes up to his alarm, but unlike before, his morning doesn't begin with an energized leap out of bed. Instead, the neurotransmitter imbalance associated with depression causes him to feel groggy and uninterested in starting his day. His reduced dopamine levels result in a diminished anticipation for the reward from his coffee. Even getting out of bed seems overwhelming, demonstrating how mental health can profoundly impact our decision-making capabilities.

As he moves towards the kitchen, he faces the decision between a healthy breakfast and a donut. This time, his impaired serotonin regulation fails to effectively suppress the impulsive behavior, resulting in him reaching for the donut. Not only does this depict how our biochemistry can lead to less than optimal decisions, but it also underscores the role of our mental state in the choices we make.

Moving on to his workday, the decisions he faces seem daunting. The low levels of serotonin and dopamine make even minor tasks seem like massive hurdles. The reduced serotonin diminishes his mood, while the low dopamine levels affect his motivation. Even a simple coding problem feels like a mountain he's unable to climb.

The stress and frustration from his coworker's missed deadline trigger an overwhelming emotional response. The surge in glutamate isn't balanced by sufficient GABA (Gamma-Aminobutyric Acid), a neurotransmitter responsible for calming the nervous system. This imbalance intensifies his emotions, causing his anger to spill over into his response.

Finally, the decision of whether to work late or spend time with his family presents itself. His high cortisol levels, a consequence of chronic stress often associated with depression, push him towards staying late to avoid the anxiety of pending tasks. The low oxytocin levels, on the other hand, weaken the pull towards social bonding. His day, filled with stressful decisions, ends with him staying late at work, driven by his heightened stress response.

In this revised scenario, John's decisions are shaped differently due to the biochemical alterations associated with depression. This version of John's day underscores how our mental health state, deeply intertwined with our neurobiology, can greatly influence our decisions.

By contrasting these two scenarios, it becomes evident how our biochemical state can dramatically impact our decision-making. While we may or may not possess the ability to make choices freely, this capacity is inherently tied to our biological state. Understanding this complex interplay between our biochemistry and our decisions is key to unraveling the true nature of free will. The chemical messengers within us, both the neurotransmitters and hormones, are silent influencers, nudging our decisions in one direction or another.

In John's story, his free will is exercised within the bounds set by his biochemistry. As we understand more about these biochemical underpinnings, we can see that our concept of free will requires some reevaluation. It doesn't mean that we don't have control over our decisions, but rather our decisions are part of a complex system of interactions between our environment, experiences, and biochemistry.

Through the lens of neurobiology, we can see that our choices aren't entirely free of influences – they're guided and shaped by a dance of chemicals within us. Recognizing this doesn't restrict our freedom; instead, it allows us to understand it better. Our choices are not made in isolation, they are a result of a complex interplay of numerous factors. Understanding this complexity can enrich our perspective, helping us to navigate our decisions with greater awareness and compassion towards ourselves and others.

CHAPTER 7: EMERGENCE OF DECISION-MAKING SYSTEMS

As we dive deeper into the realm of decision-making, we encounter the complex landscape where our choices take shape. This landscape is shaped not just by our individual minds, but by countless factors: social, cultural, environmental, and biological. This complex web of interrelations forms what is known as a "complex system." The shift in perspective in this chapter moves us from the biological and neurological underpinnings of decision-making to understanding how complex systems emerge and evolve. It's about exploring the decision-making process from a macroscopic lens, to see how our individual choices converge to create larger, emergent phenomena. This, in turn, feeds back into our individual decision-making processes, influencing our perception of free will.

7.1 COMPLEXITY THEORY: A NEW LENS TO UNDERSTAND CHOICES

Complexity theory, rooted in mathematics and computer science, provides a fascinating lens through which to view and understand the process of decision-making in human beings. It challenges the linear, deterministic view of cause and effect and instead embraces the idea of nonlinearity, unpredictability, and emergent behavior.

Convergence and Divergence: In the realm of complexity, the concepts of convergence and divergence play a pivotal role. Convergence refers to how systems with different initial states but operating under the same set of rules tend to evolve towards a similar outcome. This can be observed in natural phenomena, economic systems, and even human behavior. For instance, people from diverse backgrounds may eventually develop similar behaviors or attitudes if they are subjected to similar societal rules and norms.

Conversely, divergence is the idea that slight differences in initial conditions can lead to vastly different outcomes. This is the foundation of the 'butterfly effect' - a concept in chaos theory where a minor event, like the flapping of a butterfly's wings, can potentially trigger a hurricane thousands of miles away. In the context of decision-making, divergence implies that minor differences in our thoughts, feelings, or environment can significantly alter our choices.

Emergence: Complexity theory also introduces us to the fascinating concept of emergence – the idea that complex behaviors can be coded for with the right simple rules. In the context of decision-making, emergence suggests that our choices are not random, isolated events but part of a complex, interconnected network of thoughts, feelings, and external stimuli. Just as a group of neurons team up to produce information, our decisions emerge from the interaction of various factors within and outside us.

An example of emergence in the natural world is a flock of birds. Each bird follows a set of simple rules – maintain a certain distance from other birds, match speed with the closest birds, and move towards the average position of nearby birds. Out of these simple rules, the complex and beautiful patterns of bird flocking emerge. Similarly, our decisions emerge from a set of simple, yet interconnected factors such as our genes, past experiences, and the social and physical environment we find ourselves in.

Understanding Neural Networks: The brain, a complex organ in its own right, functions much like a chaotic system, especially in terms of how it processes information and makes decisions. Each neuron in the brain is a simple processing unit, but when billions of these neurons interact, they form a neural network that exhibits complex behaviors. This is much like an impressionist painting where each individual dot of paint is simple and unremarkable, but when viewed from a distance, these dots come together to form a beautiful and complex image.

Our brain's neural networks allow us to process information in a parallel and distributed manner, enabling us to respond to a wide array of stimuli. Importantly, this process involves both convergence and divergence. Convergence occurs when different sensory inputs are processed to arrive at a single perception. For instance, our brain converges visual and auditory information to perceive a person speaking. Divergence, on the other hand, happens when a single input leads to multiple outputs. For example, the sight of a delicious meal can trigger a variety of responses - salivation, a feeling of hunger, and the decision to eat.

The Role of Associational Pathways: The associational pathways in our brain contribute significantly to our decision-making process. These pathways, formed by connections between neurons, allow us to retrieve and associate different pieces of information. For instance, the smell of freshly baked cookies might retrieve memories of your grandmother's kitchen and evoke a feeling of nostalgia. This is why the weakening of these pathways, such as in neurodegenerative disorders like Alzheimer's disease, can lead to difficulty in recalling information.

The Influence of Genetic Fractals: The principles of complexity theory and emergence extend to the level of our genes as well. Fractal genes follow simple rules that can create complex forms. For example, a simple rule like "grow this tube until it is five times longer than it is wide, then bifurcate" can lead to the creation of our complex vascular system. This fractal distribution makes it possible to supply every cell in the body with nutrients and oxygen efficiently, despite the circulatory system taking up only a small portion of the body.

At the same time, the fractal nature of our genetic structure underscores the sensitivity of our development to minor disturbances. A slight mutation in the gene can disrupt the entire process, leading to vastly different outcomes, much like the butterfly effect. This divergence can have significant implications on our decision-making processes.

Complexity Theory and Decision Making: The complexity theory thus provides us with a new perspective on the multifaceted nature of decision-making. It elucidates how our choices emerge from the complex interplay of various factors such as our genetics, environment, and social interactions. This perspective challenges the deterministic view of choices and free will and opens the door to a richer, more nuanced understanding of why we make the choices we do.

The Wisdom of Crowds: As we delve deeper into the complexities of decision-making systems, it's intriguing to consider the phenomena of collective intelligence or the 'wisdom of crowds.' This concept is based on the notion that a group's collective decision-making can, under certain conditions, outperform even its best individual members. In essence, it refers to how diverse opinions in a group can balance out individual biases or inaccuracies, leading to a surprisingly accurate collective decision.

Consider the classic example proposed by Francis Galton, a pioneer in the field of statistics and eugenics. At a country fair, Galton observed a contest where participants had to estimate the weight of an ox. He found that the average estimate of the crowd was extremely close to the ox's actual weight. This observation served as an early testament to the accuracy of collective decision-making. Similarly, in the context of decision-making, an individual may not always make the best choice, but a group's collective decision is likely to be more balanced and accurate, owing to the diversity of experiences and perspectives.

Applying Complexity Theory to Human Behavior: So how does this all apply to our everyday life and decision-making? To illustrate, let's consider a hypothetical scenario. John, a middle-aged man, is deciding whether to accept a new job offer. This decision isn't made in isolation. It emerges from a complex interplay of various factors within and outside John.

Internally, his genetic predispositions, past experiences, current mood, and physiological state all play a role. His inherent personality traits may incline him towards seeking new challenges (a manifestation of his genetic fractals). His past experiences with job changes might prime him either positively or negatively towards the new offer (the role of neural networks and associational pathways). His current physiological state, say if he is well-rested or tired, could also influence his decision (convergence of different inputs).

Externally, the specifics of the job offer, his current job satisfaction, the opinions of his family and friends, and even the current economic climate factor into his decision. The diverse opinions of his family and friends may balance out his own biases or blind spots, much like the wisdom of crowds.

The economic climate might act as a butterfly flapping its wings, causing a ripple effect on John's decision-making.

As these various elements interact in complex ways, a decision emerges. John's choice to accept or reject the job offer is not merely a deterministic output of his internal state or external circumstances. It is an emergent behavior arising from the complex system that is John in his environment.

Complexity theory, thus, gives us a dynamic and nuanced lens to understand our decision-making process. It illustrates that our choices are not simply the sum of individual factors but the product of their interaction. This perspective is invaluable in appreciating the richness and depth of human behavior and the fascinatingly complex process of decision-making.

This exploration of complexity theory sets the stage for our journey into the world of collective decision-making, emergent behavior, and the constraints on our freedom of choice. Let's move on to the next section to delve deeper into these intriguing aspects.

7.2 COLLECTIVE DECISION-MAKING: THE POWER OF THE MASSES.

Collective decision-making is a phenomenon that operates across the biological world, from microscopic cells to grand human societies. The essence of collective decision-making lies in the power of group dynamics, where every individual acts like a piece of a jigsaw puzzle, contributing uniquely to the bigger picture. The beauty of it lies in the harmony of diverse units achieving a common purpose, like notes in a symphony creating a melodic masterpiece.

The world of honeybees offers an enthralling illustration of collective decision-making in action. Eusocial in nature, honeybees operate within complex societies with division of labor, cooperative brood care, and overlapping generations. The decision about the relocation of their hive to a more advantageous nesting site is a fascinating example of their collective intelligence. This process isn't driven by the queen bee but is the cumulative outcome of the worker bees' interactions and communication, a system similar to democracy.

Here's how it works: scout bees fly out to explore potential nesting sites, assessing various factors like the size, the proximity to food sources, and the safety from predators. After the exploration, they return to the swarm and perform a unique 'waggle dance'. The more attractive the location, the more enthusiastic the dance is, thus influencing more bees to visit and validate the proposed site. This feedback process continues until a consensus is reached—a majority of bees vibrating to the same rhythmic dance, signifying collective approval for a new home. This process, termed as 'quorum sensing', encapsulates the beauty of collective decision-making, harmoniously interweaving individual perceptions into a unanimous decision.

When we shift our perspective from the world of bees to human societies, the scale and complexity of collective decision-making multiply manifold, yet the underlying principles remain the same. Let's consider the Velvet Revolution of 1989 in Czechoslovakia—a significant historical event that was the result of collective decision-making.

The Velvet Revolution wasn't a movement propelled by a single individual or party. Instead, it was the collective outcome of thousands of individual decisions. Each participant, armed with their experiences, perspectives, and emotional responses, contributed to a collective action that profoundly reshaped their political landscape. The dissatisfaction with communist rule, the longing for democracy, and the desire for freedom—these shared feelings
136

coalesced into a massive, peaceful protest that ultimately toppled a forty-year-old regime.

Just like the bees reaching a consensus for a new hive, the people of Czechoslovakia collectively decided they wanted a change. Their unified action, a peaceful protest, marked the end of communist rule and the dawn of democracy—a testament to the power of collective decision-making.

These examples, one from nature and the other from human society, showcase how collective decision-making influences the course of life and history. The principles underpinning these phenomena permeate various aspects of our lives—from the political elections where we select our leaders, to the stock markets where the buying and selling decisions of millions determine the rise and fall of economic indices.

While collective decision-making has demonstrated powerful outcomes, as seen in the hive decisions of bees and the Velvet Revolution, it is essential to understand that it also has its downsides. The same group dynamics that can bring about positive changes can also, under certain conditions, lead to unfavorable outcomes, trapping individuals within a 'mob mentality'.

The concept of 'mob mentality', also known as 'herd behavior', describes how people can be influenced by their peers to adopt behaviors, follow trends, and/or purchase items. This phenomenon is driven by the human tendency to conform to group norms, which is deeply ingrained in our evolutionary past. There's safety in numbers, and so our ancestors who stuck with the group had better chances of survival than those who ventured out on their own.

However, in modern contexts, this primal drive can lead to less than ideal outcomes. A classic example of this is the phenomenon of 'panic buying' that often occurs in times of perceived crisis. When individuals see others buying large quantities of a particular item—say, toilet paper during the COVID-19 pandemic—they fear missing out and start doing the same, even if they don't need the item in large quantities. This leads to artificial scarcity, with store shelves quickly emptying, and those who genuinely need the item unable to access it. Here, the collective decision-making process, fueled by fear and uncertainty, leads to irrational behaviors and inefficient outcomes.

In the financial world, herd behavior can result in volatile markets and economic bubbles. The dot-com bubble of the late 1990s and the housing market bubble that led to the 2008 financial crisis are stark examples of this. Investors, influenced by the collective euphoria around certain investments, began pouring money into these sectors despite warning signs of overvaluation. When these bubbles burst, the collective decision to follow the herd resulted in significant financial loss for many.

In the realm of social and political phenomena, collective decision-making can sometimes give rise to 'groupthink', a psychological phenomenon where the desire for harmony in a group leads to an irrational or dysfunctional decision-making outcome. Group members may suppress dissenting viewpoints, fail to critically analyze alternatives, or ignore possible risks in the pursuit of consensus. Historical disasters like the Bay of Pigs invasion or the Challenger space shuttle disaster have been attributed in part to the effects of groupthink.

Yet, despite these potential pitfalls, collective decision-making remains an integral part of human society. It enables diverse inputs, broadens perspectives, and shares responsibility. The key lies in managing the balance—promoting free-thinking and individual judgment, while still reaping the benefits of collective wisdom.

Educating individuals about these potential risks and encouraging critical thinking, dissent, and open discussion within groups can go a long way towards mitigating these issues. Moreover, building systems and structures that promote diversity and prevent the concentration of power can help ensure that collective decision-making serves its purpose: to synergize the many into a unified, powerful force for decision-making.

In the following section, we'll shift our focus from these group dynamics to a related but distinct concept: emergent behavior. We'll explore how individual actions can lead to patterns that are more than the sum of their parts, and how this shapes our understanding of decision-making at a larger scale.

7.3 From Social Dynamics to Emergent Behavior: Uncovering Patterns

Have you ever gazed in awe at a murmuration of starlings, that spectacular airborne ballet performed by thousands of birds, shifting and morphing across the sky in perfect harmony? Each bird individually might not appear to be doing anything extraordinary, but together, they create a living spectacle that is far more than the sum of its parts. This is a classic example of emergent behavior, a phenomenon that occurs when individual entities operate in an environment, forming more complex behaviors as a collective.

Emergent behavior is found throughout nature and society, and it exists on a spectrum of complexity. It starts with simple, patterned behaviors, such as schools of fish moving in unison to confuse predators or the seemingly chaotic yet perfectly coordinated movement of rush hour traffic in a crowded city. Then there are complex emergent behaviors such as the global stock market movements, the ebb and flow of fashion trends, or the birth of a political revolution.

To understand the concept of emergence, let's examine a ubiquitous, albeit seemingly mundane, instance of emergent behavior: city traffic. At its core, traffic is an outcome of individual drivers making localized decisions based on immediate, often incomplete information—how close is the vehicle in front, what color is the traffic signal, is there a pedestrian crossing ahead? Yet, from these millions of discrete decisions emerges a system that can be studied, modeled, and to a certain degree, predicted. Traffic jams, for instance, can ripple backward from a single point of disruption, like a car crash or construction site, even after the initial cause has been cleared.

The stock market is another prime example of emergent behavior in action. Every individual investor makes decisions based on a unique combination of factors—personal financial goals, risk tolerance, available capital, market news, and countless more. Yet, out of this swirl of individual decision-making emerges the overall behavior of the market, rising and falling in response to trends that no single investor may be able to perceive or predict.

However, it is crucial to note that predicting emergent behavior is a complex and challenging task. Even with state-of-the-art computational models and artificial intelligence algorithms, predicting the exact behavior of emergent systems with perfect accuracy is practically impossible. This is due to the 'sensitive dependence on initial conditions,' a fundamental aspect of chaotic systems. In other words, minor changes in the starting state of a system can lead to significant differences in its final state, which makes precise long-term predictions inherently uncertain.

Yet, despite its unpredictability, understanding emergent behavior is critical. It allows us to harness collective behavior for communal benefit, from coordinating traffic flow more efficiently to creating better investment strategies. Further, the study of emergent behavior can inform public policy and urban planning initiatives. For instance, understanding the factors that lead to the organic growth of neighborhoods could help city planners design more efficient, livable urban spaces.

As we navigate the labyrinth of decision-making, emergence adds another layer of complexity. Decisions do not exist in isolation. They interact, interfere, and build upon one another, generating patterns and phenomena that transcend the sum of individual choices. As we continue to probe the depths of decision-making, we must not lose sight of this broader picture, the rhythm of choices that constitutes the symphony of our social existence.

Indeed, emergent behavior serves as a poignant reminder that while our choices may seem like individual droplets in the ocean of decision-making, together they can create waves that shape the world around us.

7.4 THE DOMINO EFFECT: EXTERNAL CONSTRAINTS AND FREEDOM OF CHOICE

As we tread the path of existence, every choice we make, every action we take, sends ripples across time and space, influencing the course of events in ways that are often unpredictable. This concept is strikingly similar to a meticulously arranged sequence of dominos where the slightest nudge triggers a cascade of toppling pieces. Each domino's fall, seemingly predetermined, is influenced by the subtle forces of its predecessor, serving as a metaphor for our interconnected world.

In the grand theater of life, the domino effect signifies the extraordinary impact of seemingly ordinary decisions. A single, perhaps inconsequential choice can spark a chain reaction, crafting significant transformations in our individual and collective lives. This is similar to the snowball effect where a small ball of snow gains mass and momentum as it rolls downhill, metamorphosing from an unassuming entity into a formidable force.

However, while we bask in the freedom of our choices, we must also acknowledge the invisible constraints that nudge us in certain directions. Just as a swift gust of wind can influence a domino's fall, unseen forces in our lives can influence our decisions.

Take, for instance, an unexpected external shock like an earthquake, a global pandemic, or an economic downturn. These powerful events can dramatically limit our choices, reshaping our lives in significant ways. Such constraints exert an undeniable influence over our decisions, serving as reminders of the delicate interplay between freedom and restrictions.

Underneath this complex dynamic lurks the intriguing world of chaos theory and the butterfly effect. These concepts, although primarily rooted in the realm of physics, spill over into our understanding of decision-making and behavioral sciences. Chaos theory deals with complex, nonlinear systems that are highly sensitive to initial conditions. The butterfly effect, a subset of chaos theory, postulates that even minor perturbations can lead to drastically different outcomes.

To illustrate this further, let's turn our attention to a critical event in modern history—the 2008 global financial crisis. What started as the collapse of a single financial institution, Lehman Brothers, had repercussions that were felt around the globe. Like a line of dominos toppling one after another, the impact of Lehman Brothers' failure spread throughout the world's financial system. Confidence evaporated, leading to a reluctance among banks to lend. This resulted in businesses downsizing or closing, unemployment rates soaring, and consumer spending plummeting. The effects were far-reaching, altering the trajectory of countless lives.

Yet, life's intricacies extend beyond the predictable fall of dominos. Unlike a line of dominoes, where the outcome is largely preordained, our existence is characterized by complexity and unpredictability. This realization plunges us into the realm of chaos theory, where initial conditions can lead to vastly diverse outcomes.

This introduces us to the limitations of reductive science, which strives to understand complex systems by breaking them down into their components. Traditional scientific thought promotes reductionism, the pursuit of reality's basic units—moving from an overarching understanding to more granular levels of knowledge. In other words, if we can understand the parts, we can comprehend the whole.

Chaos theory, however, presents a different perspective. It suggests that the process of reduction has no endpoint. Beyond a certain threshold, we encounter the Heisenberg Uncertainty Principle, introducing a level of randomness and unpredictability. This reveals the limitations of a purely reductive approach, particularly in understanding complex systems such as human behavior.

Indeed, the frontal cortex—the most complex part of humans and the least constrained by genes—provides a fascinating stage for chaos theory to illuminate our understanding of human cognition. By stepping away from a strictly deterministic perspective, we allow ourselves to appreciate the unpredictable, the complex, and the chaotic aspects of our existence.

As we continue our journey through life, let us embrace chaos and complexity, understanding that the most nuanced arenas of life are populated not just from predictable threads but also from those that defy expectations and norms. The ups and downs of choice and chaos continues, shaping our lives in countless, often surprising ways. Just like the cascading fall of dominos or the growth of a rolling snowball, our decisions—both big and small—leave an indelible imprint on the canvas of life. And it is through the interplay of choice, chaos, and constraints that we continue to explore, adapt, and evolve.

CHAPTER 8: COGNITIVE BIASES & EXTERNAL CONSTRAINTS

In this chapter, we venture into the intricate maze of our minds and the invisible societal threads that subtly or blatantly direct our actions. We explore the cognitive biases, often referred to as the mind's blind spots, that distort our decision-making, alongside the unignorable impact of society and external constraints. Understanding these influences not only equips us to make better decisions but also fosters empathy for the choices of others that may seem irrational at a superficial glance. Through this exploration, we seek to unravel the complexity of the human decision-making process, deepening our understanding of the individual in relation to society.

8.1 COGNITIVE BIASES: THE MIND'S BLIND SPOTS

In the maze of our psyche lies a vast and complex mechanism that controls our perceptions, our judgments, and our decisions—our cognitive biases. As we delve deeper into the winding corridors of our cognitive landscape, we encounter the mind's myriad 'blind spots,' which subtly yet profoundly influence our decision-making processes. These cognitive biases, almost imperceptible in their operation, cast a profound impact on the judgments we form and the choices we make.

Our minds are ceaselessly inundated with an overwhelming volume of information. To cope with this, our brain relies on a variety of cognitive shortcuts, or 'heuristics.' These heuristics offer an efficient way to process information quickly, albeit not always accurately. They allow us to make rapid decisions without needing to meticulously analyze every piece of information we come across. However, these mental shortcuts can sometimes mislead us, giving birth to cognitive biases. Cognitive biases, therefore, are systematic errors in our thinking that impact our interpretations of our world and skew our decision-making processes.

One might think of cognitive biases as optical illusions of the mind. Just as an optical illusion might trick our eyes into perceiving a two-dimensional image as three-dimensional, cognitive biases warp our interpretation of information and sway our subsequent decisions. While these biases are not always detrimental—indeed, they often serve valuable functions in simplifying our decision-making processes—they can sometimes lead us to incorrect or suboptimal outcomes.

The universe of cognitive biases is diverse and expansive, with each bias carrying its unique idiosyncrasies and characteristics. Among the sea of these biases, several have been widely recognized and studied, including confirmation bias, the availability heuristic, and the anchoring bias.

Confirmation bias represents our mind's proclivity to search for, interpret, and remember information that aligns with our existing beliefs, opinions, and values. We are naturally inclined to give greater weight to evidence that supports our viewpoints while dismissing or rationalizing away evidence that contradicts them. This bias can lead us to become entrenched in our beliefs, creating a sort of echo chamber where our pre-existing views are continuously reinforced, making it difficult to consider alternate viewpoints or revise our stances in light of new evidence.
146

Imagine, for instance, a person who vehemently denies the reality of climate change. Despite the overwhelming scientific consensus supporting the existence of human-induced climate change, this individual might cherry-pick data or events that seem to support their belief while disregarding the vast body of evidence that contradicts it. This person's confirmation bias has created a mental barrier that prevents them from fully engaging with the available information and arriving at a more accurate understanding of the issue.

Next, we encounter the availability heuristic, which describes our propensity to base our decisions on information that is most readily accessible to us, rather than comprehensively reviewing all relevant data. This heuristic often guides our judgments about the frequency or likelihood of an event. For example, if someone has been frequently exposed to news stories about plane crashes, they might overestimate the danger associated with air travel. The vivid, emotionally charged images associated with plane crashes are more readily available in their memory, leading them to believe that such events are more common than they actually are. In reality, statistically speaking, flying is much safer than other forms of transport, such as driving.

The anchoring bias is another pervasive cognitive bias. It refers to our tendency to overly rely on the first piece of information we encounter—the 'anchor'—when making decisions. This anchor, once established, can significantly influence our subsequent judgments and choices. For instance, if we first see a shirt priced at $100 and then find a similar one for $60, we are likely to perceive the second shirt as a bargain, regardless of its actual value. The initial price of the $100 shirt serves as an anchor, skewing our perception of the subsequent price.

As the examples illustrate, cognitive biases can subtly but powerfully infiltrate our decision-making processes, often leading us to make less than optimal choices. Confirmation bias can cause us to become entrenched in potentially unproductive or even erroneous beliefs, stifling personal growth and learning. The availability heuristic can cause us to overlook the bigger picture, resulting in disproportionate fears or inaccurate risk assessments. Anchoring bias can render us susceptible to manipulation, particularly in situations involving negotiations or price evaluations.

However, while these biases present clear challenges, it's not an entirely pessimistic scenario. The first step toward mitigating the influence of these biases is awareness—recognizing their existence and understanding their impact on our decision-making. With this awareness, we can begin to take deliberate steps to counteract these biases.

To mitigate the impact of confirmation bias, for example, we can make a conscious effort to seek out diverse perspectives and expose ourselves to information that challenges our pre-existing beliefs. This approach forces us to consider viewpoints that differ from our own, potentially leading to more balanced and accurate judgments.

To counteract the availability heuristic, we can strive to gather and assess information from a broad range of sources before making decisions. By considering data beyond what is immediately available or salient, we can form more accurate perceptions of situations and make better-informed decisions.

In the case of the anchoring bias, being aware of its potential influence allows us to be more critical of the initial information we receive and encourages us to make decisions based on a more comprehensive evaluation of available data. For instance, if we know that a seller might set a high initial price to anchor our perception, we can consciously strive to evaluate an item's value independently of this anchor.

While it might seem like a daunting task to navigate the murky waters of our cognitive biases, understanding these biases and their influence on our decision-making processes is a crucial part of our cognitive journey. Recognizing these 'blind spots' allows us to make more conscious, deliberate decisions. As we delve deeper into the complexities of our cognitive processes in this chapter, we will continue to uncover the many layers of our decision-making processes, enriching our understanding of ourselves and the world around us. Understanding our cognitive biases doesn't just enrich our individual decision-making processes—it can also have profound implications for our collective existence. Whether in our personal lives, our professional spheres, or broader societal contexts, this understanding empowers us to navigate our world with greater consciousness and clarity.

8.2 THE SOCIAL FABRIC: HOW SOCIETY INFLUENCES CHOICES

The fabric of society is rich and complex, woven from innumerable threads. Each thread represents an element of the cultural, economic, political, and social environment in which we live. They intertwine and intersect, influencing and shaping our decisions and choices in ways we may not always recognize. This societal influence is so omnipresent and so deeply woven into our lives that it often goes unnoticed. Yet, it is pivotal in determining our behaviors, perceptions, and attitudes.

Cultural norms form one of the most potent threads in the social fabric. These are shared expectations and rules that guide behavior within a group. They dictate what is considered acceptable or unacceptable, right or wrong, important or unimportant. These norms can range from seemingly trivial matters, like what to wear or how to greet others, to life-altering decisions like what careers to pursue or whom to marry. Our choices are significantly shaped by these norms, as straying from them can lead to social disapproval or even ostracism.

For instance, consider the impact of gender norms on career choices. In many societies, traditional gender norms prescribe that men should engage in "masculine" occupations such as engineering, law enforcement, or construction, while women are nudged towards "feminine" careers such as teaching, nursing, or social work. Even though these norms have been challenged and have evolved over time, they still influence many people's career choices. The social sanctions associated with violating these norms can be substantial, reinforcing their power.

Additionally, social structures – systems of socioeconomic stratification, institutions, networks, and roles – shape our choices by dictating what opportunities are available to us and how we are perceived by others. Take, for example, the role of educational institutions in shaping our career paths. The quality of education we receive and the subjects we are encouraged to study can greatly affect our career choices. Or consider the influence of socioeconomic status. Children from wealthier families often have access to better education, more extensive networks, and more opportunities than those from poorer backgrounds, which can significantly influence their life trajectories.

This concept is not limited to just economic and career decisions. It extends to our beliefs, values, and personal preferences. For instance, our food choices are often significantly influenced by the society we live in. In cultures where vegetarianism is prevalent due to religious or ethical beliefs, individuals are more likely to choose vegetarian diets. Conversely, in societies where meat consumption is the norm, people may be less likely to consider vegetarian or vegan diets.

While societal influence is powerful, it is not deterministic. Individual agency and the ability to question, resist, or modify social norms and structures mean that there is always room for choice. However, these choices are rarely free from the influence of the social fabric we are part of.

The societal influences described above can shape our preferences and decisions in ways that are not always aligned with our best interests. Social pressure and the desire to conform can lead to choices that are not optimal for our well-being or happiness.

This pressure to conform can manifest in various ways. Consider, for instance, the phenomenon of "keeping up with the Joneses". This phrase describes the tendency to compare ourselves with others and to match or exceed their lifestyle. If our neighbors or colleagues acquire a new car, the latest smartphone, or a bigger house, we may feel pressured to do the same, even if it strains our finances. Such choices, driven by societal pressure rather than personal need or satisfaction, can lead to financial stress and decreased well-being.

Another manifestation of societal influence is the prevalence of stereotypes and prejudices, which can lead to biased decision-making. Stereotypes are generalized and simplified beliefs about certain groups of people. When these stereotypes are negative or discriminatory, they can result in unjust decisions and behaviors. For instance, an employer might unconsciously favor a male candidate over a female candidate for a leadership role due to ingrained gender stereotypes, even if the female candidate is equally or more qualified.

Furthermore, societal influence can sometimes lead to groupthink, where the desire for harmony or conformity in a group results in an irrational or dysfunctional decision-making outcome. Groupthink can cause individuals to suppress dissenting viewpoints, overlook potential risks, and ignore alternative solutions, leading to poor decisions.

It's important to note that while society significantly influences our choices, it doesn't mean we are helpless puppets being manipulated by social forces. Recognizing these influences can help us make more informed and conscious choices. It can enable us to challenge biases, question norms, and resist harmful pressures, enabling us to make decisions that better align with our personal values and goals.

We've seen how social and cultural factors can guide and shape our decisions. However, these are not the only influences. External constraints, often outside our immediate control, can also significantly impact our choices.

The concept of external constraints refers to conditions or circumstances that limit our options and influence our decisions. These constraints can be physical, economic, legal, or even temporal.

Physical constraints include factors such as geography and environment. For example, someone living in a rural area may have limited access to certain types of employment, education, or healthcare services, thus constraining their choices in these areas. Similarly, someone with a physical disability may have their choices constrained by accessibility issues.

Economic constraints include factors such as income, wealth, and market conditions. Someone with low income may have limited choices when it comes to housing, food, education, or leisure activities. Similarly, market conditions can impact choices related to investments, employment, or business.

Legal constraints refer to laws and regulations that limit what choices are legally available or impose costs on certain options. For example, laws can limit who can marry, what
152

substances are legal to consume, or what business practices are permissible.

Temporal constraints refer to the limitations imposed by time. We all have a limited amount of time in our day, our week, and our life. This finite nature of time constraints our choices – we cannot do everything, so we have to choose how we spend our time.

All these external constraints shape and limit our choices, sometimes in ways that can be frustrating or lead to suboptimal outcomes. However, recognizing these constraints can also lead to creative problem-solving and the search for alternatives. It can lead us to challenge and try to change the constraints that we find unjust or harmful.

In understanding the theory of how societal influences and external constraints shape our choices, real-life examples can be illuminating. These tangible instances allow us to see the concepts in action, reinforcing our understanding of their significance.

One powerful example of societal influence comes from the field of fashion. Fashion trends can be seen as a manifestation of societal pressure to conform. When a particular style becomes trendy, many individuals feel compelled to adopt it, often irrespective of their personal taste or the practicality of the clothes. This societal pressure can drive individuals to make purchasing decisions that they might not make independently.

On a more serious note, the influence of socioeconomic status on educational choices provides a stark example of how social structures and external constraints can shape decisions. Children from low-income families often face limited educational opportunities, not due to a lack of talent or ambition, but because of economic constraints. This limitation can impact their career choices and future earnings potential, perpetuating a cycle of poverty.

Yet another example can be seen in the impact of legal constraints on personal choices. The prohibition of same-sex marriage in some countries is a clear example of how laws can limit the choices available to individuals.

These examples underline the pervasive influence of societal factors and external constraints on our choices. However, they also highlight the potential for change. By recognizing these influences and constraints, we can strive to challenge and alter them, creating a society that offers more equitable and liberating choices for all.

The exploration of these concepts is not merely an academic exercise. It has practical implications for how we understand our own decisions and those of others. It can foster empathy, as we recognize how the choices of others may be shaped by forces beyond their control. It can also empower us to make more informed and conscious choices, resist harmful societal pressures, and challenge unjust constraints.

The exploration of societal influences and external constraints in decision making provides a nuanced understanding of human behavior. By recognizing these factors, we are better equipped to make informed decisions that align with our values and goals and to create societies that offer equitable opportunities for all.

While this concludes our detailed exploration of "The Social Fabric: How Society Influences Choices," it is just one piece of the broader puzzle. As we continue our journey through this text, we will delve into more aspects of decision making, each adding another dimension to our understanding.

8.3 Unseen Chains: The Impact of External Constraints on Choice

To begin, it is essential to understand what we mean by 'external constraints.' These are factors that exist outside of us, independent of our control, which affect our decision-making processes and ultimate choices. These can be broad, such as the state of the economy or the cultural norms of our society, or more personal, like our immediate physical environment or financial status. It is these constraints that often act as unseen chains, shaping and guiding our choices in directions we may not consciously realize.

One way to visualize these constraints is to consider our lives as paths through a landscape. This landscape is filled with various barriers and obstacles, each representing a different external constraint. Our job is to navigate through this landscape, choosing our paths based on our internal desires, needs, and cognitive processes, all the while negotiating with these external constraints.

Physical constraints are one of the most basic forms of external factors that influence our choices. The physical condition of our bodies, our geographical location, and our environmental conditions all play a significant role in our decision-making. A person with a physical disability might have to consider their mobility and accessibility when choosing their career or place of living. Similarly, someone living in a rural area might have limited access to certain types of jobs or education, which could significantly affect their choices in these areas.

In addition to physical constraints, economic constraints are another significant external factor that influences our decisions. Our economic status and financial conditions can dictate our choices in many areas of life, such as what kind of education we can afford, what job we take, or even what we eat. A person living in poverty, for example, may have to prioritize basic survival needs over other considerations, which could affect their choices in many areas of life.

Moving on to legal constraints, these represent the laws and regulations at the national and international level that influence our decision-making. These laws can affect everything from our personal freedoms to our financial decisions, and even to the choices we make about our bodies. For instance, in places where abortion is illegal, women might not have the freedom to make choices about their own bodies. Similarly, in countries with strict internet censorship laws, citizens might not have access to the same information as those living in countries with freedom of the press.

Societal constraints, or social norms and cultural expectations, are another powerful force shaping our choices. These norms and expectations often operate subconsciously, subtly guiding our decisions to align with societal values and avoid social stigma. For instance, someone from a culture that places a high value on family might prioritize decisions that favor maintaining close family ties, even at the expense of personal desires or ambitions.

Lastly, temporal constraints refer to factors such as age, time availability, and life stages, which can limit our choices in various ways. For instance, a person nearing retirement age might have different priorities and constraints compared to a young adult just entering the workforce. A parent with young children might have time constraints that affect their career choices, and so on.

Now that we've outlined these different types of external constraints, let's examine how they play out in real-life scenarios.

One powerful illustration of the interplay of physical, economic, and societal constraints is visible in the phenomenon of "food deserts." These are areas, often in low-income neighborhoods, where access to affordable, nutritious food is limited due to a lack of grocery stores within convenient traveling distance. In such a scenario, the physical constraint of geography, economic constraint of limited financial resources, and societal constraint of systemic inequality converge to limit the choices available to residents. Even if they wish to make healthier dietary choices, the external constraints make it exceedingly difficult, if not impossible.

Another example can be seen in the domain of career choices. A young adult from a lower socio-economic background, despite having a deep interest in the arts, may choose to pursue a degree in a more "practical" field such as business or engineering due to societal and economic constraints. The societal norm perceives arts as a risky career path with low financial stability, and the economic constraint of needing a stable income further reinforces this decision.

Legal constraints play a massive role in shaping choices in societies worldwide. One can consider the case of countries with strict internet censorship laws, where citizens' choices and ability to access a wide range of information are significantly limited. Despite the growing digital age, their decision to explore various aspects of knowledge, culture, or even entertainment are impacted by this unseen chain.

Temporal constraints can also be impactful. Take, for instance, the case of a single parent who works full-time. They might wish to pursue further education or personal hobbies, but the lack of time due to work and parenting responsibilities serves as a powerful constraint that restricts their choice.

These examples underline how our choices are seldom made in a vacuum. They are often the result of a complex interplay between our internal cognitive processes and a host of external constraints.

In conclusion, recognizing and understanding these unseen chains is crucial. It can help us make more informed decisions and potentially find ways to mitigate their restricting influence. It can also cultivate empathy, as we understand the constraints others may be operating under and the choices they make as a result. Moreover, it can guide societies and policymakers to create environments that reduce harmful constraints and provide a more level playing field for all.

8.4 CONCLUDING CHAPTER 8

To exemplify the intertwined impacts of cognitive biases, social influence, and external constraints on decision-making and perceived free will, let's construct a case study. We will delve into the life of an individual named Alex, a recent graduate from a prestigious university with a degree in Software Engineering. Alex's life offers a rich tableau of intermingling factors which demonstrate how these elements factor into our perception of free will.

Raised in a middle-class family, Alex was conditioned by societal and parental expectations that stressed the importance of a successful career. His decision to study software engineering was driven, in part, by the cognitive bias of 'social proof,' reflecting the trend of increasing interest in technology-related fields, and the societal narrative equating success with careers like software engineering, medicine, or finance. This societal influence, subtly yet effectively, narrowed down his perception of viable career choices.

After graduation, Alex found a well-paying job in a tech firm. Here, his decisions were significantly influenced by the 'bandwagon effect,' a cognitive bias where he tended to align his choices with those of his peers. If his colleagues used a particular programming language or advocated a specific work methodology, Alex was more likely to adopt these too. The thought of being an outlier was uncomfortable, leading to conformity and perpetuating social influence.

The impact of external constraints is also apparent in Alex's life. The need to repay his student loans, an economic constraint, influenced his decision to continue in his job, despite realizing that his passion lay in environmental conservation. In addition, temporal constraints played a role too. The demanding hours of his job left him little time to explore opportunities in environmental work or go back to school.

All these factors combined present a potent image of how perceived free will operates. Alex believed he was making free, independent choices – choosing his major, his job, his daily decisions at work. However, beneath the surface of these choices, the invisible threads of cognitive biases, societal influences, and external constraints were continually at play.

This is not to say that Alex's choices were completely devoid of free will. After all, he could have chosen to resist societal expectations, overcome his biases, or take drastic measures to change his career. However, the interplay of cognitive biases, societal influences, and external constraints can sometimes subtly nudge or even forcefully push us towards particular paths, creating a landscape where the exertion of pure, unadulterated free will can become an increasingly complex endeavor.

In understanding this, we can strive to become more conscious of the biases we hold, the influences we yield to, and the constraints we operate under, giving us a clearer picture of how free our free will truly is. In acknowledging these factors, we may also be able to navigate them better, increasing the space for truly free choices in our lives.

CONCLUDING PART II

Let's embark on an explorative journey, retracing our steps through the complex maze of Alex's life, as we weave together the threads of his narrative with the newfound fabric of our understanding of free will.

This tale begins with the force of evolution, the silent architect of behavior that crafted Alex's predispositions and traits over millennia. Our protagonist, Alex, is the product of relentless natural selection, inheriting genetic predispositions that equipped him with an analytical mind, critical for survival in an environment that values problem-solving and innovation.

But genes alone do not tell the full story; the environment acts as a co-author in this narrative. The interplay of nature and nurture is evident in the way Alex's early experiences shaped his preferences and strengthened his analytical abilities, reinforcing his inherited traits.

As we transition from animals to humans in our exploration, we encounter an increasing complexity in our cognitive apparatus. The brain's mechanical cognitive machinery underpins our perceived free will. It's within this labyrinth of neurons that Alex's decision to pursue software engineering was formulated, a choice driven by conscious and unconscious processes.

Alex's brain, the command center of his decisions, contains specific regions that are hotspots for decision-making. Neural networks interact to evaluate options, forecast outcomes, and select actions. The intricate web of neurons, neurotransmitters, and hormones intricately organize this cognitive performance. Every dopamine rush Alex experienced while solving a complex problem or receiving approval from his peers nudged him further along his chosen path.

Underlying all this is a deterministic shadow cast by genetic and neurobiological factors, acting as unseen puppeteers guiding his choices. His genetic makeup, combined with his neurobiology, steers his behaviors and preferences, making certain paths more attractive than others.

The environmental imprint on Alex's life is also evident. The external constraints—economic, societal, temporal—limited his scope of choices. These constraints, invisible chains tethering Alex to specific pathways, were primarily economic. The necessity to pay off his student loans and maintain his lifestyle led him to remain in a high-stress job, further influenced by hormonal responses to stress, such as increased cortisol levels.

Yet, understanding the neurobiology of choice and acknowledging deterministic influences doesn't equate to negating free will. As we delve into the illusion of free will, we encounter a spectrum of perspectives. Even if some factors influencing Alex's decisions are beyond his control, it doesn't mean he's devoid of agency. Instead, his free will might operate within the boundaries set by these influences.

A key revelation comes from exploring the emergence of decision-making systems. Drawing from complexity theory, we understand that individual decisions, including Alex's career choice, are part of a more significant pattern that emerges from collective behavior. His choice to pursue software engineering didn't occur in isolation; it's influenced by societal trends favoring certain professions.

In conclusion, Alex's life story offers a comprehensive illustration of the myriad forces shaping our perceived free will. The interplay of evolutionary forces, cognitive machinery, deterministic influences, neurobiology, and external constraints weave an intricate tapestry that tells a unique story of human decision-making.

By understanding these forces, we can hope to navigate them better, allowing us to exert more control over our lives, despite the constraints. We might not have absolute free will, but understanding the elements influencing our choices can help us exercise the freedom we do possess more effectively.

PART III: MORALITY AND THE LACK OF FREEWILL

Part III of our book delves into a topic of paramount importance that dwells on the intersection of philosophy, ethics, and cognitive science: Morality, Responsibility, and the Lack of Free Will. These elements come into play when we move beyond the pure mechanics of decision-making and venture into the societal and moral implications of those decisions.

This part navigates the complex relationship between moral judgment, legal implications, mental illness, and constructing morality, all intertwined with the nuances of free will, or the potential lack thereof. It forces us to pose and ponder a challenging question: If our choices are bound by the deterministic forces of nature and nurture, what does it mean to be morally responsible?

In the preceding chapters, we've dissected the concept of free will from various angles, encompassing biological, psychological, and social perspectives. We've peeled back layers of cognitive functions, neurobiological mechanics, and the influence of societal constructs on our decisions, all the while questioning the true extent of our freedom in making choices. We have navigated the territories of determinism and pondered the illusion of free will.

As we move into this part, we will carry forward these insights and interrogate how they interact with our understanding of morality and responsibility. Each chapter within this part delves into a specific facet of this complex interaction.

Chapter 9 will explore moral judgment, with a focus on the evolutionary origins of morality and the unsuspected role free will plays in our moral decisions. Chapter 10 will cast a lens on the legal implications, contemplating the intricate role of free will in law, order, and punishment. In Chapter 11, we turn our attention to the link between mental illness and free will, tracing how altered neurological conditions impact decision-making. Finally, Chapter 12 will round out this section by constructing an understanding of morality in a deterministic world.

As we embark on this part of the journey, we shall challenge our understanding of free will further. The question we keep at the back of our minds is: "How does morality and responsibility stand up to scrutiny when the autonomy of our decisions might be called into question?"

This exploration may not necessarily end with clear-cut answers, but it will certainly provoke thought and enrich our understanding of these complex interrelations. As we delve deeper, we carry with us the knowledge and insights gained from our exploration of the origins, neurobiology, and cognitive workings of free will, and their shadows.

We'll start our investigation with an examination of moral judgment, a subject that intrinsically hinges on the notions of decision-making and free will. Let's take a step into this fascinating world of morality, responsibility, and the intriguing concept of free will.

Chapter 9: Moral Judgment and Freewill

In this chapter, explore the intrinsic connection between moral judgment and the concept of free will. It lays the groundwork by connecting the dots between our evolutionary past and morality, then unravels the unsuspected yet critical role of free will in shaping our moral compass. As we transition from theories to the tangible world, we dive into the burgeoning field of neuroethics and its implications. Lastly, we revisit philosophical debates to engage in thought-provoking discussions on moral responsibility in the light of our newfound knowledge on free will.

9.1 Evolution and Morality: Unearthing Connections

The topic of morality and its evolution over time is indeed fascinating, rich, and intricate. As we unravel the story, we embark upon a journey through time, taking us back to our ancestors and their struggle for survival, laying the groundwork for the morality we know today.

To begin with, let's first understand what we mean by morality. In a broad sense, morality refers to principles or rules of conduct that govern the behavior of individuals within a society. It involves a sense of right and wrong, fairness and unfairness, justice and injustice. But here's an interesting question - is morality exclusive to humans? Or can we trace its roots back to our evolutionary past, possibly even to other social species?

There's strong evidence suggesting that elements of morality, such as empathy, cooperation, and fairness, are not just confined to humans but are widespread among social animals. For instance, consider the case of wolves hunting in packs, or bees working collectively for the welfare of their hive.

Could these behaviors, reminiscent of our own moral norms, be the precursors of human morality? Could they have evolved through the ruthless mechanism of natural selection, favoring behaviors that increase the chances of survival and reproduction? It appears quite plausible. Let's explore this notion in further depth.

To delve deeper into this topic, let's consider an example that most readers can identify with: the common behavior of sharing. Sharing resources, be it food, territory, or knowledge, is a critical part of human society, and is considered a moral virtue in virtually all cultures worldwide. Now let's turn to the animal kingdom and look at how sharing behaviors manifest there.

Observations and studies have shown that many social animals display a form of sharing behavior. For instance, vampire bats, which feed exclusively on the blood of other animals, are known to regurgitate blood and share it with other bats who have failed to feed. The recipients are usually relatives or previously generous donors. This behavior, known as reciprocal altruism, demonstrates a primitive form of sharing and cooperation, and the social norms that enforce it.

Similarly, among primates, grooming is a common behavior where an individual will clean the fur of another, picking out parasites and dead skin. This not only helps to keep the recipient healthy but is also a way to form and maintain social bonds. Oftentimes, grooming is reciprocal, with the groomed individual returning the favor either immediately or at a later stage. This reciprocity, akin to the idea of 'tit-for-tat', is a primitive form of fairness and justice, the cornerstones of human morality.

So, where does evolution fit into this narrative? These behaviors are hypothesized to have evolved through natural selection because they offer survival advantages. In the case of the vampire bats, sharing blood helps to reduce the risk of starvation in the group. If a bat fails to feed, it can rely on the generosity of others to get through the night. By sharing their resources in times of abundance, bats ensure their own survival in times of scarcity, thus increasing their overall chances of survival and reproduction. Similarly, grooming among primates not only helps maintain health but also strengthens social bonds, providing access to allies in times of conflict or danger.

This discussion indicates that some aspects of morality, such as sharing, cooperation, and a sense of fairness, have likely evolved as survival strategies among social animals, eventually becoming more complex and sophisticated in humans. However, this is only a part of the story.

With these examples of sharing and grooming among animals, we see the basic tenets of social contract theory in play: individuals forgo certain liberties (in this case, sole possession of a resource or personal time spent for self-benefit) to receive mutual benefits. This cooperative behavior underscores the evolution of moral norms that dictate how individuals within a group should interact to maximize collective wellbeing.

But morality extends beyond cooperation and sharing. Many animals exhibit empathy, the ability to understand and share the feelings of another. Elephants are known to console one another in times of distress, gently touching the other with their trunk. Rats have been shown to free other rats from cages, choosing to do so even when there's a chocolate treat they could indulge in instead. This willingness to put others' needs before their own immediate desires showcases an elementary form of empathy and selflessness, both key ingredients of moral conduct.

Through evolution, these rudimentary moral behaviors observed in animals have been woven into the social fabric of human societies, expanded, and refined. Human morality includes a wide array of virtues such as honesty, integrity, loyalty, respect, and many others. We have developed complex moral and legal codes that govern our behavior, set out rights and responsibilities, and provide mechanisms for dealing with transgressions.

All these behaviors and norms point to a critical aspect of morality: choice. Whether it's a bat choosing to share its food, a primate deciding to groom another, or a human choosing to tell the truth in a difficult situation, free will appears to be an integral part of morality. The exercise of choice, guided by internal moral compass and societal norms, is the thread that ties together our actions, decisions, and interactions.

In the context of evolution, it can be argued that free will and the ability to make choices are survival strategies that have been favored by natural selection. Being able to weigh options and make decisions that enhance personal and collective wellbeing would confer a survival advantage. Over millions of years, this decision-making capacity, powered by a progressively complex brain, has become an integral part of who we are as a species.

With this perspective, we realize that morality isn't an abstract concept imposed on us by society or religion, but rather a natural product of our evolutionary history. It's woven into our biological and psychological makeup. In the next section, we will delve deeper into the role of free will in shaping our moral judgments and actions. For now, ponder on the evolution of morality and its implications for our understanding of human nature.

9.2 FREE WILL: THE UNSUSPECTED BACKBONE OF MORALITY

Free will is often viewed as an isolated construct, something that stands alone and independent. However, when we dive into the complex mechanisms of the mind, we find that it acts as an unseen backbone supporting many constructs of our cognition and behavior - none more so than morality. Moral decision-making is a complex process, a dance between our ethical understanding, societal norms, and individual judgment. Free will, in this regard, steps in as the choreographer, subtly but significantly influencing our moves.

In recent decades, researchers have started unraveling the complex relationship between free will and morality. One groundbreaking research that stands out was conducted by Rebecca Saxe and colleagues at MIT. Their studies focused on the temporoparietal junction (TPJ), an area of the brain known to be active during moral decision-making. Through innovative experiments involving magnetic stimulation of the TPJ, they discovered that when the TPJ was disrupted, participants' moral judgments of attempted harm (where intention was present, but the outcome was harmless) were significantly affected.

This experiment provides a fascinating example of how our neurobiology can influence our moral decisions and, by extension, our perceived free will. The researchers used a technique called transcranial magnetic stimulation (TMS), which involved stimulating the TPJ with magnetic fields. Participants in the study were then asked to judge a series of moral dilemmas. Interestingly, when the TPJ was temporarily disrupted, participants were less able to condemn attempted harm. They seemingly failed to consider the perpetrator's harmful intent when the outcome was neutral.

The implication of this study on our understanding of free will and morality is immense. If a physical intervention can alter our moral judgment, it suggests that our decisions, often attributed to free will, are in part, a result of the neurobiological processes within our brain. It hints at the intriguing prospect that what we consider to be a product of our independent will might be more influenced by our brain's biology than we previously thought.

The findings from Saxe's experiment contribute to an evolving debate: if our decisions can be influenced by physical changes in our brain, where does free will come into play, and to what extent does it influence our moral judgments? To answer this, we must explore the intricate network of factors that come into play when we make a moral decision.

When faced with a moral dilemma, our brain embarks on a complex cognitive journey. It weighs the pros and cons, considers societal norms, personal beliefs, potential consequences, and emotional implications. Then, it arrives at a decision that, to us, seems like a product of our free will. However, if we dissect this process further, we realize that each of these factors is linked to a tangible process in our brain, involving specific regions and biochemical reactions.

Delving deeper into this journey, let's explore the role of societal norms in our decision-making process. Society, with its rules and norms, exerts a powerful influence on our behaviors. We tend to align our actions and decisions with what is deemed acceptable in our society to maintain harmony and avoid conflict. Our brain, in an attempt to comply with these norms, often nudges our decisions in a particular direction. This suggests that even though we might feel that we are making a decision out of our free will, it might be significantly guided by societal influences, undermining the 'free' in our free will.

Next, let's consider our personal beliefs. Each of us holds a set of beliefs and values that guide our actions. These beliefs, shaped by our experiences, learning, and genetic predispositions, act as a personal compass. When faced with a moral decision, our brain automatically aligns the decision with our beliefs. However, the intricate process that shapes our beliefs is influenced by genetic and environmental factors, raising the question of the extent of freedom in our free will.

Further, our brain also considers potential consequences when making a decision. If an action leads to negative consequences, our brain will usually steer clear of it. However, this process of weighing consequences is not entirely free from influence. Neurotransmitters like dopamine, known for their role in reward processing, play a crucial part in this. If our brain anticipates a rewarding outcome, dopamine release motivates us towards the action, suggesting that our neurochemistry might be influencing our perceived free will.

Finally, our emotions play a vital part in our decisions. Our brain has a dedicated limbic system to process emotions, which significantly sways our decisions. However, our emotions are deeply intertwined with our biology, with neurotransmitters and hormones playing a key role in their regulation. This implies that our emotional decisions, often deemed a product of our free will, might be more grounded in our biology than we realize.

In short, each factor that we believe to be independently influencing our moral decisions under the guise of free will has a biological counterpart. This doesn't deny the existence of free will but rather suggests that it might not be as 'free' as we think it is. Our free will, in this context, seems to be a product of a complex interplay between our neurobiology, cognition, and environment. It becomes clear that our free will might be subtly guided by these factors, acting as an unsuspected backbone of our morality.

An excellent real-world example of this is the story of Phineas Gage, a railroad construction foreman who in 1848 survived a severe brain injury when an iron rod shot through his skull, damaging his frontal lobes. Gage experienced a dramatic personality shift post-accident, becoming impulsive, erratic, and irresponsible. His moral compass seemed to have been skewed. This case provides a unique insight into the deep-rooted neurobiological influences on our morality, suggesting that our moral decisions may not be as freely willed as we think.

Similarly, modern neuroimaging studies have revealed fascinating insights into the neurobiological aspects of our morality. For instance, research has shown that the right temporoparietal junction (TPJ), an area of the brain involved in understanding others' perspectives, plays a crucial role in moral judgments. Remarkably, researchers were able to manipulate participants' moral decisions by using transcranial magnetic stimulation (TMS) to temporarily disrupt the functioning of the right TPJ. These studies again raise the question: if our moral decisions can be manipulated by altering our brain activity, how 'free' is our free will?

These neurobiological influences on our morality also spark ethical debates. For example, if our actions are heavily influenced by our neurobiology, how do we assign responsibility for one's actions? If someone commits a crime because of an underlying brain disorder, should they be held accountable in the same way as someone without such a disorder? These are complex issues that provoke considerable discussion and have substantial implications for our legal systems, which we will explore in subsequent chapters.

In summary, it is clear that our moral judgments, which seem to be products of our free will, are deeply intertwined with our neurobiology. While this does not negate the existence of free will, it certainly adds layers of complexity to it and urges us to rethink our understanding of it. Free will, rather than being an independent entity, seems to be an intricate product of our biology, cognition, and environment - making it the unsuspected backbone of our morality.

We've journeyed from the evolutionary roots of morality to the interplay between free will and moral judgments, seeing the pervasive influence of neurobiological factors. Let's continue our exploration into this captivating world, where neuroscience, philosophy, and ethics converge, to further unravel the mysteries of free will.

In our next section, 9.3 From Theory to Reality: Neuroethical Implications, we will delve into the ethical considerations stemming from our expanding knowledge about the neural underpinnings of free will and morality. We will discuss how the studies mentioned earlier, along with other groundbreaking research, are not just altering our understanding of free will and morality but are also presenting us with profound ethical challenges.

In this realm of neuroethics, we will discuss questions such as, "If our moral decisions are influenced by our neurobiology, to what extent can we be held accountable for them?", "Should the knowledge about a person's neural predispositions be admissible in court?", and "Could this knowledge be used to manipulate people's moral decisions, and if so, should it?"

We will also discuss how this knowledge could potentially be used to develop novel treatments for mental disorders associated with impaired moral judgments, such as psychopathy. However, this potential benefit also raises its own set of ethical questions: "Could such treatments inadvertently alter a person's identity?", "Who gets to decide what constitutes 'normal' moral judgments?", and "What might be the societal implications of such treatments?"

By discussing these neuroethical implications, we aim to demonstrate the profound societal and personal implications of the science of free will. This complex dance between free will, morality, and neurobiology does not exist in a vacuum but rather in the rich tapestry of our lives, shaping our laws, healthcare systems, and personal identities.

We will then conclude Chapter 9 by revisiting philosophical debates on moral responsibility, in light of the knowledge we have gained about the neurobiological influences on our morality. We will discuss various perspectives on how to assign moral responsibility in a world where free will is not as 'free' as we once thought, providing a philosophical grounding to our scientific journey.

9.3 FROM THEORY TO REALITY: NEUROETHICAL IMPLICATIONS

The fusion of neuroscience and ethics, known as neuroethics, presents a fascinating landscape for the exploration of the relationship between free will and morality. With the increasing ability to peek into the human brain and understand the neurobiological underpinnings of our decisions, we find ourselves standing on the precipice of myriad ethical questions. How do we navigate this novel terrain where our understanding of the neural mechanisms behind free will could fundamentally shift our societal norms, legal principles, and individual identities?

Our understanding that decisions, moral or otherwise, arise from a neural orchestra is undeniably influencing our notions of personal accountability. If we consider that our choices are the result of complex neural computations, the deterministic echoes resonate strongly, raising questions about moral responsibility. To illustrate, let us revisit the case of Alex we introduced in Chapter 2. If we find that his transgressions were partially a result of a dysfunctional neural circuitry, could we still hold him fully responsible for his actions? From a neuroethical perspective, this question probes into unchartered territories, questioning our traditional views on personal accountability.

Taking this argument a step further, we encounter a contentious debate – the admissibility of neurobiological evidence in courtrooms. If neuroscience can provide insights into the brain that could potentially explain certain behaviors, should such information be utilized in the legal process? Here, we step into the sphere of 10.1 Law and Order: The Implicit Role of Free Will, a preview into our exploration in Chapter 10.

The potential manipulation of moral decisions, too, presents a significant ethical challenge. As we have discovered, certain brain regions play a crucial role in moral decision-making, and external influences can alter the activity in these regions. This reality thrusts us into a domain of potential ethical breaches where such knowledge could be exploited for manipulation, leading us to question if there should be regulations in place to prevent such occurrences.

The implications of neuroethics are not confined solely to law and societal norms; they reach into healthcare systems and individual identities as well. Let us consider the potential development of treatments for mental disorders associated with impaired moral judgments, like psychopathy. If neuroscientific advances could help 'normalize' the moral decisions of those with such conditions, it raises questions about the definition of 'normal' moral judgments. Who holds the authority to define this 'normalcy'? What happens to the individual's identity when their moral decision-making is altered?

From this vantage point, the implications of neuroethics stretch beyond the personal sphere, potentially influencing societal norms and legislation. In the following subsection, we will delve deeper into the intertwining paths of neuroscience, morality, and law.

We stand at the forefront of a brave new world where neuroscience, morality, and free will intermingle, and navigating this terrain requires a robust ethical compass. As our knowledge expands and the neuroethical landscape broadens, we must tread with caution and respect, considering the profound societal and personal implications of our quest to understand free will.

Tracing back the historical evolution of neuroethics is much like embarking on a journey through a time tunnel, where the changing perceptions about the mind-brain interface provide a fascinating insight into the evolution of our understanding of free will. The discipline of neuroethics, emerging at the intersection of biomedical ethics and neuroscience, has undergone significant evolution, mirroring our growing knowledge of the brain and the complexities of human behavior.

The origins of neuroethics can be traced back to the philosophical debates about the nature of the mind and its relationship with the body, a theme that was explored by Descartes in the 17th century. However, the term 'neuroethics' itself was coined only in the early 21st century, reflecting the increasing recognition of the ethical implications of our expanding knowledge about the brain. The contemporary domain of neuroethics encapsulates not just the ethical issues arising from neuroscientific research, but also the investigation of how neuroscientific facts can illuminate traditional philosophical questions.

One crucial domain where neuroethics intersects with our understanding of free will is in the realm of moral and legal responsibility. As neuroscience advances, we have gained unprecedented insights into the biological basis of our actions. This has brought about radical changes in how we perceive free will, and consequently, our concepts of moral and legal responsibility. Historical perspectives on neuroethics reveal that the correlation between an individual's neural architecture and their capacity for decision-making was not always so apparent. However, as our understanding of neuroscience has expanded, it has become clear that our brain's architecture plays a substantial role in our decision-making processes and, in turn, our actions.

The implications of neuroscience on our concepts of free will have profound effects on the legal domain. Historically, legal systems have largely operated on the premise that individuals possess free will and, hence, can be held accountable for their actions. However, as neuroscience increasingly reveals the underlying biological mechanisms influencing our decisions, it begs the question – to what extent can we truly hold individuals accountable for their actions?

Reconciling the concepts of free will and determinism in the legal landscape requires a careful evaluation of neuroethical considerations. Courts around the world are beginning to witness the introduction of neuroscientific evidence, ranging from genetic predispositions to specific brain abnormalities, to influence verdicts and sentencing. This raises a plethora of neuroethical concerns that need to be thoroughly evaluated before such practice becomes commonplace.

For instance, the use of neuroscientific evidence could potentially lead to a 'neurological exceptionalism,' where individuals with specific neurological conditions may be absolved of their responsibility, thus creating a disparity in the justice system. Moreover, it might foster a deterministic view where individuals are seen merely as the products of their neurobiology, thereby undermining the principles of justice.

On the flip side, neuroethical considerations might provide a fresh perspective on punishment and rehabilitation. If our actions are indeed heavily influenced by our neurobiology, it opens up avenues for rehabilitating offenders through neuroscientific interventions, thereby focusing more on reform rather than retribution.

To truly grasp the profound implications of neuroethics in our everyday lives, let's consider some hypothetical scenarios.

Imagine a situation where a man with no prior history of violent behavior suddenly starts exhibiting aggressive tendencies. On examination, it is revealed that he has a tumor in his brain's frontal lobe, a region associated with impulse control. If this man commits a violent crime, to what extent should he be held responsible? Would his sentence differ if the tumor were removed and his aggressive tendencies diminished? Such a scenario brings the neuroethical considerations of responsibility and punishment to the forefront.

In another scenario, consider a futuristic society where neurotechnology has advanced to the point where devices can accurately predict an individual's likelihood of committing a crime based on their neural patterns. Should such individuals be subjected to preemptive interventions or surveillance? This scenario presents a significant neuroethical dilemma, balancing the prevention of potential harm against individual rights and freedoms.

The neuroethical implications of our understanding of free will and morality are subject to interpretation, varying significantly across different cultures, societies, and philosophical schools of thought. For instance, Western philosophical traditions have often gravitated towards the concept of free will, grounding moral and legal responsibility in the individual's capacity to make free choices.

On the other hand, many Eastern philosophies, such as Buddhism and Hinduism, espouse a more deterministic view, emphasizing the influence of karma or the law of cause and effect on our actions. From these perspectives, our actions are not solely a product of our free will but are influenced by our past actions and their consequences.

Moreover, different societies might place varying degrees of emphasis on individual responsibility versus collective responsibility. For example, individualistic societies might favor a concept of free will where individuals are seen as autonomous agents responsible for their actions. In contrast, collectivist societies might perceive actions as the product of broader social and environmental factors, thereby espousing a more deterministic view.

Neuroethics, therefore, is not a monolithic entity but is subject to interpretation and adaptation based on cultural, societal, and philosophical contexts.

Neuroethical considerations are an essential part of our understanding of free will and morality. The exploration of neuroethical issues offers a fresh lens through which we can reevaluate our concepts of moral and legal responsibility, societal norms, and cultural perspectives. As we move forward, it is crucial to navigate these neuroethical issues with sensitivity and open-mindedness, fostering a dialogue that is both inclusive and forward-thinking.

9.4 PHILOSOPHY REVISITED: DEBATES ON MORAL RESPONSIBILITY

As we embark on the exploration of this section, we find ourselves at the confluence of the ideas of determinism, free will, and morality. This section, imbued with philosophical musings and concrete examples, will shine a spotlight on the intricate knot of moral responsibility.

The keystone of moral responsibility in philosophical discourse is the idea of "free will". An assumption operates underneath this concept – the idea that individuals, empowered with the capacity of choice, have the capability to discern right from wrong, and thus should be held accountable for the consequences of their actions. This forms the crux of our societal understanding of justice, fairness, and morality. As such, it's crucial to underline this principle in our discussion.

We have traversed this territory before in our exploration of free will, where we've studied it as an isolated concept. Now, we must reassess its role in the broader picture, as a primary pillar holding up the edifice of moral responsibility. Thus, let's revisit the nuances of the concept and its contentious standing in philosophical debates. In this section, we will delve deep into philosophical discussions, studying varied viewpoints, and finding the impact these have on our understanding of morality.

This first interaction has set the stage for an in-depth exploration of the philosophical landscapes that form the backdrop of moral responsibility. As we further delve into the topic, we shall discuss various schools of philosophical thought, scrutinize their arguments, and attempt to connect the dots that lead us back to the heart of moral responsibility.

We shall also draw upon previous knowledge established in this book and enrich our current understanding, painting a holistic picture of moral responsibility in the grand tableau of determinism and free will.

The first aspect to examine in our philosophical journey through moral responsibility is the association between free will and determinism. From an objective standpoint, these concepts seem incompatible. Determinism implies a world where actions and decisions are dictated by an unbroken chain of causes and effects, leaving no room for the unpredictability and freedom of choice that free will advocates.

This is where the debate branches out into two main philosophical camps: compatibilism and incompatibilism. Compatibilists argue that determinism and free will can coexist. They suggest that even though our actions might be determined by past events, we are still acting according to our desires and intentions – we are still exercising our will. This viewpoint could align with a perspective we've touched upon earlier, the deterministic view of free will.

On the other hand, incompatibilists hold that determinism and free will are entirely incompatible. If our actions are predetermined, how can we genuinely exercise free will? They assert that moral responsibility requires an agent to have real alternatives to choose from, a possibility nullified by determinism.

In our previous discussions, we've encountered a similar divide while debating the concept of free will. Now, it is the same chasm, except viewed from the other side – the side of moral responsibility.

This forms the basis of our philosophical discourse on moral responsibility. As we move forward, we will delve deeper into these perspectives, exploring their implications and criticisms, and how they tie into the broader debates on moral responsibility.

Our discussion wouldn't be complete without addressing the problem of moral luck, a thought-provoking issue that plays a crucial role in our discourse on moral responsibility. Moral luck refers to the notion that our moral responsibility could be significantly influenced, if not entirely dictated, by factors beyond our control. This concept might seem disconcerting, as it throws into question our basic notions of fairness and justice.

Take, for instance, the case of two drivers. Driver A, while driving home after a party, slightly swerves into the oncoming lane but quickly corrects his course. There are no other vehicles in sight, and he reaches home safely. Driver B, in a similar situation, swerves and collides with another vehicle, leading to fatal consequences. The only difference in their actions was the presence of another vehicle, an external factor they had no control over. Yet, society's moral and legal judgment of them will drastically differ.

This example illustrates the moral luck dilemma. If determinism is true, and our actions are predestined, aren't we all, in a sense, subjects of moral luck? Can we genuinely be held morally responsible for actions dictated by factors beyond our control?

This question, too, has divided philosophers. Some argue that moral luck exposes a fundamental flaw in our judgment system, leading us to assign praise or blame unfairly. Others contend that moral luck is an inherent part of life, and our moral judgments should reflect this reality.

Essentially, moral responsibility is a complex terrain, with the crisscrossing paths of free will, determinism, compatibilism, incompatibilism, and moral luck. However, it is vital terrain to traverse, as it allows us to better understand the nature of human morality, the implications of our actions, and the principles of justice we uphold in society.

Having discussed these philosophical debates, let's now turn our attention to the implications they bear on our societal structures, mainly legal and ethical systems. Our legal system, for instance, relies heavily on the notion of moral responsibility. The idea of 'just deserts,' that one should be rewarded or punished in proportion to their actions, is a cornerstone of many justice systems around the world.

If determinism threatens the concept of moral responsibility, it likewise throws into question the basis of our justice systems. If our actions are entirely dictated by factors beyond our control, is it then fair to punish or reward individuals based on those actions? This question is not just theoretical but has practical implications, influencing how we structure our societies and legislate our laws.

On the other hand, if compatibilism holds true, we may continue to assign moral responsibility, albeit with a nuanced understanding of free will. Recognizing that our actions are influenced, but not entirely determined, by external factors allows us to maintain a sense of justice while also being more compassionate and understanding of the circumstances that shape people's choices.

In the ethical domain, these debates have significant implications as well. They influence our understanding of right and wrong, our judgment of others' actions, and our perception of our own moral agency. They shape our personal and collective moral codes and inform how we navigate ethical dilemmas.

In conclusion, philosophy doesn't merely provide theoretical debates about moral responsibility; it critically informs our societal, legal, and ethical structures. While we may not arrive at a definitive resolution to these debates, understanding them enriches our perspective on human nature, morality, and free will. It illuminates the complexities of human choice and behavior and highlights the nuances of our moral judgments.

In the next chapter, we will delve deeper into one such critical area of application, exploring the intricate relationship between free will, morality, and law. As we transition from theory to practice, we will encounter new challenges and revelations, further deepening our understanding of these profound concepts.

CHAPTER 10: LEGAL IMPLICATIONS OF FREEWILL

As we journey through the maze of free will and determinism, we arrive at the doors of the law - an institution that reflects our societal values, moral principles, and beliefs about human behavior. Throughout history, law has been one of the crucial pillars guiding societal interactions, asserting a semblance of order in our diverse and complex human existence. It has also been one of the areas most influenced by our understanding of free will. The concepts of guilt, innocence, responsibility, and punishment that underpin the legal system are deeply intertwined with our assumptions about free will. This chapter, therefore, aims to explore this fascinating intersection of free will, determinism, and legality.

10.1 LAW AND ORDER: THE IMPLICIT ROLE OF FREE WILL

The notion of 'law and order' has served as a cornerstone of organized societies throughout history. Laws, the codified set of rules governing behavior, and the broader concept of order, the social harmony resulting from adherence to these laws, are foundational elements of any society. They operate on the tacit assumption of human agency and choice - the idea that individuals are free to make decisions and are therefore accountable for their actions. This is where the concept of free will is intrinsically embedded in our legal systems.

Free will, as we have discussed earlier in this book, is the ability to make choices that are genuinely one's own and not the outcome of causal chains of events that trace back to the dawn of time. In this context, law serves to guide these choices along paths that society deems acceptable, establishing norms of behavior that serve to protect individual rights and maintain social harmony. The assumption of free will is critical in this equation because it underpins the idea of responsibility. If individuals were not free to make choices, it would be fundamentally unfair, not to mention impractical, to hold them accountable for their actions.

However, it is crucial to note that this relationship between law and free will is not explicit. There is no statute or legal document explicitly stating that the legal system operates under the assumption of free will. Rather, it's an implicit principle woven into the very fabric of law and order. It can be seen in the way we approach guilt and innocence, in the method we assign responsibility, and even in the way society reacts to the pronouncement of judgments.

The legal system's reliance on free will is so deeply ingrained that we often don't even notice it. However, when viewed through the lens of free will and determinism, the law's many intricacies become fascinating subjects of exploration. That's precisely what we aim to do in this section.

If we consider the law as a means of deterring 'unwanted' behavior, the implicit role of free will becomes even more evident. Deterrence operates on the assumption that individuals have a choice in their actions. When faced with a potential decision to commit a crime, the fear of legal repercussions is supposed to serve as a deterrent, discouraging that choice. In other words, laws are designed to 'nudge' our free will in the right direction.

Take, for example, the law against theft. The premise is simple: if you steal, you will face legal consequences, which might include a fine, imprisonment, or both. This law, like any other, is intended to deter potential thieves by presenting a clear consequence for their actions.

The key factor here is the presentation of a choice. The potential thief can choose to steal and face the punishment or choose not to steal and avoid the consequences. This simple scenario is a perfect illustration of how free will is implicitly woven into the fabric of our legal system.

It's worth noting, however, that this paradigm of law and order may seem overly simplistic in the face of real-world complexities. Human behavior is rarely motivated by a single factor, and choices are not always as clear-cut as our theoretical example. The socioeconomic status, education, upbringing, and countless other factors play a role in shaping our decisions, often blurring the lines between 'free' will and determinism. This is precisely why our exploration of the legal implications of free will must delve deeper.

As we dig deeper into this intricate topic, it's important to consider another pivotal aspect of our legal systems - the intersection of law and morality. One could argue that laws serve not just as a deterrent for antisocial behaviors, but also as a moral compass, guiding individuals towards 'right' actions and away from 'wrong' ones. This moral aspect of the law underscores the implicit role of free will even further.

Consider the laws concerning human rights, such as those prohibiting discrimination or hate speech. These laws do more than just punish transgressions; they make a moral statement about the values that our society holds dear - values such as equality, respect, and dignity for all. By adhering to these laws, individuals are not just avoiding punishment; they are aligning their actions with the moral values upheld by the law.

The role of free will becomes evident here as individuals are supposed to freely choose to act in alignment with these values, influenced not just by the fear of legal repercussions, but also by their moral compass. In essence, the law is believed to provide an environment where people can exercise their free will to make morally right decisions.

Yet, this brings us to another dimension of the law-free will conundrum: What if an individual's moral compass doesn't align with the law? What happens when the exercise of free will leads to actions that, while legally sound, are morally questionable? Such instances underscore the delicate balance between free will, morality, and the law - a balance that often treads on a tightrope.

One of the most profound areas where the concept of free will subtly resides within the legal system is in the realm of punishment and rehabilitation. How a society decides to punish its wrongdoers or work towards their rehabilitation is intimately tied to its belief in free will.

If we assume free will, it becomes reasonable to administer punitive measures as a response to criminal actions. The belief here is that individuals, having freely chosen their actions and having been aware of the laws they were breaking, should face consequences. This perspective aligns with retributive justice theories that see punishment as a deserved consequence of wrongdoing.

On the contrary, rehabilitation takes a different view. Here, the goal isn't to simply punish the wrongdoer but to change their behavior and reintegrate them into society. This approach often goes hand-in-hand with the acknowledgment that external factors beyond an individual's control can influence their actions, somewhat challenging the concept of free will.

In essence, whether our legal systems lean towards punishment or rehabilitation might reflect our collective belief, or disbelief, in free will. A legal system rooted in retribution might imply a stronger belief in free will, while a rehabilitative system might suggest recognition of determinism.

The concept of free will doesn't just manifest in lawmaking or court rulings, but also significantly shapes the creation and application of legal precedents. A precedent, a legal case that establishes a rule or principle that courts follow when deciding later cases with similar issues or facts, heavily leans on the assumption of free will.

Precedents hinge on the belief that individuals, given the same set of circumstances, have the free will to choose similarly. That's why, for instance, if a court decides that under particular facts it is a violation of equal protection to award damages on the basis of race, future courts will follow that decision. The underlying assumption is that individuals, fully aware of the potential consequences of their actions (such as a violation of equal protection), would refrain from such behavior. It suggests that individuals could have chosen differently under the same circumstances, reinforcing the idea of free will.

But what if this isn't the case? What if determinism holds, and our actions, even in similar situations, are the result of our unique genetic makeup and life experiences? That would challenge the very basis of legal precedents, making room for the argument that every case is unique, given the unique deterministic paths of each person involved.

Once we recognize the deep-seated role of the assumption of free will in our legal system, it forces us to ask the difficult questions: What if our understanding of free will is flawed? What if deterministic forces have more say in our actions than we give them credit for?

In the face of such inquiries, the legal system may have to reorient its understanding of responsibility, guilt, and punishment. If deterministic factors significantly influence our behavior, our legal paradigm, based on the idea that individuals could have acted differently under the same circumstances, may need to be reassessed.

Such a reformulation doesn't necessarily mean a disintegration of our current legal system, but it would certainly call for a more nuanced understanding of human behavior. This could potentially involve greater emphasis on rehabilitative justice, considering the deterministic influences on behavior. A shift from retribution to rehabilitation could change the way we view the role of the legal system, focusing more on the prevention of harmful behaviors rather than merely punishing them.

An understanding of deterministic influences on behavior could also lead to a more compassionate legal system, one that understands that people sometimes make bad decisions because of factors beyond their control. This could lead to the development of programs that aim to mitigate these influences, providing support to individuals who might be more susceptible to making harmful decisions due to their circumstances.

However, any significant change in the legal system would require a societal shift in understanding, which would undoubtedly be a long, contentious process. Nevertheless, it's a conversation worth having if we want a legal system that truly reflects our understanding of human behavior.

This concludes our exploration of the implicit role of free will in our legal system, but it's just the beginning of our journey into the legal implications of free will and determinism.

10.2 ASSIGNING RESPONSIBILITY: A JUDICIAL TIGHTROPE WALK

The complexity of assigning responsibility within the justice system is analogous to a high-wire balancing act. It's a topic that is rooted in an intricate interplay of determinism and free will. The legal system assumes that individuals possess free will and are capable of making independent decisions. This foundational assumption is the basis on which consequences for actions are determined.

At first glance, it appears relatively simple. Someone commits an action deemed illegal, they are apprehended, tried, and if found guilty, they are punished in line with the legal standards for such a crime. However, as we've explored earlier in the book, the underpinnings of our decision-making processes are more complex than they initially appear.

To illustrate this complexity, let's revisit some of the foundational concepts we've covered in the previous chapters. In Chapter 1, we delved into the evolutionary origins of free will. Our actions are influenced not only by our momentary desires and decisions but also by the intricate interplay of our genetic makeup and our environment. This biological and environmental determinism can significantly shape our behavioral traits, sometimes in ways that predispose us to certain actions.

This raises an intriguing question: to what extent should we consider these deterministic influences when assigning legal responsibility? For instance, if an individual's genetic predisposition or environmental circumstances drive them towards committing a crime, are they entirely at fault? Or should we consider the determinism that shaped their decision-making process?

On the other hand, we can't completely absolve individuals of responsibility based on deterministic influences. We can think of numerous cases where people from similar genetic or environmental backgrounds have made different choices – some leaning towards unlawful behaviors, others conforming to societal norms. This showcases the element of free will in action, guiding our decisions and actions despite the determinism inherent in our biology and environment.

This concept ties back to Chapter 2, where we analyzed the cognitive machinery of free will. Our brains are complex decision-making machines, processing information from our surroundings and our inner thoughts to direct our actions. Free will, in this context, can be seen as a manifestation of this intricate neural processing. While determinism sets the stage and provides the script, our brains – our 'selves' – are the directors, making decisions based on the available information.

Here, we find ourselves in a conundrum. We can't deny the role of deterministic factors, but neither can we ignore the role of free will in our decision-making processes. Our choices aren't wholly predetermined, but they aren't completely free either.

This perspective poses challenges for the legal system, which largely operates on a binary understanding of responsibility. In most jurisdictions, an individual is either found guilty or not guilty, and there's little room for nuanced considerations of the deterministic influences on their actions.

We may find some answers in the legal principle of "mens rea" or "guilty mind." This principle holds that an individual's mental state at the time of the criminal act – their intentions, knowledge, and beliefs – plays a critical role in determining their legal responsibility. This idea is strongly tied to the concept of free will – that we are conscious agents, making deliberate choices based on our thoughts and intentions.

On the other hand, deterministic influences come into play in the form of "mitigating factors" or "extenuating circumstances," where the court may consider aspects like the individual's background, upbringing, mental health, and other environmental influences that could have significantly impacted their decision-making ability. Such considerations can sometimes result in reduced sentences, portraying an intersection of free will and determinism in the law.

But where do we draw the line? If we consider every deterministic influence, won't every action be justified in some way? On the contrary, if we rely solely on the concept of free will, won't we overlook the critical influences that drive people to commit certain acts?

The legal implications of the free will versus determinism debate bring us face-to-face with these challenging questions. Our legal systems, as they stand, aren't fully equipped to address this intricate interplay of factors. This necessitates a thoughtful reconsideration of our legal principles, keeping in mind the nuances of the free will versus determinism debate we've explored throughout the book.

Remember the experiment discussed in Chapter 4 where participants were subjected to transcranial magnetic stimulation, which influenced their moral judgments. What if such a person commits a crime under this influence? Can they be held responsible for their actions? While this may seem like a plot from a sci-fi movie, it's not entirely implausible, given the rapid advances in neuroscience.

Our current understanding of neurology also brings us face-to-face with challenging questions. Consider the case of Charles Whitman, a man who murdered his wife and mother, and then killed 14 more people in a shooting spree at the University of Texas in 1966. Upon autopsy, it was discovered that Whitman had a brain tumor pressing against his amygdala, the part of the brain associated with emotions, especially fear and aggression. Could it be possible that Whitman was not exercising free will when he went on his rampage, but was instead being compelled by a brain tumor?

Moreover, the case of Phineas Gage, a railroad construction foreman who survived an accident in which a large iron rod was driven completely through his head, gives us more insight. Before the accident, Gage was well-liked and responsible. After the accident, he became erratic, irritable, and irresponsible. Clearly, the accident had changed Gage. His case tells us that our brains determine our personalities and behavior to a great extent. So, to what extent was Gage responsible for his post-accident behavior?

Such cases force us to reconsider the concept of responsibility in light of our growing understanding of the brain. If certain actions are driven by deterministic influences that are beyond our control, it becomes complex to assign responsibility. And the law, as a system of assigning responsibility, might need to reconsider its approach.

These are complex, multifaceted issues that do not lend themselves to simple answers. However, recognizing and exploring these challenges can help us better understand the complexity of human behavior and the importance of considering both free will and determinism in our attempts to make sense of it.

Thus, assigning responsibility is indeed a judicial tightrope walk. The law attempts to balance the idea of free will, which places the individual at the center of their actions, and the idea of determinism, which acknowledges the broader influences that shape an individual's behavior. The balance is delicate, and our understanding is evolving, just as our understanding of free will & determinism continues to evolve.

As we proceed, we need to rethink the concept of responsibility, not just in the courtroom but in our daily lives as well. It is important for us as a society to understand and empathize with the various influences that shape an individual's actions, without absolving them of responsibility for their actions. The paradox of free will and determinism compels us to seek a nuanced understanding of responsibility, one that takes into account the complex interplay of various factors that drive our actions.

The philosophy of law, or jurisprudence, provides an excellent platform for understanding how responsibility is assigned and what role free will plays in this process. Classical jurisprudence considers an individual responsible for his or her actions unless the individual was forced to act against his or her will or if the individual was not in a mental state to understand the nature and consequences of his or her actions.

However, our expanding knowledge about the brain and the role of determinism could add another layer of complexity to this issue. A person's actions could be influenced by deterministic forces, such as their genetic makeup, upbringing, or even an undiagnosed brain condition, as in the case of Charles Whitman.

In this regard, the legal system may need to update its understanding of responsibility to account for deterministic influences. For instance, should a person with a proven predisposition towards violence be held to the same standard of responsibility as a person without such a predisposition? The answer to this question is not straightforward and calls for a careful reconsideration of the concept of responsibility.

The assignment of responsibility in the legal system is indeed a tightrope walk. It must find a balance between acknowledging free will and understanding deterministic influences on human behavior. As our knowledge of the human brain and its influence on our actions grows, we may need to develop a more nuanced understanding of responsibility that can account for the complex interplay of free will and determinism.

10.3 RETHINKING PUNISHMENT: IS THERE A BETTER WAY?

We commence Section 10.3 with an exploration of the theme, "Rethinking Punishment: Is There a Better Way?" under the umbrella of legal implications related to the debate on free will. We tread into this section with the cognizance that our understanding of punishment has been shaped, to a great extent, by the conventional outlook of the legal system, where punishment is seen as an outcome of retributive justice. This notion of punishment weaves itself into the societal fabric, not as an isolated legal principle, but as a widely accepted moral axiom deeply rooted in our collective consciousness.

The conventional view of punishment is twofold, primarily considering it a means of retribution for a wrongful act and secondarily as a deterrent for potential future acts of similar nature. The foundation of such a perspective is built on the principle of "just deserts" or the moral philosophy of "an eye for an eye." In this philosophy, punishment is seen as a deserved response to an act deemed morally or legally wrong. Such a perspective necessitates the presence of free will, which allows individuals the ability to make a choice between right and wrong actions. The deterrent effect of punishment is perceived as a mechanism that discourages individuals from committing wrongful acts, thereby fostering a sense of societal order and security.

Examining this perspective within the context of determinism opens up the discourse for critical debate. If our actions are the result of deterministic processes, can we claim that punishment as a form of retribution is justified? The central question here is the morality and effectiveness of punishment in a deterministic paradigm. If determinism holds, then the very idea of retribution could be fundamentally flawed. Individuals, as per determinism, act as they do because of a series of causal influences outside their control. Therefore, the notion of "just deserts" becomes questionable, and the moral justification for punitive responses is undermined.

This segment of the chapter takes us into the crosshairs of conflicting ideologies, and it becomes imperative to tread these waters carefully, giving due respect to all perspectives. With this introduction, we've set the foundation for an elaborate and explorative discourse on rethinking punishment. The journey we embark on from here shall take us through the nuances of traditional views on punishment, criticisms, exploration of alternatives, and the role of neuroscience in understanding punishment.

To begin our deep dive, we must first understand the conventional perspective on punishment. Rooted deeply in our collective consciousness, these conventional views find their genesis in religious, cultural, and legal contexts. The Judeo-Christian concept of divine justice, for instance, significantly influenced Western legal thought. The idea that punishment serves a dual purpose: retribution for the wrong committed and deterrence for potential future misconduct, is as old as human civilization itself. The notion of free will is deeply intertwined in this paradigm, with individuals deemed morally accountable for their actions based on the presumption of their free choice.

This presumption of free will is what upholds the principle of "just deserts," where punishment serves as a morally justified response to a wrong act. It is this perspective that forms the bedrock of our legal systems and societal norms, and it is this perspective that we now scrutinize under the lens of determinism.

Determinism challenges the traditional view of punishment by questioning the very premise on which it stands - the freedom to choose. If our actions are causally determined by factors beyond our control, can punishment still be morally justified? Under a deterministic view, the notion of retribution appears fundamentally flawed as individuals are acting not out of free choice but due to deterministic forces.

This contradiction between determinism and the traditional view of punishment raises critical questions about the morality and efficacy of our punitive systems. It prompts us to explore the consequences of retributive justice and its alignment, or lack thereof, with the principles of determinism.

Diving deeper, we also need to explore alternatives to the traditional approach of punishment, focusing on more rehabilitative and restorative justice models. Simultaneously, we need to critically assess these models' compatibility with determinism, gauging whether they offer a more ethical and effective approach to punishment. In parallel, Neuroscience also enters the conversation as we discuss how insights from brain science could shape our understanding of punishment. We'll explore studies linking neurological factors to behavioral outcomes and how this could influence our approach to punishment, particularly in the legal context.

Now, it's important to understand that the punitive systems across the world vary drastically, shaped by each society's unique history, culture, and legal traditions. Despite these differences, the common denominator remains the notion of "free will" underpinning the justifications for punishment. Thus, the potential shifts in perspective prompted by determinism have global implications.

To explore these implications, we must begin by analyzing the legal systems that prominently embody the philosophy of retribution. The United States, for instance, has a notably punitive justice system, heavily reliant on incarceration. Here, punishment often serves the dual purpose of retribution and deterrence. The idea is that severe penalties would both penalize the wrongdoer and deter potential offenders. But if determinism holds, these principles may crumble, as punishment becomes less about moral culpability and more about societal control and reform.

It is worth noting, however, that even within a deterministic framework, deterrence retains some validity. Although people might not possess absolute free will, they can still be influenced by the prospect of punishment. Here, however, the purpose of punishment shifts. It is less about penalizing an individual for a past wrong and more about manipulating behavioral patterns in the future. The question that arises then is whether this approach would lead to a more pragmatic, utilitarian justice system, and whether such a system would align with our moral intuitions and principles of justice.

To consider the alternative models of justice, we veer away from retribution. For instance, the restorative justice model, practiced by several indigenous communities worldwide and gaining recognition in the formal justice systems, emphasizes repairing the harm caused by criminal behavior. It involves the perpetrator, victim, and often community members, in a process aimed at reconciliation and restoration.

Similarly, the rehabilitative model emphasizes the reintegration of the offender into society through treatment and social support. These models inherently acknowledge that an individual's criminal behavior might be a product of societal or personal circumstances rather than free choice, thereby resonating with the deterministic perspective.

We must examine the theoretical and practical implications of these models, analyzing their effectiveness and compatibility with determinism. This examination shall not merely be a theoretical exercise but shall involve real-world case studies and legal precedents, focusing on the societal and individual impacts of different justice models.

Despite the theoretical appeal of restorative and rehabilitative justice models, their practical implementation raises several concerns. Firstly, the determinism-inspired shift from retribution to reform must contend with the inherent complexities of human behavior. Rehabilitation programs are not a panacea; they require significant resources, expertise, and long-term commitment, with the outcome far from guaranteed. Even if we accept that criminal behavior is the product of determinable factors, the interplay of these factors – ranging from genetics to social environment – is so intricate that manipulating them to predict or alter behavior presents a significant challenge.

Secondly, there is a potential danger of determinism being used to justify overreach by the state. If criminal behavior is viewed purely as a product of deterministic factors, it could pave the way for increasingly invasive measures under the guise of prevention or reform. There are moral and legal concerns around the potential misuse of predictive policing technologies and preemptive detentions, creating a paradox where determinism, originally a challenge to the morality of punishment, becomes a basis for arguably immoral practices.

Another concern arises from the victims' perspective. A justice system underpinned by determinism might focus heavily on offender reform, possibly overlooking the victims' needs for closure and justice. It is crucial, therefore, that any shift towards determinism-based justice models incorporates mechanisms to ensure that victims' rights and dignity are not compromised.

To illustrate these considerations, we'll refer to real-life examples. The Norwegian justice system, for example, is renowned for its focus on offender rehabilitation. Even for serious offenses, the emphasis is on providing the offender with the skills and support to lead a law-abiding life post-release. However, despite these efforts, recidivism rates remain a concern, underscoring the complexities involved in modifying human behavior.

On the other end of the spectrum, the predictive policing algorithms used in some US jurisdictions offer a glimpse into the potential dangers of determinism-based crime prevention measures. These algorithms use historical data to predict future crime hotspots or potential offenders, but they have been criticized for perpetuating systemic biases, intruding on privacy, and potentially punishing individuals for crimes not yet committed.

The third issue pertains to the social and psychological impacts of a reformed justice system. Society, for centuries, has been acclimated to a punitive justice system where retribution is not only seen as just but also serves a purpose – it deters potential criminals, appeases victims and their families, and reinforces societal norms. Hence, transitioning to a deterministic model, where punishment is largely seen as an outdated concept, could trigger considerable resistance, mistrust, and unrest.

For instance, let's consider a hypothetical case of a serial killer who was shaped into a violent predator by an unfortunate combination of genetic predisposition, child abuse, and subsequent exposure to violence. Under a deterministic model, he would be seen as a victim of his circumstances rather than an architect of his atrocities. Society, however, might struggle to accept this view, finding it unjust that the killer's punishment is reduced or replaced with treatment. Such scenarios could create societal backlash, leading to vigilante justice or a complete rejection of the justice system.

On the psychological level, a significant aspect of current penal philosophy is its role in satisfying the instinctive human desire for retribution. This 'just deserts' principle is deeply ingrained in many cultures, with its roots in religious texts and traditional wisdom. Studies in cognitive psychology suggest that humans are intuitively retributivist and feel satisfaction upon seeing wrongdoers receive their 'deserved' punishment. Thus, an abrupt shift towards a deterministic justice model may cause cognitive dissonance and dissatisfaction among the public.

Finally, it is worth noting that there is a balance to be struck between determinism and retribution. The binary framing of retributive versus rehabilitative justice may not be the most constructive approach. Instead, an integrative model that acknowledges both deterministic factors and personal accountability might be more practical and socially acceptable. This model would advocate for proportional punishment combined with efforts to reform the offender and address the deterministic factors influencing their criminal behavior.

The fourth element of this discussion revolves around the practicality and feasibility of a rehabilitative model. Implementing such a system requires a radical shift in many aspects of the current justice system. For instance, legal personnel would need extensive training to comprehend and apply complex neurobiological knowledge in court proceedings. The court would also need to gain access to reliable neuroscientific tools capable of assessing an individual's capacity for change, which currently don't exist. Furthermore, designing suitable rehabilitation programs would be an immense challenge due to the vast diversity of criminal behaviors and their corresponding causal factors.

Take, for instance, the case of a convicted felon found guilty of multiple instances of violent assault. In a rehabilitative system, the court would need to assess the root causes of the individual's aggressive tendencies. These could range from genetic predisposition to anger issues, exposure to violence during formative years, substance abuse, mental health conditions, or a combination of these factors. Designing an effective rehabilitation program would necessitate a nuanced understanding of these root causes, reliable methods of monitoring progress, and robust mechanisms to prevent recidivism.

Further complicating matters is the ethical question of forced rehabilitation. If an individual is determined to lack the capacity for free will, do authorities then have the right to enforce treatment or therapy? This could potentially lead to problematic scenarios, akin to the dystopian notion of "thought policing", where the state has the power to modify individuals' behaviors to conform to societal norms, even if these behaviors have not yet manifested in criminal acts. This would open a Pandora's box of potential human rights abuses and threats to personal freedom.

Lastly, the transition to a rehabilitative model of justice also poses substantial financial implications. Shifting from a punitive to a therapeutic model could involve significant costs associated with training, development of neuroscientific assessment tools, creation and management of personalized treatment plans, and long-term monitoring of rehabilitated individuals. This raises the question of whether society is willing and able to bear these costs, especially when the current punitive system is already perceived as an economic burden.

10.4 THE FUTURE OF LEGAL SYSTEMS: A NEUROSCIENTIFIC APPROACH

As we venture further into the 21st century, the fields of neuroscience and law are finding themselves intertwined in an unprecedented manner. With the advancements in neuroscientific techniques and our improved understanding of the human brain, it is becoming increasingly clear that neuroscience may hold profound implications for legal systems worldwide. These implications aren't just mere theories, but they have practical relevance that could potentially influence how justice is served and perceived in society. The integration of neuroscience into legal practice isn't a radical proposition but a logical next step in the evolution of law.

In this section, we will examine the role neuroscience might play in shaping the future of legal systems. It's important to remember that the notions of determinism and free will will continue to be the underlying themes as we traverse this fascinating territory. What you will find here is a continuation of the dialogue we have been engaged in throughout this book. While the legal landscape is vast, we will focus on several key aspects, each significant in their own right.

The frontier of neuroscience and law is a burgeoning field, often called 'neurolaw'. The potential for this interdisciplinary field is immense, yet the path forward is layered with intricate ethical, moral, and practical considerations. However, the prospect of a legal system that takes into account the intricacies of the human brain is compelling.

Neuroscience has already started providing us with valuable insights into the human condition. For instance, we now understand that certain neurological disorders or brain injuries can lead to significant changes in a person's behavior and decision-making abilities. This knowledge begs the question - how should the legal system respond to such individuals? Are our current practices of assigning guilt and meting out punishment sufficient, or do they need an overhaul? The field of neuroscience doesn't merely introduce these questions but offers us tools to find suitable answers as well.

A critical area in the legal system where neuroscience could play a crucial role is in evaluating the competence of defendants. The traditional legal perspective posits that all individuals possess an equivalent capacity for rational thought and decision-making. However, neuroscience tells us a different story. It elucidates that our brains are complex, unique, and subject to a multitude of influences, both internal and external.

In some cases, defendants may have cognitive or neurological impairments that impact their ability to fully understand their actions or the consequences thereof. Neuroimaging and other neuroscientific tools could assist in objectively assessing these impairments, leading to more accurate evaluations of a defendant's competency to stand trial or their criminal responsibility. It might be the case that some individuals, due to certain neurological conditions, are incapable of conforming their behavior to the law. Here, neuroscience provides us with a tangible way to identify these conditions and consider them in a court of law.

However, it's not just about identifying neurological conditions. Neuroscience also gives us the ability to understand how these conditions affect an individual's behavior and decision-making. It helps us look beyond the symptoms to the underlying cause, ensuring a more nuanced and fair assessment of the defendant's situation.

Another area where neuroscience could revolutionize the legal system is in rethinking our approach to punishment. As we've explored in previous sections, the traditional retributive model of punishment is based on the idea of free will. It assumes that individuals freely choose to engage in criminal activity and hence should be punished accordingly.

Neuroscience, however, brings a new perspective. If our understanding of human behavior is influenced by our brains' neurobiology, it implies that our choices might not be as free as we've traditionally assumed. This understanding necessitates a shift in our approach to punishment - from one that is primarily retributive to one that is rehabilitative.

A neuroscientific approach to punishment would focus more on understanding the underlying causes of criminal behavior and addressing them. This approach might involve a combination of therapy, medication, or even neurosurgical procedures in extreme cases. The goal here is not just to punish but to rehabilitate, to ensure that the individual can return to society as a productive member. This perspective aligns with our discussion on determinism and the implications it holds for moral and legal responsibility.

Delving deeper into the neuroscience-law nexus, it becomes essential to address the question of privacy. As neuroscientific techniques become more advanced, they potentially provide a window into the inner workings of our minds. This possibility raises profound questions about the right to cognitive liberty and mental privacy.

If the legal system were to leverage neuroscience to its full extent, it could mean that defendants are required to undergo neuroimaging or other brain-based tests. This could open up a Pandora's box of privacy issues, as these techniques might reveal information about the individual that goes far beyond the scope of the case at hand. It's one thing to know someone's actions; it's entirely another to have a glimpse into their thoughts, feelings, and memories.

This issue extends beyond the courtroom and into everyday life. If neuroscientific methods became commonplace, it could create a society where our thoughts are no longer private, leading to serious ethical and privacy concerns. This scenario is reminiscent of dystopian fiction, where mind-reading technology leads to totalitarian regimes. While this might seem far-fetched, it's a potential reality that we must consider as neuroscience continues to advance.

The integration of neuroscience and the law is a complex and multifaceted issue that goes far beyond the scope of a single section in a book. It requires us to reevaluate our fundamental assumptions about human nature, responsibility, and justice. But despite the challenges it poses, the convergence of these two fields also offers promising opportunities.

By leveraging the insights from neuroscience, we can develop a legal system that is more fair, accurate, and compassionate. It can help us move away from a one-size-fits-all approach to justice and towards a more individualized and nuanced system that takes into account the complexities of human behavior and decision-making.

However, to make this a reality, it is crucial to tread with caution. The implementation of neuroscience in the law should be guided by rigorous scientific standards and ethical considerations. We must ensure that neuroscience does not become a tool for invasion of privacy or deprivation of rights, but rather a means to enhance our understanding of human behavior and improve the justice system.

As we continue to explore this fascinating convergence of neuroscience and law, we can look forward to a future where science and justice go hand in hand, enhancing our collective pursuit of truth and fairness.

When it comes to the fusion of neuroscience and law, we must also consider the critical role of ethics and policy. Advancements in neuroscience often outpace the evolution of ethical guidelines and legal regulations, creating a gap that needs to be filled.

At the heart of this issue is the question of how we can ensure that the integration of neuroscience and law is carried out ethically and responsibly. This requires us to strike a delicate balance between leveraging the potential benefits of neuroscience for the legal system, and protecting individuals' rights and privacy.

We must also consider the implications of this convergence for social justice. For instance, if only the wealthy have access to advanced neuroscientific defenses, it could exacerbate existing inequalities in the legal system. Policymakers must work towards ensuring that the benefits of neuroscience are accessible to all, regardless of socioeconomic status.

Finally, it's crucial to have a robust system of checks and balances in place. This includes establishing guidelines for the admissibility of neuroscientific evidence in court, as well as creating ethical codes of conduct for neuroscientists working in the legal realm.

It's clear that the marriage of neuroscience and law is not just a scientific and legal issue, but also an ethical and policy one. As we move forward, we must navigate these uncharted waters with care and foresight, shaping the future of this exciting interdisciplinary field in a way that is fair, equitable, and just.

The Journey Ahead

The convergence of neuroscience and law is an exciting frontier that promises to revolutionize our understanding of human behavior and the concept of responsibility. However, it is also a journey filled with uncertainties and challenges.

As we continue to explore this new landscape, we must do so with an open mind, recognizing the potential benefits and pitfalls that lie ahead. We must also remember that while neuroscience can provide valuable insights, it does not hold all the answers. The complexities of human behavior and decision-making extend beyond what can be explained by our brain's biology alone.

Above all, we must ensure that our pursuit of knowledge and justice is guided by a deep respect for human dignity and the fundamental rights of individuals. After all, at the heart of both neuroscience and law, lies the human being - a complex, multifaceted entity driven by a myriad of factors that are as much social, cultural, and psychological as they are biological.

The journey ahead is long and uncertain, but it is one that we must undertake. For at stake is nothing less than our understanding of ourselves, our actions, and the very concept of justice.

As we delve deeper into the world where neuroscience interacts with law, we can't overlook the ethical dimensions of how we interpret and apply this new knowledge. Neuroscience could provide insights that are potentially revolutionary, but how we interpret those insights is crucial. There's a risk that our interpretations could be biased or simplistic, leading us to draw overly deterministic conclusions about human behavior based on the brain's biology.

Moreover, it's also critical to remember that while neuroscientific evidence might illuminate certain aspects of a defendant's behavior, it doesn't offer a comprehensive picture. A brain scan can't tell us about a person's childhood, their relationships, or the myriad of other factors that shape their behavior. Over-reliance on such evidence could lead to an oversimplified understanding of human behavior, ignoring its complexity and richness.

As neuroscience makes further inroads into the legal system, it becomes essential to develop standardized guidelines for its application. This might involve creating rules about which types of neuroscientific evidence are admissible in court, and in what circumstances. Additionally, guidelines could be established on how to present and interpret such evidence in a manner that is fair and accurate.

It's also important to ensure that these policies are flexible and adaptable. Given the rapid pace of progress in neuroscience, any guidelines we create today may need to be revised or updated in the future. Therefore, a static policy won't be sufficient; instead, we need dynamic, evolving guidelines that can keep pace with scientific advancement.

The intersection of neuroscience and law presents both enormous potential and significant challenges. Harnessing the power of neuroscience could revolutionize our legal system, but doing so ethically and responsibly requires careful thought and ongoing dialogue.

In this journey, the scales of justice and the microscope of neuroscience must be held in equilibrium. While neuroscience can shine a light on the inner workings of the brain, it must not eclipse the broader social, psychological, and environmental factors that play a crucial role in shaping human behavior. The integration of neuroscience into our legal system must be done in a way that respects individual dignity, upholds justice, and strives for truth.

As we navigate these uncharted waters, it is our moral compass - our deep-seated commitment to justice, equity, and human rights - that must guide us. Only then can we chart a course that truly integrates the worlds of neuroscience and law in a manner that benefits us all.

10.5 Looking Ahead: Future Implications

As we stand on the precipice of this unprecedented amalgamation of neuroscience and law, it becomes imperative to think about the future implications of this nexus. What challenges will we face as we dig deeper into the mysteries of the human brain, unraveling layers of information about human behavior, decision-making, and culpability? How will these revelations influence our understanding of justice, fairness, and retribution?

For one, the advancements in neuroscience could potentially lead to a more personalized system of justice. By having a better understanding of an individual's brain functioning, we might be able to devise more effective rehabilitation programs, tailored to the specific needs and circumstances of each offender. This could pave the way for a system where punishment is not merely about retribution but about transformation and reform.

Yet, this personalized approach might bring its own set of challenges. For instance, how do we strike a balance between acknowledging individual differences and maintaining a sense of universal fairness? Would it be just to mete out different punishments to two individuals for the same crime, based on differences in their brain functioning? These questions would necessitate us to reconsider our notions of equality and fairness.

Furthermore, as our understanding of the human brain and behavior becomes more nuanced, we may need to redefine our legal concepts. Notions of culpability, responsibility, and free will might need to be reframed in light of neuroscientific findings. This could mean a significant overhaul of our legal principles and frameworks, leading us into uncharted territories.

Moreover, the integration of neuroscience into law could also raise important questions about privacy and consent. Neuroimaging techniques that provide insights into an individual's brain might be seen as intrusive or violating an individual's right to privacy. The legal system would have to devise ways to protect these rights, even as it seeks to utilize the benefits of neuroscience.

Lastly, it's crucial to remember that neuroscience, like any other scientific field, is not infallible. Its findings are subject to revisions and updates, as new research emerges. Therefore, while neuroscience can provide valuable insights, we must be cautious about the weight we give these findings in legal contexts. The law deals with matters of profound significance – guilt, innocence, justice – and we must tread this path with due diligence and caution.

As we venture into this brave new world, the journey promises to be as challenging as it is exciting. The intersection of neuroscience and law offers immense potential, but also demands from us a commitment to ongoing learning, reflection, and dialogue. As we move forward, let's hold on to our quest for truth, our pursuit of justice, and our belief in the dignity and worth of every individual.

The journey continues, and it is one that we must undertake with open minds, compassionate hearts, and a steadfast commitment to justice.

In addition to the questions and challenges previously raised, it is also essential to discuss the potential influence on the public perception of free will and the consequent repercussions on social order. If the notion that our decisions are wholly predetermined by neural mechanisms takes root, it might inadvertently lead to an increased tolerance for antisocial behaviors. In an attempt to reduce the stigma around criminal activities, we might unintentionally propagate a narrative that justifies these actions based on an individual's neurological makeup. We must, therefore, be cautious about how we communicate these concepts to the public and ensure that we don't oversimplify the complex interplay between the brain, free will, and moral responsibility.

Additionally, as we dive deeper into the intricate world of neuroscience, we might discover that there are numerous factors – both genetic and environmental – that contribute to an individual's predisposition to commit crimes. How we handle this information could have significant social implications. For instance, would a person's knowledge of their increased susceptibility to criminal tendencies, based on their genetic makeup or upbringing, influence their behavior? And if so, how should society and the legal system respond?

Also, we must consider the potential misuse of neuroscientific findings. In a world where information is power, the knowledge gleaned from brain studies could potentially be used to manipulate individuals or groups. Safeguards need to be in place to prevent the misuse of this information and to protect the rights and liberties of individuals.

Furthermore, if neuroscience advances to a point where we can accurately predict an individual's future actions, this might lead us down a morally dubious path. Would it be justified to incarcerate someone for a crime they are predicted to commit, even if they haven't yet committed it? Such a scenario seems more suited to a dystopian science fiction novel than to real life, but it's a possibility we cannot ignore.

As we embark on this endeavor to intertwine neuroscience and law, we must keep in mind the profound moral, ethical, and social implications. We are treading on a path filled with both promise and peril. The challenge lies in harnessing the potential of neuroscience to improve our legal system, without losing sight of our fundamental values of justice, fairness, and respect for individual autonomy. The future might be uncertain, but it is in our hands to shape it in a way that respects the dignity of every individual while striving for a just and equitable society.

Diving further into the abyss, we now need to address another crucial query that emerges when dealing with the new subsection - the implications on the healthcare system. If our understanding of the brain and its workings advances to a point where we can accurately predict the likelihood of an individual engaging in criminal behavior, it would significantly impact our approach to mental health. A possible pathway that emerges from such knowledge is the early intervention and treatment of individuals at risk, which could potentially prevent a considerable number of crimes.

A shift from a reactive to a proactive stance in dealing with crime, however, brings forth its own set of ethical dilemmas. On one hand, the identification of at-risk individuals could be instrumental in curbing crime rates and rehabilitating potential offenders. On the other hand, such a practice could lead to the stigmatization of these individuals, who may face discrimination and ostracization, which might push them further down the path of crime.

There is a delicate balance to strike here, which is further complicated by the question of consent. If an individual is identified as being at risk but has not yet committed a crime, to what extent can interventions be enforced? Are mandatory interventions justified, and if so, under what circumstances? These are crucial questions that need to be addressed as we proceed with this integration of neuroscience into the legal framework.

On another note, as neuroscience advances, it might challenge our current understanding of mental illness. The Diagnostic and Statistical Manual of Mental Disorders (DSM), the bible of psychiatry, categorizes mental illnesses based largely on symptoms rather than underlying neural mechanisms. However, as we gain more insight into the workings of the brain, we might discover that what we now categorize as different disorders might have the same neural underpinnings, or vice versa. This could lead to a complete overhaul of how we diagnose and treat mental illnesses, with significant implications for the legal system.

For instance, consider the legal doctrine of 'insanity defense,' where an individual is considered not guilty by reason of insanity if they were unable to understand the nature of their actions due to a severe mental disease or defect. As our understanding of mental illness evolves, so will our application of the insanity defense, potentially leading to more accurate and fair judgments.

Finally, as we step into the future of neuro-legal integration, we must consider the possible implications of emerging neurotechnologies. Brain-computer interfaces (BCIs), neurofeedback, deep brain stimulation, and other such technologies that can alter brain function have the potential to dramatically reshape our society. While these technologies hold great promise, they also present significant ethical and legal challenges. For instance, who owns and controls the data generated by these devices? How do we ensure the privacy and security of this sensitive information? And importantly, to what extent can these technologies be used to alter an individual's behavior, and under what circumstances?

In conclusion, as we delve deeper into the world of neuroscience, we are confronted with numerous questions and challenges that need to be addressed thoughtfully and responsibly. As we progress, it is crucial to ensure that our pursuit of knowledge and innovation does not compromise our ethical principles and commitment to justice and fairness.

CHAPTER 11: MENTAL ILLNESS AND FREEWILL

As we traverse further into the labyrinth of neuroscience, we approach another crossroad. Here, we meet the convoluted and often misunderstood world of mental health. This chapter aims to navigate the intricate connection between mental illness and free will, and the profound implications it has on our understanding of human behavior and the way our society functions.

11.1 THE LINK: MENTAL DISORDERS AND FREE WILL

The intricate interplay between mental disorders and the concept of free will forms a fascinating and complex narrative, one that lies at the intersection of various fields - neuroscience, psychiatry, philosophy, ethics, and even law. This narrative necessitates a deep dive into our understanding of both these elements and an examination of their interaction. So, we embark on this journey, appreciating the diversity and spectrum of mental disorders, their impacts on decision-making capabilities, and how they shape our perspectives on free will.

A mental disorder, by its inherent nature, disrupts the normal functioning of an individual's cognitive processes, often distorting their perception of reality and affecting their ability to make decisions. The World Health Organization defines mental disorders as "generally characterized by a combination of abnormal thoughts, perceptions, emotions, behavior, and relationships with others." This definition itself indicates a potential conflict with the principles of free will - if thoughts, perceptions, and emotions are abnormal, how can decisions stemming from them be considered free?

However, simplifying mental disorders to mere disturbances in decision-making would be an oversimplification. Mental disorders encompass a wide range, each with unique symptoms, triggers, and impacts. For instance, consider the stark differences between Major Depressive Disorder (MDD), characterized by persistent feelings of sadness and loss of interest, and Schizophrenia, a chronic mental disorder characterized by distortions in thinking, perception, emotions, language, sense of self, and behavior. The nature and extent of the impact on free will differ significantly between these disorders.

At this juncture, we need to introduce the concept of a free will matrix in the context of mental disorders. This matrix is a framework to understand the varying degree and aspects of free will affected in different mental disorders.

For instance, in MDD, the free will could be compromised in making decisions that bring joy or require a positive outlook. On the other hand, in schizophrenia, the free will might be compromised due to the inability to perceive reality as it is. In personality disorders, the long-standing and enduring pattern of behavior might suggest a lack of free will to change. However, when one delves deeper, it is clear that these disorders alter the environment (internal and external) in which the will operates, rather than negating the presence of free will.

Here, we should remember that the free will matrix doesn't just apply at a disorder level, but also at an individual level, since the same disorder could affect different individuals differently.

To fully appreciate the link between mental disorders and free will, it is necessary to take a closer look at environmental factors and their influence on mental health. We know that both genetic and environmental elements play crucial roles in the onset and progression of mental disorders. Factors such as childhood trauma, stress, exposure to violence, substance abuse, and even socio-economic conditions have a marked impact on an individual's mental health.

The notion of free will becomes particularly complex when we consider these environmental influences. For example, a person born into adverse conditions may develop a mental disorder as a result of continuous exposure to stress or violence. In this case, to what extent was their will free in determining their mental health outcome? The environmental constraints that shaped their mental disorder have surely influenced their ability to make decisions - a cornerstone of free will.

This does not imply that individuals with mental disorders have no free will or are entirely victims of their circumstances. It's more nuanced. The environment shapes the context in which our free will operates, but it doesn't eliminate the capacity for decision-making entirely. However, it does compel us to reevaluate how much weight we assign to free will when it comes to managing mental disorders.

When we step into the realm of mental disorders, we begin to realize that free will is not an all-or-nothing phenomenon. Rather, it operates on a spectrum, influenced by the type and severity of the mental disorder and the unique circumstances of the individual.

For example, a person with mild anxiety might experience some limitations in their decision-making capacity, such as a propensity to avoid certain situations due to fear or worry. However, their overall ability to make decisions - their free will - is not significantly impaired. On the other end of the spectrum, an individual with severe schizophrenia might experience substantial constraints in their ability to make decisions, particularly if they're experiencing acute symptoms such as hallucinations or delusions.

This spectrum of free will within the context of mental disorders helps us appreciate the complexities and intricacies of the relationship between free will and mental health. It also underscores the need for a nuanced and compassionate approach when dealing with individuals with mental disorders, particularly in areas such as legal responsibility and societal expectations.

Neuroscience and brain imaging studies have significantly contributed to our understanding of mental disorders and free will. The brain, being the hub of our cognitive processes, is inevitably implicated in the discussion of free will. This is further complicated when disorders afflict the brain, skewing the exercise of free will.

Schizophrenia, for instance, is characterized by structural and functional changes in the brain. Studies have shown abnormalities in both the gray and white matter of schizophrenic patients, which are associated with the disorder's typical symptoms, like hallucinations and delusions. These aberrant perceptions and beliefs undoubtedly influence the decision-making process, posing questions about the extent of free will in such individuals.

Depression, another common mental disorder, is linked with altered brain activity, especially in regions like the prefrontal cortex and the amygdala, which are involved in emotional regulation and response. A depressed individual's ability to make decisions or exert their will might be influenced by these changes in brain function. Prolonged feelings of sadness, hopelessness, or lack of interest could restrict their perceived range of choices, thus impacting their exercise of free will.

Brain imaging studies in individuals with addiction have also shown changes in areas related to reward, stress, and decision-making, such as the prefrontal cortex and the basal ganglia. The compulsion to use substances can override an individual's self-control mechanisms, leading them to make decisions that align with their addiction, even when they understand the harmful consequences. This challenges the conventional perspective of free will and necessitates a more comprehensive view that incorporates neuroscience.

The process of therapy and treatment in mental disorders also raises questions about the link between free will and mental health. Cognitive-behavioral therapy (CBT), for example, aims to help individuals recognize and challenge their unhelpful thought patterns and behaviors. The very premise of CBT is that our thoughts influence our feelings and behaviors, suggesting a certain deterministic aspect. But CBT also implicitly assumes the existence of free will. It relies on the individual's ability to consciously choose different thoughts and behaviors once they recognize the unhelpful ones. Hence, the paradox of free will and determinism also exists in the realm of therapy and treatment.

The role of medication in treatment presents a similar paradox. Psychiatric medication alters the brain's neurochemistry to mitigate the symptoms of mental disorders. Antidepressants, for instance, increase the levels of certain neurotransmitters like serotonin in the brain to improve mood. This mechanistic action may seem deterministic as it prompts a direct change in the individual's feelings and behaviors. However, the decision to adhere to medication, cope with side effects, or combine it with therapy involves the exercise of free will.

Moreover, the impact of psychiatric medication on free will is multifaceted. While medication can potentially restrict free will by inducing certain changes in mood and behavior, it can also enhance free will by alleviating the debilitating symptoms of mental disorders. For instance, an individual with severe depression might feel so hopeless and fatigued that they see suicide as their only choice. By mitigating these symptoms, antidepressants could broaden their perceived range of choices, thus enhancing their sense of free will.

In sum, the relationship between mental disorders and free will is far from straightforward. It involves a complex interplay of various factors, including the nature and severity of the disorder, the individual's self-perception and worldview, and the societal and cultural context. The deterministic aspects of mental disorders do not negate the existence of free will but highlight the necessity for a nuanced understanding of this fundamental concept.

Delving further, it is important to acknowledge the potential implications of this nuanced understanding for how society perceives and responds to mental disorders. The deterministic aspects of mental disorders could elicit greater empathy and reduce the stigma associated with these conditions. Recognizing that mental disorders are not a matter of choice, but often the result of a complex interplay of genetic, neurobiological, and environmental factors, could shift the societal narrative from blame to understanding. This perspective could foster more supportive societal attitudes and policies, such as better funding for mental health research and services, and stronger protections for individuals with mental disorders in various domains, including education and employment.

On the other hand, emphasizing the deterministic aspects of mental disorders may have some unintended consequences. For instance, it could lead to a fatalistic mindset where individuals with mental disorders see themselves as helpless victims of their condition. This mindset could hinder their recovery process as it negates the role of personal agency and resilience. Moreover, it could be used to justify discriminatory practices such as forced treatment or the denial of certain rights on the grounds that individuals with mental disorders are incapable of making their own decisions. Therefore, while acknowledging the deterministic aspects of mental disorders, it is equally crucial to recognize the role of free will.

Recognizing the role of free will in mental disorders can empower individuals. It acknowledges their capacity for agency and change, fostering a sense of hope and motivation. It validates the efforts that individuals with mental disorders make every day in managing their condition, from adhering to treatment, coping with symptoms and side effects, to navigating the societal challenges posed by stigma and discrimination. This perspective can also inform therapeutic approaches that foster personal agency, such as CBT and other forms of psychotherapy.

At the societal level, recognizing the role of free will can inform policies and practices that respect and promote the autonomy of individuals with mental disorders. This can include laws that ensure their right to informed consent in treatment, policies that provide them with the necessary support to live independently, and initiatives that involve them in decisions about mental health services and policies. In short, recognizing the role of free will in mental disorders can foster a more inclusive and empowering societal approach to mental health.

However, it is equally crucial to avoid the potential pitfalls of overstating the role of free will in mental disorders. This could lead to an overemphasis on personal responsibility, which may shift the blame for the disorder onto the individual, exacerbating the stigma and discrimination associated with these conditions. Moreover, it may overlook the need for systemic changes, such as improving access to mental health services, addressing socio-economic inequalities that contribute to mental health disparities, and fostering societal attitudes and environments that support mental health.

The link between mental disorders and free will involves a complex and delicate balance. It requires acknowledging the deterministic aspects of these conditions without negating the role of personal agency, and vice versa. It demands a comprehensive and nuanced approach that considers the individual, societal, and systemic dimensions. The challenges in achieving this balance are considerable, but so are the potential benefits for individuals with mental disorders and society at large.

11.2 Neurological Conditions: Altered Landscapes of Decision Making

As we explore the fascinating field of the human mind and its multifaceted aspects of decision-making, it is worth delving deeper into neurological conditions and how they significantly influence the decision-making process, thus casting a different light on the concept of free will. The intention is not to diminish the significance of personal responsibility, but rather to emphasize the impact of brain functioning on our behaviors and choices, thus nudging the narrative of free will into a more nuanced and comprehensive discourse.

First, let's take a step back and examine the landscape that separates neurological conditions from mental illnesses. It's like comparing weather to climate. Weather refers to short-term atmospheric conditions, while climate represents the long-term patterns. Mental illnesses can be likened to weather changes, episodic, and often fluctuating, greatly affecting our mood, behavior, and thinking. In contrast, neurological conditions resemble climate, long-term and constant, primarily caused by physical changes in the brain structure or function that may significantly affect an individual's behavior, decision-making, and perceived free will.

Neurological conditions refer to a broad spectrum of disorders that affect the brain's function, the spinal cord, and the nerves that connect them. These conditions can result from genetic mutations, malformations during brain development, or acquired conditions due to a brain injury or disease. Some common neurological conditions include Alzheimer's disease, Parkinson's disease, stroke, traumatic brain injuries, and epilepsy.

Now that we've established a clear understanding of neurological conditions and their impact on the brain's functioning, let's delve deeper into specific conditions and observe their influence on the notion of free will.

Alzheimer's Disease and Decision-Making

Alzheimer's disease (AD) stands out prominently among neurological disorders due to its profound effect on cognition and decision-making. As a progressive disease that affects memory and thinking skills, Alzheimer's challenges the concept of free will by eroding the very foundations upon which we make decisions.

A person with AD experiences a gradual but inevitable loss of memory, making it challenging to recollect past experiences, which form a crucial component of decision-making. Cognitive decline also impacts an individual's ability to project future consequences of their decisions, thus making it difficult to choose the course of action that aligns best with their long-term goals.

In the context of free will, Alzheimer's raises questions about the degree of autonomy in decision-making for individuals with cognitive decline. When memory and foresight, the cornerstones of conscious choice, are compromised, to what extent can we say that a person is exercising their free will? Such questions lead us to reevaluate the traditional concept of free will, underscoring the need for a more nuanced understanding that accommodates the complexities of human cognition.

Parkinson's Disease: A Unique Perspective on Free Will

Parkinson's disease (PD) offers another enlightening perspective on free will. Characterized by the loss of dopamine-producing cells in the brain, PD primarily affects motor functions, leading to symptoms like tremors, rigidity, and bradykinesia (slowness of movement). However, the disease also has cognitive implications, with some individuals experiencing changes in memory, attention, and decision-making abilities.

An intriguing aspect of PD related to free will is the concept of "freezing." Some individuals with Parkinson's experience moments where they cannot move, often described as feeling like their feet are "glued" to the floor. This phenomenon poses an interesting question about free will. If the intention to move is present, but the ability to execute the movement is hindered, is the concept of free will purely limited to our conscious decisions, or should it extend to our capacity to act upon those decisions?

Epilepsy and Automatisms: Unconscious Actions

Epilepsy, a neurological disorder marked by recurrent, unprovoked seizures, provides yet another unique vantage point to examine the dynamics of free will. One of the intriguing aspects of epilepsy is the phenomenon of automatisms – automatic, unconscious behaviors that occur during certain types of seizures. These can range from simple actions like lip-smacking or blinking to more complex behaviors such as walking, fumbling with objects, or even driving.

During these episodes, individuals have no awareness or memory of their actions, raising compelling questions about free will. If an action occurs in the absence of consciousness, can it be attributed to free will? The concept of automatisms challenges the conventional perception that free will is an exclusive attribute of conscious, intentional actions.

Automatisms in epilepsy also bring to light legal and ethical considerations. For instance, if a person with epilepsy engages in harmful behavior during a seizure, should they be held responsible for their actions? This question blurs the line between voluntary and involuntary actions, demanding a thorough reconsideration of how free will is defined and applied in legal contexts.

Multiple Sclerosis and Decision-Making

Multiple sclerosis (MS) is another neurological condition that influences our understanding of free will. MS is a chronic disease that affects the central nervous system, resulting in a wide range of physical, mental, and psychiatric symptoms.

Cognitive impairment is common in MS, affecting approximately 40-65% of individuals with the disease. This can include changes in processing speed, memory, attention, and executive functions – a group of skills that allow us to set goals, plan, and get things done. Thus, MS can potentially impact a person's decision-making capacity, once again raising questions about free will.

The impact of MS on free will can also be explored through the lens of fatigue, a frequent symptom of the disease. Fatigue in MS might affect an individual's ability to make consistent decisions or follow through on intentions, thus potentially influencing the expression of free will.

A Brief Summary

In each of these neurological conditions – Alzheimer's, Parkinson's, epilepsy, and multiple sclerosis – we see how alterations in the brain can influence decision-making and actions, two fundamental elements of free will. While none of these conditions negate the existence of free will entirely, they do illustrate that our capacity for free will can be constrained or modified by our neurological state.

These diseases underscore that free will isn't a simple, universally defined ability, but rather a multifaceted phenomenon, deeply intertwined with the complexities of our brain and its functioning. Therefore, any attempt to understand free will requires a holistic view that accounts for the myriad ways in which our brains can shape our choices and actions.

Neurological Conditions and Ethical Considerations

The exploration of free will in the context of neurological conditions like Alzheimer's, Parkinson's, epilepsy, and multiple sclerosis, raises profound ethical considerations. One of the most pressing concerns is the impact of these conditions on informed consent, a fundamental ethical principle in healthcare and research that presupposes the exercise of free will.

Informed consent requires individuals to understand, appreciate, and voluntarily decide on a course of action. However, in neurological conditions that impair cognitive functioning or consciousness, the capacity to give informed consent may be compromised. This raises challenging questions: How should healthcare providers assess an individual's capacity for informed consent? When, if ever, should decisions be made on behalf of individuals with impaired decision-making capacities? And who should be responsible for making such decisions?

The answers to these questions are not straightforward and can vary considerably depending on the specifics of the situation. Nonetheless, the questions themselves underscore the complex interplay between free will, neurological conditions, and ethical practice.

Another critical ethical concern related to free will and neurological conditions revolves around stigma and discrimination. Stigma is a potent social force that can lead to marginalization, discrimination, and reduced opportunities for people with neurological disorders. It stems, in part, from misconceptions about these conditions – including the erroneous belief that individuals with neurological disorders lack free will.

Challenging these misconceptions and advocating for the rights and dignity of people with neurological disorders is an essential step toward promoting equity and social justice. Understanding the nuanced influence of these conditions on free will can help fuel these efforts by providing a more accurate and empathetic perspective on what it means to live with a neurological disorder.

Walking through the Complexity

Neurological conditions offer a profound insight into the intricate dance between our physical brains, our conscious minds, and the concept of free will that sits at their intersection. They reveal the flexible nature of free will, showing how it can be bent and shaped by the circumstances of our neurology without being completely broken.

However, these insights also reveal the limitations of our current understanding of free will. Much like a map that becomes less accurate as you zoom in, our broad-brush concepts of freedom will begin to fray at the edges when we dive into the details.

The challenges are indeed significant, but so too are the opportunities. Each question, each ethical dilemma, each philosophical debate pushes us to refine our understanding, to iterate on our models, and to approach the puzzle of free will with humility, curiosity, and a commitment to keep exploring. In doing so, we not only expand our knowledge but also cultivate empathy and understanding for the diverse experiences of humanity.

11.3 ETHICAL DILEMMAS: THE DIAGNOSTIC AND TREATMENT MAZE

Ethics, at its core, involves the systematization, defense, and commendation of concepts related to right and wrong conduct. In the realm of mental health, the field of ethics takes on an intricate and sensitive significance. The mental health landscape is a convoluted web woven together by a myriad of threads representing different disorders, treatment options, professional responsibilities, and personal rights and freedoms. This complexity becomes even more pronounced when the element of free will enters the fray.

When an individual's mental health is in question, their free will—or perceived free will—can be compromised. This disruption in the freedom of choice and action can be subtle or glaring, influenced by a multitude of factors such as the nature and severity of the illness, societal perceptions and stigma, the treatment approach, and even the individual's personal beliefs about their condition and ability to manage it. Therefore, it becomes evident that mental health and ethics, under the umbrella of free will, share an intimate relationship—one that demands careful exploration and understanding.

Here, we will delve into the various ethical dilemmas that exist within the realm of mental health. We'll scrutinize the way these challenges not only influence an individual's perception of their free will but also examine how these dilemmas are handled by professionals, institutions, and legislations.

Ethical Dilemmas in Diagnosis

Our initial focus will be on the ethical dilemmas that arise during the diagnostic phase. Diagnosis is the first step in the journey of mental health treatment. It is an essential process that entails recognizing and labeling the condition, which guides the treatment protocol. However, the act of labeling can give rise to numerous ethical conundrums. One such conundrum is the risk of self-fulfilling prophecies. Labeling an individual with a specific mental disorder might lead them to conform to the symptoms and behaviors associated with that disorder. This effect can be further amplified by societal stereotyping and stigma, potentially impacting their sense of free will.

Another ethical challenge is overdiagnosis or underdiagnosis. Overdiagnosis refers to a scenario where a mental disorder is diagnosed when, in fact, the individual doesn't have one. This can lead to unnecessary treatment and may significantly impact a person's perception of self and free will. Conversely, underdiagnosis occurs when a person with a mental disorder does not receive the appropriate diagnosis. In such cases, individuals may struggle with unexplained symptoms and the inability to access the necessary help and treatment.

Lastly, the diagnosis of mental disorders is often subjective, based on symptomatic presentations rather than tangible biomarkers. This subjectivity leaves room for bias and can cause ethical dilemmas. For example, two clinicians might diagnose the same individual differently, which can lead to inconsistent treatment strategies and confusion for the patient.

Ethical Dilemmas in Treatment

The ethical dilemmas extend from the diagnosis to the treatment phase as well. The decision-making process regarding treatment options is fraught with difficulties, particularly when considering issues of autonomy and informed consent.

Informed consent requires that individuals fully understand their diagnosis, the recommended treatment plan, and the potential risks and benefits of treatment before they agree to it. However, this process is complex when dealing with mental disorders. It might be challenging to ensure that the individual fully comprehends the implications of the treatment due to their cognitive state, especially in severe cases of mental disorders. For instance, in cases of severe depression or psychosis, the individual might be unable to understand the information, raising the question of whether the consent provided is truly informed.

Furthermore, there are often ethical concerns around treatment refusal. Individuals with mental disorders have the right to refuse treatment, even when it is clear that the treatment would be beneficial for them. This scenario presents a conundrum: should the individual's right to autonomy be respected, even if it means potentially endangering their well-being?

Pharmacological interventions, often a significant part of treating mental disorders, come with their ethical dilemmas. Psychiatric medications can cause side effects, sometimes severe, which can impact an individual's quality of life. They may also influence the patient's personality and behavior, giving rise to questions about authenticity and personhood. What does it mean for free will when a pill can change how you think, feel, and behave?

Treatment also often involves psychotherapy. However, the therapist-client relationship can create power dynamics that need to be carefully managed. A therapist's suggestions and interpretations can greatly influence a client's thinking and behavior, once again raising questions about free will.

Lastly, the role of societal and cultural factors in determining treatment strategies can't be ignored. The same mental disorder might be treated differently depending on the cultural context, which brings in issues of cultural competence and sensitivity. Failure to consider these factors can lead to ineffective treatment and further marginalization of the individuals.

Each of these ethical dilemmas underscores the complexity of free will in the context of mental health treatment. The intricate web that interlinks diagnosis, treatment, ethical considerations, and free will illuminates the maze that mental health professionals, patients, and caregivers must navigate.

Coercive Treatment and Free Will

Coercive treatment in mental health care is another domain where free will collides head-on with the desire to protect the individual and the public. Coercive treatment involves the use of legal mechanisms to enforce treatment or hospitalization for individuals with severe mental disorders against their will. This scenario poses significant ethical and philosophical questions. If the principle of free will is indeed sacrosanct, can such coercion ever be justified?

Legal frameworks worldwide grapple with this issue, and the balance between individual autonomy, the need for treatment, and public safety is fraught with complexities. If the person is acutely unwell and unable to make sound decisions, it could be argued that the coercion is for their benefit. On the other hand, denying someone the right to decide their treatment infringes on their autonomy and can be perceived as a violation of their human rights.

In some jurisdictions, the concept of 'mental capacity' or 'competence' is employed. This concept assesses whether the individual has the cognitive ability to understand their situation and the implications of their choices. If they're deemed incapable, coercive treatment might be considered ethically and legally permissible.

Nevertheless, even these evaluations aren't free of dilemmas. These assessments can be subjective, and their outcomes can significantly affect the person's life. Furthermore, the concept of mental capacity is underpinned by the notion of 'rationality,' which in itself is a contested concept in philosophy and psychology. What constitutes 'rational' behavior or thinking, and who gets to decide that?

Neuroethical Considerations

The realm of neuroethics, which deals with the ethical implications of advances in neuroscience, also has significant implications for our understanding of free will in the context of mental disorders. Cutting-edge developments in neuroimaging, neuromodulation (such as deep brain stimulation), and even neuroenhancement technologies can alter brain function and, by extension, cognition, emotion, and behavior.

While these technologies hold immense potential for understanding and treating mental disorders, they also raise profound ethical and philosophical questions. If we can modulate our brain activity to change our mental states, what does that mean for our free will? If a person uses neuroenhancement technology to boost their mood or cognitive performance, are they exercising their free will, or are they being controlled by the technology?

Moreover, as our understanding of the neural correlates of mental disorders deepens, we may have to revisit our concepts of blame, responsibility, and even identity. For instance, if a particular pattern of brain activity is associated with antisocial behavior, how should society treat individuals who exhibit this pattern? Are they 'guilty' of their behavior, or are they 'victims' of their neurobiology?

The exploration of these questions forms a significant part of the ongoing discourse in neuroethics. It is clear that as our understanding of the brain advances, the implications for our notions of free will, especially in the context of mental disorders, will become increasingly profound.

This complex journey through the maze of diagnostics, treatment, and ethical dilemmas surrounding mental disorders and free will illuminates the intricate dance between our brain, our mind, and our society. While we may not have clear-cut answers, the exploration of these questions is crucial for fostering a mental health care system that respects individual autonomy, promotes well-being, and aligns with our evolving understanding of human nature and free will.

11.4 MENTAL HEALTH DATA: WHAT DOES IT REVEAL ABOUT FREE WILL?

In the world of mental health research, data plays an integral role. It is the raw material from which researchers and professionals draw their conclusions, diagnose conditions, and devise treatment strategies. The collective knowledge about mental health that we possess today owes a lot to the vast amount of data gathered from various sources including hospitals, mental health surveys, research institutions, and more.

Data in mental health is as diverse as the field itself. It encapsulates an array of factors including the number of people affected by certain mental health conditions (prevalence), the rate of occurrence of new cases (incidence), the details of treatment provided (treatment data), and the outcomes post-treatment (outcome data). Each piece of data tells a story, adds to the complex puzzle of mental health, and assists in understanding the scope and impact of mental disorders.

Furthermore, mental health data serves an even greater purpose, especially when we explore it through the lens of free will. It not only helps us understand the decisions and actions of those with mental health issues but also offers insights into the limitations of free will, thus illuminating the intricate interplay between mental health and free will.

This section will provide a comprehensive overview of mental health data, its interpretation in light of free will, its contribution to our understanding of human behavior and decision-making, and a glimpse into the future of mental health data research.

Understanding Mental Health Through Data

Mental health data comes in many forms and serves various purposes. At its most fundamental level, it allows us to measure the prevalence of different mental health conditions. This prevalence data is pivotal as it helps us gauge the magnitude of mental health problems, allowing policymakers and healthcare providers to allocate resources efficiently.

Incidence data, on the other hand, tracks the number of new cases over a specific period, offering valuable insights into the emerging trends in mental health. It's particularly useful in identifying patterns, predicting future scenarios, and developing preventive measures.

Treatment data encompasses the specifics of mental health care provided to individuals, including the type of treatment, its duration, the medications used, and more. This data helps in assessing the efficacy of different treatment methods, thus guiding the development of more effective therapeutic strategies.

Outcome data is equally important as it measures the effectiveness of treatment methods by observing the improvement in patients' mental health post-treatment. By analyzing outcome data, healthcare professionals can make informed decisions about modifying treatment plans and improving patient care.

Understanding these different types of data is a prerequisite to appreciate the complex landscape of mental health. They serve as a testament to the multifaceted nature of mental health disorders and treatments, and the extensive work done by countless professionals in the field.

Data Interpretation and Free Will

In the context of free will, mental health data interpretation becomes even more nuanced. Mental disorders often impede one's ability to make decisions freely, thereby casting shadows on the concept of free will. This can be seen in individuals grappling with disorders like depression, where their ability to make conscious, willed decisions might be heavily influenced by their mental state.

The intriguing question that arises here is - To what extent does mental illness limit free will? Can data provide insights into this complex relationship?

Data interpretation can indeed provide interesting insights into this. Consider the prevalence data of depression, which suggests that it affects more than 264 million people worldwide. Each of these individuals experiences a unique relationship with their free will, influenced by their symptoms, the severity of their depression, and their personal circumstances. By studying this data in detail, we can understand the vast spectrum of ways in which depression can impact free will.

This understanding of how mental health conditions can impede free will is crucial for developing effective treatment strategies. Data shows that cognitive behavioral therapy (CBT), for example, has proven effective in treating several mental disorders. CBT is a type of psychotherapy that helps patients understand how their thoughts and feelings influence their behaviors. It's all about making individuals conscious of their decision-making process, thereby enhancing their sense of free will. The success of CBT could be seen as a testament to the potential of restoring free will in individuals suffering from mental disorders.

Furthermore, outcome data often demonstrates the restoration of an individual's decision-making abilities post-treatment, suggesting the partial or full return of their free will. Analyzing this data could help us explore the potential of different treatments in restoring free will and guide us in developing more effective therapies.

The Future of Mental Health Data

The advent of digital technologies and artificial intelligence has revolutionized the collection and analysis of mental health data. Wearable technologies and mobile applications now allow for the real-time tracking of psychological states, offering valuable insights into the human mind. Additionally, AI and machine learning algorithms can analyze vast quantities of data to identify patterns and predict outcomes that may be missed by the human eye.

This technological advancement opens a new frontier in understanding the relationship between mental health and free will. With access to real-time data, we could potentially monitor the fluctuations in a person's mental state and its impact on their decision-making capabilities. This could pave the way for personalized treatment plans tailored to the individual's specific needs and mental health condition, thereby enhancing their free will in the process.

Despite the significant progress made, the field of mental health data is not without its challenges. Privacy concerns, data security, and ethical considerations pose significant hurdles. It is imperative that as we move forward, we address these issues responsibly to protect the rights and interests of individuals.

In summation, the exploration of mental health data provides us with a nuanced understanding of the complex relationship between mental health and free will. By analyzing this data, we delve deeper into the constraints mental disorders can place on free will and the potential of treatments to restore it. As we move into a future replete with technological advancements, we look forward to a more profound understanding of this relationship, guided by responsible and ethical use of data.

CHAPTER 12: MORALITY IN A DETERMINISTIC WORLD

As we journey further into the complex web of free will, determinism, and the myriad implications they hold for our world, we find ourselves in a territory that is both deeply personal and universally relevant. The question of morality, of right and wrong, of what ought to be done - these are inquiries that have sparked debates among philosophers, theologians, and thinkers of all stripes for millennia.

In Chapter 12, "Constructing Morality in a Deterministic World", we delve into the heart of this debate, bearing in mind our exploration thus far. We've navigated the intricate landscape of the human brain in the context of neuroscience, grappled with the philosophical implications of free will and determinism, and we've waded into the realm of law and mental health, considering how these concepts of volition influence our understanding of culpability, punishment, and responsibility.

In light of all these investigations, we now turn our attention to morality. How does determinism reshape our understanding of moral responsibility? Can we construct a robust ethical system without the underpinning of free will? If our decisions are bound by the deterministic laws of nature, what place is there for moral praise or blame?

I invite you to keep an open mind as we dive into these difficult, but essential questions. Our journey continues.

12.1 RETHINKING MORALITY: ALTERNATIVES TO FREE WILL

The bedrock of our moral understandings, as deeply ingrained as they are, often rest on the premise of free will. Akin to the vast majority of our societal and judicial systems, morality, for the most part, is underpinned by the presumption of choice, of an individual's capacity to exercise control over their actions. To be virtuous, to be moral, so the story goes, is to select the 'right' choice when faced with ethical dilemmas. This prevalent perspective assumes the existence of free will, that each individual stands at the crossroads of right and wrong, independently able to decide their path.

However, as our previous discussions on determinism have highlighted, this perception of absolute freedom in our decision-making is fraught with problems. The deterministic nature of our existence, propelled by an unbroken chain of cause and effect, proposes significant challenges to this free will-based morality. If our actions are the products of pre-existing conditions, factors beyond our control, how then do we reconcile this with our notions of right and wrong, of praise and blame?

In the face of these challenges, it becomes crucial to reconsider morality without the foundations of free will. To do this, we must first consider why morality is central to our society and what it might look like in the absence of free will. Morality, at its core, acts as a system of rules or principles, guiding behaviors and actions within a social group. These moral rules help maintain social order, foster cooperation, and minimize harm among the group members. Without some form of morality, social structures could crumble, leaving room for anarchy and social disarray.

In a deterministic universe, we might posit a morality that focuses less on individual choice and more on the societal conditions that influence behavior. This perspective, often associated with 'consequentialist' theories in philosophy, emphasizes the outcomes of actions rather than the intent behind them. The focus here shifts from the actor to the act, from the internal decision-making process to the external factors shaping behavior.

With determinism in play, one could argue that rather than focusing on punishing individuals for their 'wrong' choices, society's focus should shift towards understanding the deterministic factors leading to these outcomes and making necessary changes. This approach could mean increased emphasis on education, socio-economic equality, mental health services, and a range of other social support mechanisms that can guide individuals towards making 'better' decisions.

This shift in focus doesn't imply the absolution of individual responsibility but rather frames it within a more holistic understanding of the influences on human behavior. The deterministic perspective helps us realize that the individuals we perceive as 'wrongdoers' are often themselves the products of unfortunate deterministic outcomes.

In this way, rethinking morality in a deterministic framework can lead to a more compassionate and understanding society. It's not about eliminating accountability, but about acknowledging the complex web of factors that shape our decisions and behaviors. It emphasizes a systemic perspective over an individual one. It's about recognizing that an individual's 'bad' choices are not isolated incidents that can be traced back to a singular 'bad' decision on the part of the individual. They are, instead, the result of a series of deterministically influenced events that have led the individual down a particular path.

This understanding also has implications for our judicial systems. If we accept determinism, we might rethink the purpose of punishment. If free will is indeed an illusion, then punishment as a means to deter 'bad' decisions becomes less rational. Instead, rehabilitation and societal change become more logical responses. The goal then shifts from punishment to prevention, from retribution to rehabilitation.

In a deterministic world, the question of morality becomes less about what a person should do and more about what kind of conditions we should create to foster desirable behaviors. Ethics in such a scenario could lean more heavily on social responsibility, highlighting the importance of collective actions in shaping individual behaviors. It would draw attention to the systemic and structural factors that influence our decisions, pushing for societal change as a means to improve individual behaviors.

The shift towards this perspective, however, is not without challenges. It requires a radical reframing of our current understanding and a willingness to let go of deeply held notions of personal autonomy. The idea of free will is deeply ingrained in our psyche and our societal structures, so such a shift would indeed be revolutionary.

This perspective is not without its critics. Some argue that this approach runs the risk of absolving individuals of personal responsibility, paving the way for a society where anyone can justify their wrong actions by blaming their circumstances. However, it's crucial to note that acknowledging the influence of deterministic factors on our behavior doesn't absolve us of responsibility. It simply frames that responsibility within a broader context.

It's also worth noting that these ideas aren't completely new. Many indigenous cultures around the world have long upheld similar views, emphasizing the role of the community and environment in shaping individual behavior. Moreover, there's a growing recognition in fields like psychology and sociology that our behaviors are heavily influenced by external factors. The deterministic perspective simply takes these ideas a step further, applying them to our understanding of morality and ethics.

The shift towards this new paradigm is not just philosophical but also practical. In many ways, we're already seeing the impacts of this shift in various fields. For instance, in the field of behavioral economics, researchers are finding that people's economic decisions are heavily influenced by cognitive biases and environmental factors, challenging the classical economic view of humans as rational actors.

In the realm of criminal justice, some countries are moving away from punitive justice systems towards restorative justice models that focus more on rehabilitation and reconciliation. In mental health, there's a greater emphasis on understanding the societal and environmental factors that contribute to mental illnesses, leading to more comprehensive treatment approaches.

Moving forward, the challenge will be to find a balance. A balance between acknowledging the role of deterministic factors in our behavior and maintaining a sense of personal responsibility. A balance between systemic change and individual change. A balance between rethinking morality in a deterministic world and holding onto useful aspects of our current moral frameworks.

The journey towards this balance won't be easy. It will require difficult conversations, radical changes, and a willingness to question deeply ingrained beliefs. But, as daunting as it may seem, the potential rewards are significant. A world where our moral frameworks are grounded in a deep understanding of human behavior could be a world of greater compassion, empathy, and fairness.

One of the significant criticisms of determinism is the perceived threat it poses to moral responsibility. The common argument goes that if our actions are the result of prior causes, then we can't be held responsible for them. However, some philosophers argue that determinism doesn't eliminate moral responsibility. Instead, it gives us a deeper understanding of it.

They argue that being responsible for an action doesn't mean the action wasn't caused or determined. Rather, it means that the action originated from us - it was caused by something within us. The fact that this 'something' (our desires, beliefs, etc.) was shaped by prior causes doesn't change the fact that it was still us who performed the action. This is a concept known as 'compatibilism' - the idea that free will and determinism are compatible.

For example, consider a person who steals because they're starving. The person's decision was influenced by their circumstances (hunger, poverty, etc.), but they still made the decision. The deterministic factors didn't absolve them of responsibility. Rather, they provided context for understanding why the person acted the way they did.

The same reasoning applies to more complex decisions. Suppose a person becomes a doctor because they were influenced by their parents who were also doctors. Their decision was determined by their upbringing, but they are still responsible for it because the decision originated from them, from their desires, goals, and choices, even if those were shaped by their upbringing.

Of course, this doesn't mean that we should ignore the deterministic factors. On the contrary, understanding these factors can help us better address moral issues. In the case of the starving thief, for instance, addressing the root causes (e.g., poverty, lack of access to food) can be more effective in preventing theft than simply punishing the thieves.

At the same time, the deterministic perspective doesn't absolve individuals of the need to make moral decisions. We still have to navigate the world, make decisions, and face the consequences of our actions. And while our decisions might be influenced by deterministic factors, they're still our decisions.

So, rather than negating the concept of morality, determinism provides us with a richer, more nuanced understanding of it. It shifts our focus from abstract notions of right and wrong towards a more contextual understanding of human behavior.

This shift also has profound implications for how we construct moral frameworks. Currently, most moral frameworks are based on the assumption of free will. They presuppose that individuals can freely choose between right and wrong and should be held accountable for their choices.

However, if we accept the deterministic perspective, then we need to rethink these frameworks. Instead of focusing on punishment and retribution, our moral frameworks should focus more on understanding and addressing the root causes of 'immoral' behavior. Instead of condemning individuals for their actions, we should seek to understand why they acted the way they did and how we can help them make better decisions in the future.

Such a shift would not only be more compassionate but also more effective. Studies have shown that punitive measures often don't deter crime and can even exacerbate it. On the other hand, measures that address the root causes of crime (e.g., poverty, lack of education, mental health issues) have been shown to be more effective in reducing crime rates.

As we navigate this new moral landscape, we will undoubtedly face challenges. Some people might resist the idea of determinism, seeing it as a threat to their sense of self or their religious beliefs. Others might misuse determinism to justify immoral behavior or to shirk personal responsibility.

But despite these challenges, there's a growing recognition that the deterministic perspective can provide valuable insights into human behavior. It can help us understand why people act the way they do, which in turn can help us address social problems more effectively. It can also foster greater empathy and compassion, as we realize that we're all products of our circumstances to a large extent.

As we move forward, it's crucial to approach these discussions with an open mind. Whether we ultimately embrace determinism or not, the questions it raises can only enrich our understanding of morality and ethics.

In the following sections, we'll delve deeper into these topics, exploring the potential implications of determinism for personal and societal moral frameworks, as well as providing everyday examples and analogies to help illuminate these complex issues.

The shift from a belief in absolute free will to determinism is not just a shift in belief, but also a shift in worldview. This shift is not just about acknowledging the role of deterministic factors in our actions, but also about reevaluating our moral frameworks and our societal systems. It's about realizing that we are not isolated individuals making decisions in a vacuum, but interconnected beings whose decisions are influenced by a complex web of factors. This shift in worldview invites us to reevaluate not only how we judge individual actions but also how we structure our societies.

For instance, in a deterministic perspective, it becomes difficult to justify punishing someone simply for the sake of retribution. If a person's actions were the inevitable result of their circumstances, then punishing them doesn't change those circumstances. It doesn't prevent the person from committing the same action again if they find themselves in the same circumstances.

Instead, a deterministic worldview encourages us to focus on rehabilitation and prevention. Rather than punishing someone for their past actions, we should help them change the circumstances that led to those actions. We should provide them with the resources and support they need to make better decisions in the future.

This shift in perspective also has implications for how we think about societal issues. Instead of blaming individuals for their actions, we should focus on changing the systems that influence those actions. For example, instead of blaming people for being poor, we should focus on addressing the systemic issues that lead to poverty.

This doesn't mean that we should abandon the concept of personal responsibility. Even in a deterministic universe, people still have the ability to make choices. They can still strive to improve themselves and their circumstances. But acknowledging the role of deterministic factors can help us create a more compassionate and effective approach to addressing societal problems.

In the next section, we will discuss the personal and societal implications of this shift in worldview. We will explore how adopting a deterministic perspective can reshape our moral frameworks, and how it can help us address social issues more effectively. We will also provide everyday examples and analogies to help clarify these complex concepts.

By understanding the deterministic nature of our actions, we can create a more compassionate and understanding society. We can move away from blaming and punishing, and towards understanding and helping. This is the promise of a deterministic worldview, and it is a promise that we can start fulfilling today.

12.2 FROM DETERMINISM TO ETHICS: A SHIFT IN WORLDVIEW

Let's delve into the meat of the topic. The shift from determinism to ethics has long been a subject of fascination and debate among scholars from a variety of fields, including philosophy, psychology, neuroscience, and theology. How one perceives the world around them, especially concerning the moral and ethical implications of their actions, is significantly influenced by their worldview. To appreciate this shift in worldview, we need to first understand the nuances of determinism and its implications on our sense of morality and ethical judgment.

Determinism essentially posits that all events, including human actions, are determined by previously existing causes. This standpoint offers a more mechanistic view of the universe, implying a future that is predetermined and, therefore, can be predicted based on the present. In contrast, the concept of free will postulates that humans have the power to make choices that are genuinely free, which allows us to hold individuals morally responsible for their actions.

In a deterministic world, the possibility of "choice" may seem irrelevant, but this doesn't entirely eliminate the concept of ethics. It could be argued that even in a deterministic world, individuals are driven by a set of principles or a moral compass that guides their actions, fostering an inherent system of ethics. This shift from determinism to ethics brings forth the idea that while our choices may be influenced by preceding causes, our ethical judgments and values still hold substantial weight in shaping those choices.

To further understand this shift, we can consider a practical example. Imagine two individuals, Person A and Person B. Person A firmly believes in the concept of determinism, holding the view that all their actions are a result of preceding causes, and hence they lack control over them. On the other hand, Person B adopts a more ethically-driven worldview, believing that they have the freedom to make choices that align with their personal values and principles.

Suppose both individuals are presented with a morally challenging situation – say, they find a wallet full of money lying on the street. Person A, guided by deterministic beliefs, might reason that their action – whether to take the money or attempt to return the wallet to its owner – is already predetermined, thus absolving them of any moral responsibility. In contrast, Person B, guided by an ethical framework, would contemplate the moral implications of their potential actions and make a choice that aligns with their values - most likely, the decision to return the wallet.

In both scenarios, the individuals' actions are influenced by their worldview. However, the deterministic perspective could lead to a sense of moral absolution, while the ethically-driven perspective emphasizes moral responsibility, despite both worldviews operating under the umbrella of causality.

To truly appreciate the implications of this shift, we need to delve into the evolution of ethical thought, the concept of moral responsibility, and the role of societal norms and cultural influences in shaping our ethical frameworks. By doing so, we can gain a more profound understanding of how the transition from determinism to ethics shapes our perceptions of morality and guides our actions.

Let's now explore the historical evolution of ethical thought, and how it has shaped the concept of moral responsibility within deterministic and non-deterministic frameworks.

The history of ethics is as old as human civilization itself. From the codes of Hammurabi, one of the first written laws, to the philosophical teachings of the ancient Greeks, all the way to modern theories of morality, ethical thought has continually evolved to reflect changes in societal norms, cultural values, and scientific understanding. As such, tracing this history is key to understanding the shift from determinism to ethics and its implications for our concept of moral responsibility.

In ancient cultures, morality was often tied to religion and divine laws. Ancient Egyptians, for example, believed in Ma'at, the concept of truth, balance, order, and justice, as a divine law that governed all of creation. Similarly, ancient Hindu texts like the Vedas and Upanishads laid down moral laws dictated by divine order. In these cultures, determinism and ethics were not mutually exclusive but intertwined. One's actions were seen as preordained by fate or the gods, but they also had to align with the moral laws to maintain cosmic order.

However, the ancient Greeks, particularly the philosophers, introduced a different perspective. While they acknowledged the role of fate, they also emphasized human agency and the importance of virtues. The philosopher Socrates, for instance, argued for the inherent value of personal integrity and self-knowledge. His student, Plato, believed in the existence of ideal Forms, including the Form of the Good, which he saw as the ultimate object of knowledge and the source of all virtues.

Aristotle, another Greek philosopher, further developed this line of thought by proposing a theory of ethics based on the concept of 'eudaimonia,' often translated as 'flourishing' or 'the good life.' For Aristotle, ethical behavior was not just about following rules but about cultivating virtues that enable us to fulfill our potential as humans.

These Greek philosophers emphasized the role of free will and individual responsibility, challenging deterministic views. However, they didn't completely reject determinism. Aristotle himself, in his work 'Physics,' discussed the concept of 'causality,' recognizing that our actions are influenced by multiple factors. However, he maintained that this didn't absolve us of moral responsibility.

Fast forward to the Enlightenment era, the rise of science brought new challenges and perspectives to ethical thought. Philosophers like Immanuel Kant argued for the concept of 'duty' and 'moral law,' independent of divine authority or human desires. He proposed the idea of 'categorical imperative,' a principle suggesting that we should act in such a way that our actions could be universally applied.

Meanwhile, utilitarian thinkers like Jeremy Bentham and John Stuart Mill advocated for ethics based on the 'greatest happiness principle,' suggesting that the morality of an action should be judged by its impact on overall happiness or well-being.

In the contemporary era, the interplay between determinism and ethics has become even more complex due to advances in fields like psychology, neuroscience, and social sciences. While we have gained more understanding of the factors influencing human behavior, questions about moral responsibility have also become more nuanced.

Nowadays, ethical theories range from consequentialism (judging actions by their outcomes) to deontological ethics (judging actions based on rules), virtue ethics (focused on character), and even care ethics (centered on relationships). Many of these theories accept that our actions are influenced by a variety of factors – genetic, environmental, social – reflecting a deterministic perspective. However, they also emphasize the role of moral reasoning, values, and principles in guiding our actions – indicating a shift towards ethics.

In summary, the evolution of ethical thought reflects a continuous dialogue between determinism and ethics. While our understanding of the influences on human behavior has grown, giving more weight to deterministic perspectives, the importance of ethics – the need for moral responsibility, principles, and values – has remained a constant thread.

This dialogue between determinism and ethics has significant implications for our worldview. It challenges us to rethink the foundations of our moral framework and consider how we can reconcile the apparent conflict between determinism and moral responsibility.

One key implication is the shift from a punishment-oriented justice system to a rehabilitation-focused one. If we acknowledge that people's actions are influenced by factors beyond their control, such as their upbringing, genetics, or environment, then it seems unjust to punish them harshly for their wrongdoings. Instead, a more ethical approach might be to focus on rehabilitating individuals and addressing the root causes of their behavior.

This shift in perspective can also affect how we approach issues like poverty, addiction, and mental health. Instead of blaming individuals for their circumstances, we can strive to understand the systemic and biological factors that contribute to these issues and work towards comprehensive solutions.

On a personal level, acknowledging determinism can also lead to greater empathy and understanding. If we recognize that our actions and those of others are often shaped by factors beyond our control, we can be more forgiving of ourselves and others. This can foster a sense of connectedness and shared humanity, reinforcing the importance of compassion and mutual aid in our ethical frameworks.

However, embracing this deterministic perspective doesn't mean absolving ourselves or others of all responsibility. After all, our moral frameworks also depend on the belief in personal agency – the idea that we have the ability to make choices and shape our lives. Therefore, the challenge lies in finding a balance – acknowledging the deterministic factors that influence our behavior, while also recognizing our capacity for change and moral growth.

One way to strike this balance is through the concept of 'compatibilism,' a perspective that reconciles determinism with free will. Compatibilists argue that even if our actions are causally determined, we can still act freely as long as our actions align with our desires and intentions. This allows for moral responsibility, as we can still hold individuals accountable for their actions if they act in line with their intentions, even if these intentions are shaped by deterministic factors.

To illustrate this, consider the analogy of a garden. A gardener can't control all the factors that influence the growth of her plants, like the weather or soil conditions. However, she can still make choices that contribute to their growth, like watering them regularly or providing them with adequate sunlight. Even if her actions are influenced by factors beyond her control, she can still be considered responsible for the wellbeing of her plants. Similarly, we may not have complete control over our actions, but we can still make choices that align with our moral values and contribute to our growth as individuals.

This shift from determinism to ethics, therefore, doesn't involve rejecting one perspective for the other, but rather integrating them in a way that enriches our understanding of human behavior and morality. By acknowledging the deterministic factors that shape our actions and embracing the ethical principles that guide our decisions, we can construct a more nuanced, compassionate, and effective moral framework.

In the next section, we will explore these implications in more detail and discuss how they shape our personal and societal moral frameworks.

12.3 Personal and Societal Implications: Shaping Moral Frameworks

As we dive deeper into the confluence of determinism and ethics, we also start exploring its personal and societal implications. Both these dimensions - the personal and the societal - are closely intertwined. The personal shapes the societal, and vice versa. Our personal moral frameworks contribute to socictal norms, and societal norms, in turn, shape our personal moral frameworks. This bi-directional relationship is key to understanding how a shift in worldview impacts both these dimensions.

Personal Implications: When we understand the deterministic factors that influence our behavior, we can start to let go of self-judgment. Often, we hold ourselves to high standards and judge ourselves harshly when we don't meet them. But when we understand that there are myriad factors beyond our control shaping our decisions and actions, we can start to replace self-judgment with self-understanding.

This doesn't mean we stop striving for improvement. On the contrary, understanding the deterministic factors that shape our behavior can help us better identify what we can change and how. For instance, understanding the influence of habitual patterns on our behavior can guide us to implement strategies to alter these patterns.

Societal Implications: On a societal level, recognizing the influence of deterministic factors can foster empathy and reduce judgment. For example, understanding the role of socio-economic factors in crime can shift perspectives from punitive to rehabilitative and preventative approaches in the criminal justice system.

Similarly, acknowledging the role of genetic and environmental factors in addiction can reduce stigma and facilitate supportive treatments. When society as a whole begins to appreciate the deterministic factors that influence individual behavior, it can drive systemic changes that tackle root causes rather than symptoms.

The deterministic perspective can inform policy-making as well. Policies can be designed to mitigate the adverse effects of deterministic factors. For example, social policies can aim to reduce poverty and improve educational opportunities, thus addressing some of the deterministic factors that contribute to societal issues.

Shaping Moral Frameworks: As we rethink our moral frameworks in the light of determinism, we might be tempted to think that moral responsibility becomes obsolete. But as discussed earlier, compatibility allows us to reconcile determinism with moral responsibility.

We might not have absolute free will, but we do have a degree of agency that allows us to make moral decisions. We can strive to make choices that align with our moral values, even as we acknowledge the deterministic influences on our behavior.

Moreover, our moral frameworks aren't static – they evolve over time. They're shaped by our experiences, our interactions with others, societal norms, and our growing understanding of the world. As we integrate the deterministic perspective into our worldview, our moral frameworks can evolve to become more compassionate, understanding, and effective.

Understanding the interplay between determinism and ethics, thus, has profound implications for how we perceive ourselves and others, how we interact with society, and how we construct our moral frameworks. This shift in worldview can lead to personal growth, societal progress, and more ethical ways of being in the world. In the next section, we'll delve into everyday examples and analogies that bring these concepts to life.

Now, having developed a theoretical understanding of how determinism shapes our moral frameworks and impacts our personal and societal interactions, it's time to dive into everyday examples and analogies. These real-world examples will help us grasp the concepts more concretely, allowing for a deeper understanding of the interplay between determinism and ethics.

The Case of the Unfortunate Thief: Let's start with a hypothetical scenario. Consider a young man, Tom, born and raised in poverty. He's been a victim of socioeconomic determinants that have put him in a situation where he feels compelled to steal to survive. If we view this situation from a strictly free will perspective, we might condemn Tom for his actions outright. He made the decision to steal, after all.

But, when we bring in the deterministic perspective, we see a bigger picture. Tom's actions were influenced by the environment he was raised in and the lack of opportunities he had. Understanding this, we might still not condone his actions, but our approach to handling the situation changes.

Instead of solely focusing on punitive measures, we might look towards creating better social support systems, education opportunities, and employment options that can reduce the likelihood of such actions.

Self-Control and Temptation: Here's another example - one that most of us might be able to relate to. Suppose you're on a diet and trying to avoid sugar. One day, you walk past a bakery and see a mouth-watering chocolate cake on display. You're tempted to buy a slice. If you give in to the temptation, from a free will perspective, you might blame yourself for not having enough willpower.

But let's consider the deterministic factors at play. The bakery happened to be on your way home. The cake was on display, attracting your attention. You had a stressful day at work, which is known to trigger cravings. Once we consider these factors, it's easier to understand why you were tempted to break your diet. You can then use this understanding to come up with strategies to manage such situations in the future – for instance, changing your route to avoid passing by the bakery.

These everyday examples illustrate how understanding determinism can inform our moral judgements and decision-making. They demonstrate how this understanding can foster self-compassion and empathy for others. They show us that while we do have a degree of control over our actions, we're also shaped by factors beyond our control. And in recognizing this, we can navigate the world more effectively and ethically.

This chapter opened up a new perspective on morality – one that integrates determinism with ethics. It showed us how this perspective can have far-reaching personal and societal implications, and how it can shape our moral frameworks. It offered a nuanced way of looking at moral responsibility that encourages understanding and compassion. As we move forward, we'll continue exploring the implications of determinism on various aspects of life.

The story of Rehabilitation and Recidivism: Consider the criminal justice system. Typically, individuals are held accountable for their actions based on the principle of free will. They are assumed to have had the capacity to choose between right and wrong. Consequently, when they choose wrong, they are punished. But what if we reconsider this stance from a deterministic viewpoint?

Let's look at John, a convict who's spent a significant part of his life in prison for a series of burglaries. Each time he's released, it doesn't take long for him to end up back in prison. Looking at John's life from a free will perspective might lead us to believe he's choosing to live a life of crime, despite having faced the consequences multiple times.

However, the deterministic viewpoint reveals more layers. John grew up in a rough neighborhood, his parents were absent, and the role models he had were gang members and criminals. He never had access to quality education or job opportunities. Upon release from prison, with a record, employment becomes even more challenging. The social stigma around ex-convicts doesn't ease the situation either.

In understanding John's life, the deterministic viewpoint leads us toward rehabilitation and reintegration programs. The focus shifts from punishment to correcting the course of determinants that lead to criminal behavior.

This does not mean we completely rid our systems of accountability. It means rethinking and reconstructing them to be more understanding of the human condition and the various factors at play that shape our lives and decisions.

These stories and analogies aim to ground the theoretical concepts we've discussed in real-world contexts. They highlight the practical implications of integrating determinism into our moral frameworks and emphasize the need for an empathetic approach towards ourselves and others. They underscore the fact that morality, far from being a simple matter of 'right' and 'wrong' choices, is a complex tapestry woven from a multitude of threads — our biology, our environment, our experiences, and indeed, our capacity for making choices.

As we navigate through the complexities of determinism and its implications on morality, these narratives and illustrations provide us with a more concrete understanding. They invite us to delve deeper, ask more challenging questions, and continually reassess our viewpoints. In the following chapters, we will further explore the exciting intersections of free will, determinism, and the many aspects of human life.

Concluding Part III

As we reach the conclusion of Part 3, we have embarked on a thought-provoking journey that explores the intricate relationship between determinism and ethics. We have delved into the personal and societal implications of this shift in worldview, challenging long-held beliefs and examining the multifaceted nature of moral responsibility. Throughout this exploration, we have encountered the nuances of determinism, the evolution of ethical thought, and the ways in which our moral frameworks can be reshaped in light of these concepts.

We embarked on our exploration of determinism, free will, and the interplay between the two. We examined the scientific and philosophical perspectives that underpin these concepts, recognizing the complexity of human behavior and decision-making. We learned that determinism suggests that all events, including human actions, are determined by preceding causes, challenging the notion of absolute free will. This realization set the stage for our subsequent exploration of the implications of determinism on ethics and moral responsibility.

Then we continued our journey by investigating the intersection of determinism and the law. We navigated the realm of legal responsibility, culpability, and punishment, contemplating how our understanding of determinism can shape the principles and practices of the justice system. We considered the challenges that determinism poses to traditional notions of personal responsibility, while also recognizing the importance of accountability and the need to balance rehabilitation with societal protection.

Moving forward, we delved into the realm of mental health and explored the implications of determinism for our understanding of psychological well-being. We examined the influence of biological and environmental factors on mental health, highlighting the role of determinism in shaping our experiences and behaviors. We recognized the need for a holistic approach to mental health that considers the interplay between determinism and personal agency, emphasizing the importance of support, understanding, and therapeutic interventions.

Finally, we arrived at the heart of our discussion: constructing morality in a deterministic world. We grappled with the profound implications of determinism for our understanding of moral responsibility and ethical frameworks. We questioned the traditional emphasis on individual choice and explored alternative perspectives that focus on societal conditions and outcomes. We recognized the need for a more compassionate and holistic approach to morality, one that acknowledges the influence of deterministic factors while still upholding personal agency and accountability.

Through these chapters, we have come to appreciate the complexity and interdependence of determinism and ethics. We have realized that determinism does not negate the significance of ethics but rather invites us to consider a more nuanced understanding of moral responsibility. It encourages us to shift our focus from punishment to rehabilitation, from blame to understanding, and from individual choice to systemic change.

The personal and societal implications of this shift are far-reaching. On a personal level, embracing determinism allows us to cultivate self-understanding and self-compassion, acknowledging the multitude of factors that shape our actions. It empowers us to make more informed choices and strive for personal growth while recognizing the limitations imposed by our circumstances. At the same time, it fosters empathy and reduces judgment towards others, as we recognize the complex web of influences that shape their behavior.

On a societal level, the implications are equally profound. Embracing determinism challenges us to rethink our justice systems, social policies, and approaches to issues such as poverty, addiction, and mental health. It calls for a shift from punitive measures to rehabilitation, prevention, and addressing the root causes of societal problems. It encourages us to build a more equitable and compassionate society that provides individuals with the support and opportunities necessary to make positive choices.

While this shift in worldview is not without its challenges, it holds the potential for a transformative impact on how we navigate the complexities of human existence. By integrating determinism and ethics, we can construct moral frameworks that are more nuanced, compassionate, and effective. We can strive for personal and societal growth, guided by an understanding of the deterministic factors that shape our lives while upholding the values and principles that define our humanity.

As we conclude Part 3 of our exploration, we are left with a multitude of questions and avenues for further reflection. How can we strike a balance between determinism and personal agency? How do we navigate the tension between individual responsibility and societal factors? How can we collectively build a more just and compassionate world?

These questions call for ongoing dialogue and exploration, as we continue to unravel the intricacies of determinism and ethics. In the next part of our journey, we will delve into the practical applications of these concepts in various domains of life, examining how they shape our understanding of relationships, culture, and the pursuit of meaning. As we move forward, let us carry with us the wisdom gained from this exploration, as we strive to construct a more enlightened and ethical existence.

PART IV: The Philosophy of Freewill

Welcome to The Philosophy of Free Will, an integral part of our expedition in this book. Up until now, we've journeyed through the worlds of science, law, ethics, and the human mind to understand the construct of free will and its antithesis, determinism. Part III deepened our exploration by delving into the implications of these concepts on legal systems, mental health, and moral frameworks, unraveling a tapestry of intricacies, nuances, and dilemmas.

As we transition to Part IV, it's time to steer our vessel into the waters of philosophy. Why philosophy, one might ask? Because philosophy, the mother of all knowledge, provides a unique lens to inspect and reflect upon the abstract and the concrete, the empirical and the theoretical, and most importantly, the ontological nature of free will. It furnishes us with tools to dissect the concepts we've gathered from science, law, ethics, and psychology, offering us a platform to question, reason, and understand.

This part of our journey begins with Chapter 13: Historical Philosophical Journey: Tracing Free Will, where we time-travel to witness the evolution of the concept of free will - from ancient civilizations to the medieval era, through the enlightening period of Renaissance, up to the era of Enlightenment. We consider the influential ideas of mind-body dualism proposed by Descartes and the theological interpretations of free will, particularly Augustine's profound impact.

Chapter 14: The Modern Arena: Contemporary Philosophical Debates ushers us into the present, revealing how philosophical discourse on free will continues to be vibrant and relevant. We confront and weigh two rival camps - compatibilism and incompatibilism - and understand how they reconcile free will and determinism. The daring challenges posed by libertarianism to the reign of determinism and the role of existentialism in underscoring individual freedom also form part of this dialogue.

Chapter 15: Ethical Repercussions: A World Sans Free Will takes us back to the realm of ethics, but now equipped with philosophical insights. We examine how determinism affects consequentialist and deontological views and reinterpret accountability, blame, and punishment. We also consider the weight of responsibility under the lens of determinism.

Finally, Chapter 16: In Search of Meaning: Determinism and Purpose invites us to a profound personal reflection. We discuss whether it is possible to find meaning and purpose in a deterministic framework. Can we attain psychological well-being and flourish in a deterministic world? We conclude this part with some personal reflections on navigating life without the concept of free will.

By exploring philosophy, we're not just delving deeper into free will; we're looking at how these concepts shape our understanding of responsibility, ethics, and the essence of human life. Philosophy strips bare the ontological underpinnings and the phenomenological implications of our discourse on free will and determinism.

By turning this page, you are stepping into a world of ideas that have spanned centuries and challenged some of the greatest minds. So, let's embrace this challenge and see where this final part of our journey takes us. After all, as the Greek philosopher Socrates once said, "The unexamined life is not worth living." So, let's examine.

CHAPTER 13: PHILOSOPHICAL JOURNEY THROUGH FREEWILL

As we embark on this journey through time in Chapter 13, we attempt to unravel the deep-seated and complex notions of free will. This chapter, titled "Historical Philosophical Journey: Tracing Free Will," offers us a panoramic view of how the concept of free will has transformed and evolved throughout human history. Starting from the wisdom of ancient civilizations to the theological and metaphysical enquiries of the medieval period, this chapter provides a historical backdrop against which we understand the ever-evolving narrative of free will. It offers us a critical perspective, emphasizing how each era, with its unique socio-cultural context, has shaped and reshaped the discourse around free will and determinism. Let's embark on this fascinating journey and uncover the layers of understanding that have culminated in the complex mosaic of free will that we grapple with today.

13.1 FROM ANCIENT TO MEDIEVAL: THE EVOLUTION OF FREE WILL

As we set the stage for our historical journey from the dawn of philosophical thought to the medieval period, we must remember the cultural and historical contexts that shaped these eras and their philosophical inquiries. The ancient world, rich in its diversity and cultural complexity, witnessed the emergence of many schools of thought that contributed significantly to the discourse on free will. In contrast, the medieval period was marked by a profound theological influence, leading to a distinct shift in this discourse. The transformation from ancient to medieval thought was not merely a chronological progression but a dynamic interplay of changing sociocultural narratives, intellectual discourses, and individual philosophical perspectives.

In the ancient world, philosophical inquiry was not a secluded intellectual pursuit but an integral part of life. The Greek philosophers, such as Socrates, Plato, and Aristotle, did not treat philosophy as an isolated discipline but rather as a way of life - an approach to understanding and living in the world. For them, questions about free will and determinism were not abstract theoretical concepts but crucial aspects of moral and ethical life. Let's delve into these early discourses to understand their perspectives on free will.

Socrates, often regarded as the father of Western philosophy, didn't explicitly use the term "free will," but his ideas about virtue, knowledge, and moral responsibility reflect a clear emphasis on personal agency. According to Socrates, virtue is the highest form of knowledge, and this knowledge leads to right action. He believed that "no one errs or does wrong willingly or knowingly," suggesting that individuals have control over their actions when they possess the right knowledge. While Socrates didn't use the term "free will," his emphasis on knowledge-based action resonates with the concept.

Following Socrates, Plato, his student, provided his unique insights into free will and moral responsibility. Plato believed in a well-ordered soul where the rational part should govern over the spirited and appetitive parts. He held that individuals could exercise their free will to ensure this harmony within the soul, leading to just actions. For Plato, justice and morality were intrinsically linked to the exercise of free will, emphasizing the role of personal agency in ethical decisions.

The philosophical discourse then evolved further with Aristotle, who emphasized the role of voluntary actions in moral responsibility. Aristotle argued that actions are involuntary when done under compulsion or ignorance, but if individuals act with knowledge and without external compulsion, their actions are voluntary, indicating an early understanding of free will.

The philosophical journey then takes us to the Hellenistic period, an era marked by the flourishing of various schools of thought such as Stoicism, Epicureanism, and Skepticism. The Stoics, particularly, had a deterministic view of the universe, believing in a divine reason or "logos" permeating everything. Despite this apparent determinism, Stoics like Epictetus held that while we can't control external events, we can control our responses, indicating a nuanced perspective on free will within a deterministic framework.

Shifting from the Greek to the Roman world, the philosophy of free will evolved further. The Roman philosopher and statesman Cicero, for instance, emphasized that individuals possess free will, enabling them to choose their actions, though he also recognized that these actions occur within the bounds of fate.

Upon transitioning into the Medieval period, Christian philosophers grappled with the concept of free will within the context of divine foreknowledge and predestination. Saint Augustine, an influential figure in early Christian philosophy, proposed a compelling model of free will. His argument involved the idea that human beings, though initially created with free will, were morally corrupted after the Fall of Adam and Eve, leading to a 'bondage of the will' to sin. Despite this, Augustine maintained that God's grace could restore human free will, permitting moral choices.

Thomas Aquinas, another medieval Christian philosopher, approached free will from the Aristotelian perspective, harmonizing it with Christian doctrine. Aquinas argued that, while God knows and wills all actions, this divine causality does not preclude human free will. For Aquinas, humans have a natural inclination towards the good, and our free will consists of choosing between means to achieve this ultimate end.

The philosophical journey of free will was not restricted to the Western world. The Eastern philosophies, including Buddhism, Hinduism, and Jainism, also offer diverse perspectives. In Buddhism, the doctrine of Dependent Origination holds that all phenomena arise dependent on conditions; yet, the concept of Karma upholds moral responsibility. The early Upanishadic thought in Hindu philosophy contemplated the deterministic law of Karma and its impact on free will. Meanwhile, Jainism offers the doctrine of 'Anekantavada,' or non-absolutism, emphasizing the multifaceted nature of reality, potentially accommodating both determinism and free will.

The evolution of free will's conceptualization from ancient to medieval times reflects human attempts to understand the nature of human agency within various frameworks, including metaphysical, theological, and ethical paradigms. This evolution has laid the groundwork for subsequent philosophical debates, offering a rich tapestry of ideas that continue to influence contemporary thought.

Islamic philosophy introduced its unique perspective to the discourse on free will, with significant contributions from influential philosophers like Al-Farabi, Avicenna (Ibn Sina), and Averroes (Ibn Rushd). It is important to note that in Islamic thought, philosophical explorations were often deeply intertwined with theological and ethical considerations. The tension between predestination (Qadar) and free will (Qiyas) had been a subject of rigorous debate among Islamic scholars.

Al-Farabi, following the Platonic and Aristotelian tradition, believed in the rational part of the soul's primacy. He asserted that the rational faculty is free from the bounds of deterministic celestial influence. Conversely, Avicenna offered an argument for what has been interpreted as a form of "soft determinism". He argued that although all events are predetermined, human beings possess free will insofar as their actions emanate from their internal faculties.

Islamic mysticism or Sufism also contributed a distinct perspective, where free will and predestination were seen as two aspects of a broader spiritual reality. Jalaluddin Rumi, a renowned Sufi mystic, explained this paradox using the metaphor of a bow and an arrow. The arrow (representing human beings) is shot by the bow (God's will), but it has its flight path, embodying a nuanced harmony between determinism and free will.

To understand free will, we must appreciate its cultural and historical diversity in interpretation. As we trace the philosophical journey of free will, we find our thoughts challenged, reframed, and refined by these varied perspectives. The diverse intellectual legacy of the ancient and medieval world continues to form the philosophical substrate for our modern understanding of free will, an understanding that we will continue to explore as we progress in our journey.

The culmination of the Middle Ages marked the transition into the period commonly known as the Renaissance, which signifies a 'rebirth' of classical learning and a shift in perspectives. However, before we proceed into this intriguing period of intellectual enlightenment, it's essential to reflect upon the rich philosophical heritage left by the Ancient and Medieval philosophers.

Their relentless quests to understand the mysteries of human free will have laid the groundwork for future philosophical debates. The shift from a primarily divine-centered paradigm in the Ancient period to a more balanced discourse in the Medieval era indicates the evolution of human thought over centuries. This historical perspective offers us a much-needed context to comprehend the complexity of the notion of free will and highlights the fluidity of philosophical concepts.

With an exploration spanning from the deterministic principles of Stoicism and the ethical emphasis of Aristotle to the theological debates within Christianity and Islam, the discourse on free will has been a canvas painted with diverse intellectual brush strokes. These philosophical constructs, intricate as they are, reflect a facet of humanity's perpetual struggle to understand itself, a struggle that transcends cultural and temporal boundaries.

As we move forward in our exploration of free will, we carry forward these intellectual legacies, aware of the historical weight they carry. The questions we grapple with today are not novel but a continuation of an enduring philosophical tradition. As we step into the Renaissance and the Enlightenment period in the next section, we'll explore how these historical debates have been reshaped, revised, and refashioned in light of new philosophical perspectives.

Ancient and Medieval philosophers navigated through the turbulent waters of determinism, freedom, and morality, each presenting their unique compass to guide through these perplexities. Even as their theories vary, their shared commitment to illuminate the nature of human volition provides us a cohesive narrative, one that encapsulates the central theme of free will.

As we conclude our journey through the ancient and medieval epochs, we come to understand that the concept of free will has always been much more than a philosophical debate. It has been a lens through which humanity has tried to make sense of its place in the cosmos, its relationship with the divine, and its understanding of morality and ethics.

The notion of free will carries significant weight, offering answers to some of the most profound questions about human existence. It is about freedom, autonomy, and the capacity to choose. It's about our sense of self, about our understanding of morality, about our perception of society and justice. As we move forward into new realms of knowledge, we carry forward these age-old questions - reshaped and reframed but still echoing the fundamental human quest for understanding.

13.2 RENAISSANCE TO ENLIGHTENMENT: SHIFTS IN PERSPECTIVE

The Renaissance, a period spanning from the 14th to the 17th century, was marked by a renewed interest in the cultural and intellectual achievements of the classical Greek and Roman civilizations. This 'rebirth' extended beyond art and literature and profoundly influenced philosophy, inspiring thinkers to explore human nature, the structure of the universe, and our place in it with a fresh perspective. Contrary to the Medieval worldview that painted humans as pawns in a divine cosmic play, Renaissance thinkers, influenced by the humanist movement, started to place the individual at the center of the universe, giving rise to novel ideas about free will and determinism.

However, this renewed interest in the human individual did not entirely reject the divine. Many Renaissance philosophers retained strong ties to Christian theology, resulting in fascinating explorations of the tension between divine predestination and human free will. The Dutch humanist Erasmus of Rotterdam, for example, was a firm believer in free will despite his commitment to Christianity. His work "On the Freedom of the Will" famously debated Martin Luther's deterministic view of "bondage of the will" and posited that while God's omnipotence remains a constant, humans are endowed with free will and can use it to seek God's grace.

Simultaneously, in response to the turbulence and unpredictability of the era—marked by political upheaval, religious conflict, and scientific discoveries—some Renaissance philosophers took a more deterministic stance, arguing that the world operates based on fixed natural laws, and that human actions, too, could be explained through these laws.

This debate on free will and determinism set the stage for the Enlightenment era in the 17th and 18th centuries. The Enlightenment or 'the Age of Reason,' was a period marked by a profound faith in reason, logic, and individualism. Philosophers during this period sought to use reason to understand the world and human nature, often challenging traditional religious views in the process.

Enlightenment philosophers continue to grapple with questions of free will, determinism, and moral responsibility,

276

often expressing varying, even conflicting, views. A significant figure from this period was the English philosopher Thomas Hobbes, who, in his work "Leviathan", presented a materialistic and deterministic view of the world. He argued that all phenomena, including human thoughts and actions, were the result of physical processes and could be predicted given enough knowledge of the laws of nature. In Hobbes' deterministic world, free will was an illusion stemming from our ignorance of the causes behind our actions.

However, not all Enlightenment thinkers shared Hobbes' determinism. John Locke, another influential English philosopher, was a strong proponent of the concept of the mind as a 'tabula rasa' or blank slate, emphasizing the role of experience in shaping human behavior and beliefs. His view implies a degree of freedom, as our will can be guided and changed based on our experiences.

Continuing with the discussion, another significant contributor to the Enlightenment's philosophical landscape was the Scottish philosopher David Hume. A critical skeptic, Hume scrutinized concepts such as causality, personal identity, and free will. In his view, "liberty" was consistent with "necessity". In other words, even though our actions might be determined by factors such as our character and external circumstances (necessity), we could still be considered free insofar as our actions align with our will. This view is commonly referred to as soft determinism or compatibilism.

Hume's emphasis on empirical observation and logical consistency had a profound influence on Immanuel Kant, a German philosopher of the Enlightenment who was deeply concerned with questions of knowledge, ethics, and free will. Unlike Hume, Kant did not believe that freedom could be reconciled with determinism. He argued for a dual-aspect view of reality, in which the world could be understood both from a deterministic, natural perspective (the phenomenal world) and from a free, moral perspective (the noumenal world). According to Kant, while our actions may appear determined when viewed from the phenomenal perspective, we could still regard ourselves as free agents in the noumenal sense, thus preserving the possibility of moral responsibility.

While Enlightenment philosophers engaged in these intellectual debates, significant scientific advancements were shaping the general worldview. The groundbreaking work of Isaac Newton, in particular, provided a model of a deterministic universe operating under fixed, discoverable laws of motion. These laws suggested that if one knew the position and velocity of every particle at a given moment, one could predict the future state of the universe with complete accuracy—a thoroughly deterministic outlook. Although Newton himself did not address the implications of his laws for human free will directly, his ideas had profound influences on the philosophical debates of the time.

The thinkers of the Renaissance and Enlightenment periods did not settle the question of free will versus determinism, but their contributions represent critical waypoints in the journey of this debate. Their ideas, influenced by their cultural and historical contexts, expanded the spectrum of views on free will and determinism and continue to shape contemporary philosophical discussions on these topics.

As we move into the 19th and 20th centuries, the debate over free will vs determinism took another dramatic turn. The advent of psychology and sociology as formal disciplines, the profound influence of Charles Darwin's evolutionary theory, and the development of quantum mechanics each posed new questions and challenges to the understanding of free will and determinism.

The notion of free will took a blow with the rise of behaviorism in psychology. Behaviorists like John Watson and B.F. Skinner championed a deterministic view of human action based on observable behavior, not mental states. According to Skinner, the idea of free will was an illusion. In his view, all actions could be traced back to previous conditioning; that is, all behavior was a product of an individual's history of reinforcement and punishment. This perspective has had a significant influence on many areas of psychology, from learning theory to therapies aimed at behavior modification.

The philosophical implications of Charles Darwin's evolutionary theory were profound and far-reaching. The idea that species evolved over time due to natural selection challenged the religious beliefs and worldview of many people. It implied that humans, like all other species, were subject to the deterministic laws of nature, leaving less room for the concept of free will. While Darwin himself did not delve deeply into the philosophical debate of free will, his work undoubtedly added another layer to the discussion.

The 20th century also witnessed a transformative moment in the scientific understanding of the universe: the development of quantum mechanics. In contrast to Newtonian physics' deterministic view, quantum mechanics introduced a level of inherent randomness and uncertainty at the microscopic level. Some interpretations of quantum theory suggest that determinism might not fully apply at the quantum level, leading some to argue that this might leave room for free will. However, it's crucial to note that the relationship between quantum theory and the concept of free will is still heavily debated and not entirely understood.

It's clear that each historical period, with its unique scientific, philosophical, and cultural milieu, has contributed to the evolving discourse on free will and determinism. As we move from the ancient world to the medieval period and through the Renaissance and Enlightenment to modern times, the conversation doesn't become simpler but rather more complex and multifaceted. With this historical context in mind, we are now better equipped to tackle the specific contributions of some pivotal figures in the free will debate.

In the modern era, one name stands out in the debate about free will - Jean-Paul Sartre, a prominent figure in the existentialist movement. He adamantly advocated for the existence of free will, expressing his belief that humans are 'condemned to be free.' His assertion suggested that human beings are not just free but utterly responsible for their actions, feelings, and existence. This freedom is a heavy burden for individuals to carry, and it's often tempting to escape it, a phenomenon Sartre called 'bad faith.'

In contrast to Sartre, the determinism inherent in psychoanalysis and behaviorism gained substantial traction in the 20th century. Sigmund Freud, the founder of psychoanalysis, proposed that individuals' behaviors are largely determined by unconscious forces. Similarly, the behaviorist school of psychology, led by figures such as B.F. Skinner suggested that human behavior could be predicted and controlled through understanding the patterns of stimulus and response.

Simultaneously, the rise of cognitive science in the late 20th century has brought new perspectives. These disciplines, such as cognitive psychology, cognitive neuroscience, and artificial intelligence, have provided us with tools to investigate the processes that underpin decision-making and choice, key components of free will.

Modern technology has also shed light on the relationship between the brain and mind, providing materialistic explanations for mental processes. Brain imaging techniques, for example, have demonstrated a link between brain activity and decisions made by individuals, further complicating the debate around free will and determinism.

From a religious perspective, the 20th century saw considerable debate about free will and determinism within Christian theology. The idea of predestination, which has roots in the teachings of St. Augustine and later Martin Luther and John Calvin, posits that God has already decided who will achieve salvation. This notion stands in contrast to the idea of free will, where individuals have the freedom to choose their actions and are therefore responsible for their salvation or damnation.

As we trace the development of free will from ancient times to modernity, it's apparent how the discourse has evolved. It's a journey marked by philosophical reflection, religious debates, scientific discoveries, and technological advancements. Each era has shaped and refined our understanding of this complex and deeply personal concept, contributing to a rich tapestry of thought that continues to challenge and intrigue us today.

13.3 DESCARTES AND AUGUSTINE'S PROFOUND IMPACT ON PHILOSOPHY

The tale of free will does not exist in isolation from the philosophers who dared to question and explore the human capacity for choice. Among the multitude of contributors, René Descartes stands out as an influential figure whose ideas reverberate throughout the discourse on free will.

René Descartes, a philosopher and mathematician of the 17th century, known as the father of modern philosophy, provided a radically different perspective on the relationship between mind and body that would come to shape the discussion of free will for centuries. Prior to Descartes, philosophers mainly believed in monism - the idea that the mind and body are not distinct. Descartes, however, proposed a groundbreaking theory known as 'mind-body dualism', suggesting that the mind and body are two separate entities, fundamentally different in nature. In his philosophy, the body is a mechanical entity governed by physical laws, while the mind or soul is non-physical and autonomous. This dualistic approach serves as the foundation for his beliefs on free will, which Descartes regarded as the unique faculty of the mind.

Within Descartes' framework, the mind, or the thinking thing ("res cogitans"), is the source of consciousness and rational thought. Free will, Descartes argues, resides in this non-physical mind. This conception of free will as an inherent attribute of the conscious mind contrasts with the mechanistic worldview associated with the body ("res extensa"), where everything is determined by the laws of physics and causality. In this setup, the mind, with its capacity for free will, can affect the body's actions, representing a form of interactionist dualism. In other words, Descartes postulated that despite our bodies being subject to deterministic laws, our minds – and hence our capacity for free will – exist in a realm where such laws do not apply.

This radical perspective of Descartes can be further elucidated by his famous dictum, "Cogito, ergo sum" - "I think, therefore I am." This statement underscored the primary importance of the thinking self, which was, for Descartes, the indubitable proof of existence. The ability to doubt, to think, to reason - these were hallmarks of the free mind, a distinct entity from the physical body. This positing of a non-physical realm of thought and consciousness was revolutionary in its implications for free will. If the mind, the seat of consciousness, exists independently from the deterministic physical world, then it could, theoretically, be free from the shackles of causality, offering a space for free will to operate.

However, Descartes' mind-body dualism has not escaped criticism. Many philosophers and scientists have found his proposition of two fundamentally different substances interacting in the human being difficult to digest. How can a non-physical mind cause physical actions in the body? This is known as the mind-body problem, a significant challenge to Cartesian dualism. Despite Descartes' attempts at explaining this interaction through the human brain's pineal gland, his explanation was not satisfactory for many.

The deterministic science of the post-Descartes era also raises questions about mind-body dualism. How can a non-physical mind exist in a universe where everything seems to be made of physical stuff? Despite these criticisms, it's impossible to deny the impact of Descartes' revolutionary idea on the discourse of free will. His framing of the mind as an independent entity provided a basis for the possibility of free will, even within a deterministic view of the physical world.

Even in the contemporary era, echoes of Cartesian dualism persist. Modern discussions about free will often grapple with the relationship between the deterministic laws of nature and the subjective experience of making choices - a dilemma that harkens back to Descartes' mind-body dichotomy. Advances in neuroscience, cognitive science, and psychology have added new dimensions to this debate. Today, we know that our mental processes are deeply intertwined with the workings of our brains - a fact that may seem to counter Descartes' theory. Yet, the problem of how subjective experience (or consciousness) arises from the brain's physical processes, known as the 'hard problem of consciousness', still puzzles scientists and philosophers alike, much like the mind-body problem that Descartes' dualism introduced.

Regardless of the criticisms and challenges, Descartes' philosophy continues to be a reference point in the discourse of free will. The dichotomy between the mental and the physical, the free and the determined, continues to shape our understanding and discussion of human autonomy.

With the conclusion of this segment on Descartes' contributions to our understanding of free will, we pave the way for the exploration of another influential perspective - that of Saint Augustine and his theological impact on the free will debate.

Saint Augustine, a towering figure in the history of Christian theology and western philosophy. Born in 354 A.D. in Roman Africa, Augustine's early life was marked by spiritual struggle before he converted to Christianity in 386 A.D. His subsequent role as a bishop, his copious writings, and his deep philosophical and theological insights have continued to influence Christian doctrine and western thought for more than a millennium.

In examining the idea of free will, Augustine grappled with complex spiritual, ethical, and metaphysical concepts. His concept of 'will' was not simply about the ability to make choices, but it also encompassed the spiritual dimensions of human desires and intentions. Augustine believed that humans do possess free will. Yet, he also maintained that humanity, after the original sin, had lost its ability to will what is truly good without divine assistance.

That brings us to one of the cornerstones of Augustine's theology - the concept of original sin. Original sin refers to the fallen state of human nature inherited from Adam and Eve's disobedience in Eden. Augustine believed that because of this original sin, our free will was damaged, not destroyed. We retained the ability to choose, but our choices were predisposed towards sin. Our will, while still free in a sense, was in bondage to sin, unable to break free without divine intervention.

Therefore, Augustine's concept of free will cannot be discussed without touching upon his understanding of grace. Divine grace, according to Augustine, was not merely God's favor but an active force that intervened in human lives, healing the will and enabling it to choose the good. It's through God's grace, Augustine argued, that humans can attain true freedom of will - a will not just free to choose, but free to choose the good.

However, Augustine's conception of free will, original sin, and divine grace did not go without criticism. Many questioned the compatibility of divine predestination with human free will. If God, as Augustine suggested, predestined some for salvation and others for damnation, then where did human free will stand? Critics also pointed out that the concept of original sin, as articulated by Augustine, could lead to a kind of moral fatalism, undermining human responsibility.

Yet, despite these criticisms, the impact of Augustine's views on free will, original sin, and grace can hardly be overstated. His ideas have left an indelible imprint on Christian doctrine and western philosophical thought, shaping our understanding of human nature, morality, and divine intervention. While his views have been elaborated, modified, or rejected by later thinkers, they remain a crucial reference point in discussions about free will.

Saint Augustine's theological perspective provides a deep, nuanced understanding of free will that brings to the fore the intertwined nature of human freedom, morality, and divine grace. It emphasizes that our quest to comprehend free will must go beyond the confines of purely secular philosophy and probe the rich insights offered by spiritual and theological traditions.

We find ourselves at an intersection where two influential thinkers, Descartes and Augustine, provide us with contrasting yet compelling insights into the free will debate. Their perspectives, though shaped in different historical and philosophical contexts, hold valuable lessons.

Descartes, an emblem of the Enlightenment period and one of the founders of modern philosophy, ushered in the idea of mind-body dualism. This radical concept, which diverged from the widely accepted Aristotelian metaphysics, placed the mind (or soul) outside the physical realm of determinism, and thus positioned free will as an intrinsic quality of the mind. Descartes saw humans as autonomous agents capable of shaping their destinies through rational deliberation and conscious decision-making. In essence, his philosophy endorses a robust sense of free will, rooted in the supremacy of reason.

On the other hand, Augustine, a theological giant of late antiquity, offered a nuanced perspective on free will framed within a Christian worldview. Unlike Descartes' secular approach, Augustine viewed free will through the lens of theology, focusing on the spiritual dimensions of human desires and intentions. He maintained that while humans do possess free will, our ability to will what is truly good is hampered by the original sin. For Augustine, true freedom of will, that is, the freedom to choose the good, is only attainable through God's grace.

These perspectives present us with two different narratives. Descartes' view implies that free will is inherent, immutable, and independent of external factors, encapsulating the Enlightenment's faith in human reason. Augustine's view, however, portrays free will as conditional and transformative, influenced by our moral and spiritual condition, and ultimately reliant on divine intervention.

Yet, both views reinforce the significance of free will in our understanding of human nature, morality, and responsibility. They propose that free will, whether secular or spiritual, is integral to how we perceive ourselves, interact with the world around us, and navigate the intricate maze of moral dilemmas. However, they differ in their interpretations of determinism and its relationship with free will. While Descartes places the mind outside deterministic laws, Augustine suggests a deterministic worldview where free will operates within divine preordination.

While these views may seem discordant, they collectively broaden our understanding of the multifaceted concept of free will. They encourage us to appreciate the complexity of the free will debate and to engage with it in a multifarious manner, keeping in mind the myriad cultural, philosophical, and theological lenses through which it can be examined. By doing so, we enrich our dialogue around free will and determinism, and more importantly, we continue the centuries-long philosophical journey towards understanding the depths of human freedom.

CHAPTER 14: CONTEMPORARY PHILOSOPHICAL DEBATES

As we step into the modern era, the intellectual landscape of free will debate expands and evolves. A wealth of new perspectives emerge, challenging old notions and stirring fresh dialogues. From reinterpreting the relationship between free will and determinism to redefining the notion of individual freedom, contemporary thinkers have significantly enriched this discourse. This chapter will delve into these contemporary debates, exploring how they shape our current understanding of free will.

Our journey will begin with an examination of the age-old conflict between free will and determinism, viewed through the lenses of compatibilism and incompatibilism. We will then examine the libertarian standpoint that pushes back against determinism. Existentialist views, which assert the primacy of individual freedom, will also find space in our discourse. Finally, we will conclude with an exploration of philosophical counterarguments that question the very concept of free will.

14.1 RECONCILING FREE WILL AND DETERMINISM: COMPATIBILISM VS. INCOMPATIBILISM

In the grand theater of philosophical debates, few discourses are as gripping and contentious as the one surrounding free

288

will and determinism. Since the dawn of philosophical thought, scholars have grappled with the apparent conflict between humanity's belief in its power to make free choices and the deterministic laws of nature that govern the universe. It's in this very crucible of conflicting ideas that two philosophical schools of thought have emerged, proposing their ways of reconciling this contradiction - Compatibilism and Incompatibilism.

Compatibilism, as the term suggests, is a belief in the compatibility between free will and determinism. In contrast, Incompatibilism posits that free will and determinism are fundamentally incompatible. Understanding these perspectives is not just about comprehending abstract philosophical ideas. It has far-reaching implications for how we perceive moral responsibility, ethics, and our sense of agency.

So, let's journey into the heart of these debates and dissect each position, starting with Compatibilism.

Compatibilism: A Union of Opposites

Compatibilism, a term coined by the British philosopher F. H. Bradley in the late 19th century, suggests that free will and determinism, two seemingly opposing forces, can indeed coexist. This philosophical viewpoint is not about watering down the definitions of free will or determinism but is an attempt to redefine the nature of free will in a deterministic universe.

Compatibilists argue that free will doesn't necessarily imply the ability to do otherwise - termed "principle of alternate possibilities." Instead, they posit that free will has more to do with voluntariness and non-coercion. In other words, an action is free if it aligns with one's desires and motivations and is not imposed by external coercion. This notion is referred to as "hierarchical compatibilism," based on the idea of higher-order desires - desires about desires.

To better understand the concept of hierarchical compatibility, consider an analogy. Suppose a smoker is trying to quit smoking. They have a primary desire to smoke, fueled by their nicotine addiction. However, they also have a higher-order desire not to want to smoke, stemming from the aspiration to lead a healthier life. In a situation where the smoker gives in and smokes a cigarette, the action is arguably not "free" according to hierarchical compatibilism. This is because, while it aligns with their primary desire, it goes against their higher-order desire. Conversely, if the smoker resists the urge to smoke, aligning their action with their higher-order desire, the action is seen as "free."

Thus, the compatibilist view does not necessarily challenge the deterministic universe's concept but proposes a refined understanding of what constitutes free will within it.

Incompatibilism: A Direct Conflict

Contrary to the harmonious union proposed by Compatibilism, Incompatibilism argues that free will and determinism are inherently incompatible. Incompatibilists posit that if determinism holds, then our feeling of possessing free will is nothing but an illusion. They believe in the "principle of alternative possibilities' ' that the Compatibilists refute.

Incompatibilism: Types and Perspectives

There are two principal types of Incompatibilists: the libertarians and the hard determinists. Libertarians argue that we do possess free will, implying that determinism must be false. On the other hand, hard determinists argue that determinism holds, implying that we do not possess free will.

This divergence of views within Incompatibilism underscores the complexity of the free will vs. determinism debate.

The Libertarians and Hard Determinists

Libertarians believe in the existence of free will and maintain that determinism is incorrect. This belief stems from our personal experiences, our feelings of freedom and control over our actions, and our ability to reason and make choices. These experiences, they argue, are so integral to our understanding of ourselves that any theory that denies them, such as determinism, must be rejected.

Hard determinists, on the other hand, argue that all events, including human actions, are the result of previous events and the laws of nature. Since determinism holds, they argue, free will does not exist. The feelings of freedom that we experience, according to hard determinists, are simply illusions – we may feel free, but our actions are predetermined.

The Concept of Moral Responsibility

The debate between compatibilists and incompatibilists extends into the realm of moral responsibility. If we don't have free will, can we be held morally responsible for our actions? Compatibilists would argue yes, as they believe that even in a deterministic world, we can still be free as long as our actions align with our desires and are not forced. In contrast, incompatibilists might argue that without genuine freedom, moral responsibility is undermined.

Compatibilism: A Middle Ground

Compatibilism offers a middle ground in this dichotomy, allowing for both determinism and moral responsibility. Compatibilists argue that free will is not necessarily incompatible with determinism, hence the name. They posit that free will involves making choices according to one's desires, beliefs, and character traits. If an action is consistent with these aspects, it is considered free—even if those desires, beliefs, and character traits were themselves determined.

A famous analogy used by compatibilists is a water stream's path. The water will naturally flow along the path of least resistance, determined by the shape of the land. However, we would still say that the water "chooses" its path—albeit determined by the landscape.

Incompatibilism: Freedom and Determinism Can't Coexist

Incompatibilists, however, hold the view that free will and determinism cannot coexist. Two primary subgroups within this view are libertarianism and hard determinism. As mentioned, libertarians believe in the existence of free will and categorically deny determinism, while hard determinists assert the truth of determinism and the illusion of free will.

A poignant analogy to understand incompatibilism could be imagining life as a book where all the pages have already been written, and we're merely reading it page by page, mistaking it as writing our own story.

Proponents and Critics

Famous proponents of compatibilism include philosophers like David Hume and Thomas Hobbes. Hume, for instance, argued that 'liberty' should be understood as the absence of constraints on actions, thereby reconciling it with causal determinism. Hobbes, on the other hand, proposed that free will lies in the absence of external impediments.

The school of incompatibilism also had its own significant thinkers. For instance, Peter van Inwagen, an influential contemporary philosopher, suggests that free will involves a kind of 'mystery' that makes our decisions undetermined.

Critics of compatibilism often argue that it fails to address the root issue – if our actions are ultimately determined by factors outside our control, how can we genuinely claim moral responsibility for our actions?

Incompatibilists, on the other hand, face the criticism of being unable to satisfactorily explain the existence of moral responsibility in the absence of determinism. If our actions are truly random and uncaused, how can we be held morally responsible for them?

A Case Study: A Compatibilist Response to a Dilemma

To better understand the position of compatibilism and how it plays out in real-world situations, let's consider a case study.

Suppose a person is placed in a controlled environment where their options are manipulated in such a way that they always choose to perform a specific action, say, choosing a red box over a blue one. According to a deterministic viewpoint, the person's decision is influenced by a host of preceding factors such as their past experiences, inherent preferences, and the manipulation of the environment.

Incompatibilists argue that this person isn't truly exercising free will, because their decision is essentially preordained due to the controlled circumstances.

Compatibilists, however, might argue that the person is indeed exercising free will. They would assert that although the decision may be influenced by external factors, the individual is not externally coerced into making it. The decision comes from within the individual's own mind, not from an outside force compelling them against their will.

This case illuminates the central argument of compatibilism: determinism doesn't necessarily eliminate free will, provided the individual's actions stem from their own internal desires and intentions, rather than being forced by external factors.

Incompatibilist's Viewpoint: Challenging Compatibilism

While compatibilists contend that free will and determinism can coexist, incompatibilists stand firm on the notion that they are mutually exclusive concepts. From the perspective of an incompatibilist, even though the individual in our case study made a choice according to their internal desires and intentions, they could not have acted otherwise due to the preordained nature of their decision.

The incompatibilist might further argue that the influence of external factors over our choices is so pervasive and deeply ingrained, that it is impossible to say that we are genuinely making a free choice. If our decisions are the product of predetermined factors, then we are merely acting out a script written by the circumstances of our existence.

On the other hand, some incompatibilists argue for the existence of free will and propose that it is determinism that is flawed. This viewpoint, known as libertarianism, posits that we have the power to make truly free choices, unbound by the shackles of causality. This argument, however, raises questions about the nature of randomness and chaos in human decision-making, which will be discussed later in the book.

While both viewpoints present compelling arguments, it is essential to recognize that the debate between compatibilism and incompatibilism is still an ongoing one. Both positions challenge us to think deeply about the nature of our existence, our actions, and our moral responsibility.

In the next section, we will delve into the concept of libertarianism, a philosophy that dares to challenge the reign of determinism.

This tug-of-war between compatibilism and incompatibilism is a dynamic that is central to our understanding of free will. The fact that both theories, each of which seems to present valid arguments, cannot simultaneously be correct demands that we take a closer look at the assumptions and implications of each perspective.

Compatibilists might suggest that incompatibilists' strict interpretation of determinism, which seemingly leaves no room for free will, overlooks the complexity of human decision-making processes. They might argue that, even within a deterministic framework, the myriad influences that come into play when we make a decision—our values, desires, knowledge, and the specific circumstances at the moment of choice—leave ample room for what we can reasonably consider free will.

Incompatibilists, on the other hand, could contend that compatibility neglects the full impact of determinism. In a truly deterministic universe, they might argue, the very values and desires that influence our decisions are themselves the product of prior causes, leading back in an unbroken chain to the beginning of time. Even the seemingly spontaneous choices we make are simply the result of complex causal chains that we can't fully perceive.

To sum up, the debate between compatibilism and incompatibilism is not merely an academic one. It strikes at the heart of our understanding of ourselves and our place in the universe. As we continue our exploration of the philosophical dimensions of free will, it's essential to keep these arguments in mind, bearing in mind that our interpretations of them may be influenced by our own preconceived notions and biases.

14.2 LIBERTARIANISM: CHALLENGING THE REIGN OF DETERMINISM

Continuing from where we left off, it's crucial to mention the notable Libertarian philosophers such as Robert Kane, who have contributed significantly to this debate. Kane argues that free will is indeed possible in an uncertain world and that humans have the capacity to shape their future despite the existence of indeterminism. He also introduced the idea of "self-forming actions," which are particular moments in life when individuals are torn between competing desires, and the choice they make significantly shapes their character and future. These decisions, Kane argues, embody the core concept of Libertarian free will.

Another influential figure in the Libertarian school of thought is Roderick Chisholm, who argued for a "non-causal" theory of freedom. In Chisholm's view, free acts are caused by the individual, not by any event or state of affairs. Such a perspective offers an interesting redefinition of causality and emphasizes the active role of the individual in the course of their life.

The question of responsibility also arises within Libertarianism. The perspective fundamentally argues for moral responsibility. If we, as individuals, genuinely shape our actions independent of any deterministic factors, then we are entirely accountable for them. This thought can have profound implications for our justice systems, ethical judgments, and individual behavior.

But despite the compelling propositions of Libertarianism, the philosophy has not gone without criticism. Many philosophers and scientists have questioned its feasibility, given our current understanding of the physical world. They argue that Libertarianism may rely too heavily on a somewhat mystical, uncaused 'agent-causation' which doesn't seem to fit within our current understanding of causality in the physical world. Additionally, critics point out that uncaused actions could be perceived as random, and randomness doesn't seem to offer any more control or 'free will' than determinism.

Yet, it is essential to remember that Libertarianism fundamentally arises from a deep-seated intuition that people have about their ability to make meaningful, free choices. This intuition cannot be easily dismissed and could indeed be hinting at an aspect of our reality that we do not yet fully understand. Quantum physics, for instance, has introduced the notion that indeterminism may be a fundamental aspect of the physical world, and some have suggested that this could open up a space for free will.

The rise of Libertarianism, then, could be seen as a sort of intellectual rebellion against the deterministic implications of an increasingly mechanistic worldview. By asserting the existence of free will and highlighting the limitations of Determinism, Libertarians challenge the pre-eminence of physical determinism in philosophical discourse.

In short, Libertarianism is not merely an academic exercise; it is a reflection of a deeply rooted human experience – the experience of freedom. Whether this feeling is illusory or reflective of a deeper metaphysical truth is a question that continues to inspire philosophical debates and fuel ongoing research in fields as diverse as neuroscience, quantum physics, and artificial intelligence.

Libertarianism's challenge to the reign of determinism remains one of the most exciting and essential debates within the philosophy of free will. It forces us to grapple with fundamental questions about human nature, responsibility, ethics, and the very nature of the universe itself.

This philosophical tradition, therefore, doesn't only challenge determinism, but also continually provokes us to refine our understanding of free will and its implications for our lives and society. And in doing so, it plays a crucial role in shaping our worldviews and personal philosophies.

The influence of Libertarianism has also seeped into various disciplines, such as law, politics, and psychology. For instance, in the legal realm, Libertarian notions of free will underpin systems of responsibility and punishment. If an individual couldn't have done otherwise, can they truly be held accountable for their actions? This perspective significantly influences our concepts of justice, retribution, and rehabilitation.

Similarly, in the political sphere, Libertarian ideals often drive discussions about individual rights and freedoms. From debates on civil liberties to arguments on economic policy, the belief in free will plays a crucial role in shaping our societies and political systems.

Moreover, Libertarianism has also left a profound impact on psychological and cognitive sciences. Various therapeutic approaches, such as Cognitive Behavioral Therapy (CBT) and Positive Psychology, operate under the assumption that individuals possess the free will to change their thoughts, emotions, and behaviors. This approach can have potent effects, and the belief in one's capacity for change can often be a self-fulfilling prophecy.

However, it's important to note that despite these vast implications, Libertarianism doesn't provide a conclusive resolution to the problem of free will. There remain substantial criticisms and counter arguments, which point towards the theory's potential shortcomings. And as our scientific understanding progresses, these debates continue to evolve, prompting constant re-evaluation and reinterpretation of this complex issue.

In the grand scheme of things, Libertarianism's challenge to the reign of determinism can be seen as an essential part of a broader dialectic on the nature of free will. It's a dynamic conversation that has been ongoing for centuries, evolving with each new philosophical, scientific, and technological development.

As we delve further into the world of free will and determinism, it's crucial to bear in mind the importance of these philosophical debates. They not only influence our intellectual landscape but also have significant implications for how we perceive ourselves, others, and the world around us.

In the next section, we will delve into another philosophical movement that has deeply influenced the discourse on free will – Existentialism. As we transition from the exploration of Libertarianism, we carry with us an appreciation of the depths and complexities involved in this philosophical journey, recognizing the nuances and layers within these theories.

14.3 EXISTENTIALISM: THE CLAIM OF INDIVIDUAL FREEDOM

Existentialism, a philosophical movement that flourished primarily during the mid-20th century, proffers a distinct perspective on the question of free will. Unlike other philosophical frameworks, Existentialism does not attempt to reconcile free will and determinism or to navigate their paradoxes. Instead, it emphasizes the experiential reality of individual freedom and the inherent subjectivity of human existence. Existentialism's motto might be said to be that existence precedes essence, underlining that individuals are free to define their own nature or essence through their actions and choices.

Indeed, existentialism amplifies the weight of free will by eliminating any preconceived plan or divine orchestration that might alleviate the burden of choice. Unlike deterministic theories that posit our choices as a product of environmental or genetic factors, or theistic beliefs that imbue our lives with divine meaning and direction, existentialism places the responsibility of our actions squarely on our shoulders. This existential freedom, though empowering, also invokes feelings of angst, dread, and despair, known as existential anxiety.

In existentialist thought, existential anxiety arises from the realization that we are free to choose, but these choices can be irrevocable and can significantly impact the course of our lives. This understanding imbues our existence with a profound sense of seriousness. Our actions are not just ephemeral or insignificant; they carry a deep personal and ethical weight. According to Sartre, the choices we make are a declaration of what we believe should be the ideal human nature - a concept known as 'bad faith.'

In the context of 'bad faith,' individuals deceive themselves into thinking they are not free to avoid the dread that freedom entails. By blaming their actions on external factors or social roles, individuals evade the responsibility and the moral weight of their choices. However, existentialists insist that such self-deception is a violation of our authentic self. It's a disservice to our inherent freedom and potential to create meaning in our lives.

Existentialism's approach to free will also has significant implications for ethics and morality. By asserting the primacy of individual freedom, existentialism posits that we create our moral codes based on our choices rather than any universal ethical law. This perspective resonates with moral relativism, where morality is not absolute but a construct of individual or societal choices.

Yet, the existentialist emphasis on freedom should not be misconstrued as a promotion of hedonism or selfishness. While existentialists celebrate individual freedom, they also acknowledge the interconnection between individual freedom and collective responsibility. Your freedom, according to Simone de Beauvoir, is inextricably linked to the freedom of others. Thus, the existentialist vision of a moral life is one where individuals exercise their freedom in a way that respects and enables the freedom of others.

Interestingly, existentialists argue that acknowledging our freedom and the subsequent responsibility towards others is a pathway to leading an authentic life. Authenticity, in existentialist terms, involves acknowledging the truth of our condition, namely our freedom and its accompanying anxiety, and still having the courage to act and make decisions. Such authenticity is not a given state, but a continuous process. An authentic individual fully embraces their freedom, their potential to shape their life's course, and accepts the inevitable anxiety associated with such freedom.

We should not see the existentialist portrayal of freedom and authenticity as a path of bleak despair or nihilism. On the contrary, it presents an empowering perspective of human existence. In a deterministic universe, where all our actions could be predicted and are caused by preceding events, our choices lose their value, and our lives may seem insignificant. However, the existentialist perspective posits that our choices matter, and through them, we can create our unique, individual essence.

Let's delve a little deeper into some of the key existentialist figures to understand how they developed and articulated these views on freedom. Jean-Paul Sartre, arguably the most famous existentialist, made the concept of freedom central to his philosophy. In his seminal work, "Being and Nothingness," he asserts that humans are "radically free." For Sartre, this freedom is both our blessing and our curse – it allows us to define our essence, but it also induces a profound sense of angst.

For Sartre, as for all existentialists, freedom is not merely a theoretical concept. It has profound implications for how we live our lives and how we understand ourselves. By asserting our freedom, we assert our subjectivity against a world that often tries to reduce us to objects. In his famous lecture, "Existentialism is a Humanism," Sartre argued that we are "condemned to be free." We cannot escape our freedom, even when it terrifies us. By accepting this freedom and the inherent responsibility it entails, we can lead an authentic life and defy the objectifying tendencies of modern society.

Simone de Beauvoir, a prominent feminist and existentialist philosopher, offers a nuanced perspective on existential freedom. In "The Ethics of Ambiguity," de Beauvoir acknowledges that while we are fundamentally free, our freedom is limited by our facticity - the circumstances of our life that we did not choose. These can include our birthplace, the era we're born into, our physical attributes, etc. Despite these limitations, de Beauvoir argues that we still maintain our existential freedom, the ability to transcend our facticity by making choices that shape our future.

The acknowledgment of freedom's limitations doesn't diminish existentialist thought but adds more depth to it. Recognizing these restrictions allows us to understand our situatedness within the world better and negotiate our freedom in a more informed manner. Yet, existential freedom still asserts the possibility of transcending our facticity through our choices and actions. The recognition of these constraints also serves to underscore the importance of fighting for social justice and equality. De Beauvoir, in particular, used her existentialist framework to argue for women's rights and gender equality, further reinforcing the social dimensions of existential freedom.

The existentialist notion of freedom diverges significantly from both the libertarian and deterministic viewpoints. Unlike libertarians, existentialists don't assume an inherent self that's endowed with free will. They contend that the self is an ongoing project shaped by one's chosen actions. Unlike determinists, they don't see individuals as passive products of antecedent conditions. They emphasize our ability to transcend these conditions through our choices.

However, existentialism is not without its critics. Some have argued that existentialism places too much emphasis on individual freedom and neglects the influence of social, cultural, and biological factors on our behavior. Others have criticized it for its seeming indifference to the empirical realities of the human condition, including the findings of psychology and neuroscience. These criticisms reflect the ongoing tension in the free will debate between acknowledging human freedom and recognizing the constraints on that freedom.

Despite these criticisms, existentialism continues to hold a significant place in contemporary philosophy and psychology. Its emphasis on freedom, authenticity, and personal responsibility resonates with many individuals seeking to make sense of their lives in the face of uncertainty and change. Moreover, it offers a powerful counter-narrative to deterministic perspectives that can sometimes lead to a sense of disempowerment and resignation.

The existentialist perspective provides a compelling viewpoint on the concept of freedom. It doesn't shy away from the anxieties and responsibilities that come with freedom but instead encourages us to embrace these as integral aspects of the human condition. By doing so, it allows us to assert our individuality, shape our essence, and lead lives of authenticity and meaning. It paints a picture not of individuals bound by the chains of determinism, but of individuals capable of transcending their facticity to shape their future.

14.4 COUNTERARGUMENTS: PHILOSOPHICAL RETORTS AGAINST FREE WILL

As we progress further into the intricacies of the philosophical discourse on free will, it's crucial to address counterarguments that challenge the concept's very existence. These philosophical retorts, some of which may resonate with scientific determinism, question the soundness of the doctrines we've so far explored, including libertarianism and existentialism.

To contextualize, it's worth noting that the issue of free will doesn't exist in a philosophical vacuum. The topic straddles various domains of philosophy, including metaphysics (the study of reality's fundamental nature), epistemology (the study of knowledge and belief), and ethics (the study of moral values and principles). Therefore, the counterarguments we'll discuss inherit their richness and complexity from these intersections.

One prominent counter argument comes from a branch of metaphysics known as "hard determinism". Championed by philosophers like Baron d'Holbach, hard determinism contends that every event, including human actions and decisions, is the inevitable result of preceding events and laws of nature. If hard determinism holds, then free will becomes illusory—a mere sentiment of control while we're inexorably bound by causality's chain.

Proponents of hard determinism argue that the subjective feeling of being "free" to make decisions doesn't necessarily translate into genuine free will. This sensation, they claim, might be a mere psychological construct, which makes sense given our limited knowledge of all factors influencing our decisions. To hard determinists, the belief in free will is a comforting illusion obscuring the deterministic nature of the universe.

Another counter argument comes from epistemology, with skeptics questioning whether we can genuinely know we have free will. This line of inquiry, known as "epistemic skepticism", argues that because our knowledge is inherently limited—by our finite lifespan, imperfect memory, and potential for error— we can't be sure our choices aren't predetermined or influenced by unknown factors.

Epistemic skeptics don't necessarily refute the existence of free will but highlight the practical difficulties in claiming absolute knowledge about it. This stance introduces a significant element of uncertainty into the free will debate, challenging both the libertarian and existentialist assumptions of absolute individual freedom.

From the ethical domain, we encounter the counterargument of "moral luck". This concept, explored by philosophers like Thomas Nagel, suggests that many outcomes over which we claim moral responsibility are largely influenced by factors outside our control—our upbringing, cultural background, genetic makeup, or even the era we're born into.

Moral luck undermines the claim of individual moral responsibility, a cornerstone of free will, by highlighting the role of uncontrollable factors in our actions. It questions whether we can ever truly be deserving of praise or blame when our actions, and their consequences, are so deeply entwined with luck.

Critics of moral luck, however, argue that its acceptance could lead to moral nihilism (the denial of the existence of inherent moral values), which in itself opens a new Pandora's box of philosophical and ethical issues. Balancing these concerns remains an active area of philosophical investigation.

As we dive deeper into the realm of counterarguments, we encounter another formidable philosophical standpoint — the stance of illusionism, which suggests that our perception of free will is a grand illusion orchestrated by our cognitive architecture.

The central claim of illusionists is that we are programmed to feel a sense of agency, decision-making, and control over our actions, while in reality, these might be outcomes of deterministic processes. Neuroscientific studies, some of which we touched on earlier in this book, lend some credibility to this viewpoint, as they demonstrate the neural origins of our decisions often precede our conscious awareness of making them. This unsettling evidence challenges the traditional intuitive understanding of free will and proposes that free will might be, fundamentally, an epiphenomenon of our complex brain machinery.

However, illusionism is not without its critics. Critics argue that illusionism falls prey to an overly reductionist view of human agency. They claim that equating complex human decision-making processes to mere physical reactions undermines the nuances and complexities of human consciousness and experience. A deterministic interpretation of these neuroscientific findings, they argue, is not the only plausible interpretation.

Another popular counter argument stems from the philosophical position known as eliminativism. Eliminativists argue that the concept of free will should be entirely discarded as it doesn't correspond to any actual, real-world phenomenon. They contend that free will is a relic of pre-scientific thinking, much like the concept of the "ether" in physics.

According to eliminativists, in a world governed by laws of physics, there is no room for something as metaphysically extravagant as free will. This viewpoint often associates with physicalism – the idea that everything that exists is no more extensive than its physical properties. From a physicalist perspective, any phenomena, including free will, that can't be explained within the physicalist framework, might as well be discarded.

On the other hand, opponents of eliminativism warn of the potential ethical and societal ramifications of discarding the concept of free will entirely. They fear that doing so might lead to moral nihilism, anarchy, or even tyranny, as it could strip people of their sense of personal responsibility, motivation to improve themselves, and respect for others' rights.

One of the most intriguing counter arguments against free will comes from the realm of quantum mechanics. Quantum indeterminacy, the idea that at a fundamental level, the universe is not deterministic, has been proposed as a potential escape from hard determinism. Could quantum phenomena introduce an element of randomness that allows for free will?

But randomness is not freedom, critics contend. Even if quantum phenomena could introduce a degree of randomness into our actions, this randomness doesn't equate to control or agency. We would be at the mercy of quantum randomness, which does not make us freer or our actions more voluntary. Instead, it substitutes one form of determinism with another, namely, randomness.

Moreover, detractors of quantum free will argue that quantum mechanics is likely irrelevant to the functioning of the brain. As a warm, wet, and noisy environment, the brain is thought to be a poor host for the delicate quantum states needed for quantum computation. Therefore, it's more plausible that classical physics, rather than quantum physics, governs our brain's operations.

Another prevalent counterargument against free will involves challenging the coherence of the very concept of free will. Some philosophers, known as "free will skeptics," argue that free will, as commonly understood, is an incoherent concept.

Free will is traditionally defined as the ability to act differently in a given situation. In other words, if we rewound the universe's tape and replayed it, we could make a different choice than the one we made initially. But skeptics argue that this concept is incoherent. They claim it either requires an inexplicable form of causation (causation that is neither deterministic nor random) or is equivalent to randomness, which does not align with our common understanding of free will.

The skeptics' argument highlights the apparent paradox of free will: it must somehow sit outside the domains of both determinism and randomness. Yet, the more we scrutinize this idea, the more elusive it becomes. How can an action be neither predetermined nor random? This question drives skeptics to challenge the conventional concept of free will, suggesting it may be ill-defined or misconstrued.

Another powerful counter argument comes from philosophers who contend that free will is incompatible with the causal closure of the physical world. The principle of causal closure posits that every physical event has a physical cause. If this principle holds, then it's hard to see how non-physical entities (like souls or minds conceived dualistically) could causally influence our actions. This view seems to cut against the notion of free will, as traditionally understood.

Despite these counterarguments, many philosophers have not abandoned the concept of free will. Instead, they have endeavored to refine and reinterpret it in ways that sidestep these criticisms. These modified views of free will, such as compatibilism, semi-compatibilism, and various forms of libertarianism, attempt to preserve our intuitions about free will while accommodating the discoveries of science and the insights of rigorous philosophical analysis.

Intriguingly, the ongoing debates on free will bear an uncanny resemblance to the ancient philosophical paradoxes. Just as Zeno's paradoxes of motion led to fruitful discoveries in mathematics and the philosophy of space and time, so too might the paradoxes of free will pave the way to new insights in the domains of neuroscience, ethics, law, and human self-understanding. The conflict isn't a sign of intellectual stagnation but rather a testament to the richness and complexity of the subject.

Beyond the realm of philosophy, it's important to acknowledge that the concept of free will has significant implications in other areas such as law, ethics, and politics. Many of our societal systems and norms rest on the idea that individuals can freely choose their actions and should be held accountable for them. As such, the critiques and counter arguments around free will are not just intellectual games; they carry substantial practical import.

Having concluded our exploration of contemporary philosophical debates on free will, we now turn our attention to the practical, ethical implications of a deterministic worldview to illustrate how these complex philosophical discourses translate into real-world dilemmas and guide our decisions, beliefs, and societal structures.

CHAPTER 15: ETHICS OF A WORLD SANS FREEWILL

The debate around free will and determinism doesn't stop at abstract philosophical discourses. It plunges us into the heart of our ethical, legal, and social frameworks, raising critical questions about the way we think about morality and justice. The impact of determinism on our moral and ethical constructs form the basis of this chapter.

It acts as a bridge between the philosophical and practical, shedding light on the implications of determinism on our ethical beliefs, societal rules, and systems of law and justice. It builds upon the philosophical debates discussed earlier by examining how these intellectual arguments shape our ethical conceptions and societal norms.

Chapter 15 is geared towards providing readers with a multi-dimensional perspective on the interplay between determinism and ethics, and thus enhancing our collective understanding of the profound and far-reaching consequences of this philosophical debate.

15.1 Consequentialist and Deontological Views: The Impact of Determinism

In this section, we aim to examine how determinism could affect two prominent ethical theories: consequentialism and deontology. These theories, each with their distinctive attributes, offer us a foundation to understand morality and ethics. The question we seek to answer is: how might these theories be impacted if the world is deterministic as opposed to free-willed?

Consequentialism refers to the ethical theory where the morality of an action is judged based on its consequences. This philosophy proposes that an action is right if it results in a positive outcome, and wrong if it leads to a negative one. It places value on the end result rather than the intention behind the action. In consequentialist thinking, the ends justify the means, and moral rightness is defined by the optimality of consequences. Utilitarianism, one of the most well-known consequentialist theories, advocates for the greatest good for the greatest number of people. However, consequentialism does not specifically provide guidance on how to determine what outcomes are 'good' or 'bad,' leaving room for subjective interpretation.

Deontology, on the other hand, posits that the morality of an action is determined by its adherence to rules or duties, regardless of its outcome. This philosophy argues that certain actions are inherently right or wrong, independent of their consequences. Under deontological ethics, morality is tied to duty and obligation – actions are moral if they respect the rights of individuals and adhere to socially defined rules. The philosopher Immanuel Kant is a notable proponent of deontological ethics, asserting that actions must respect the autonomy and rationality of human beings.

If we were to view these theories through a deterministic lens, what changes could we anticipate?

Under a deterministic framework, consequentialism could be challenged in significant ways. If every action and its outcome are determined by pre-existing conditions, the very notion of consequences would require a consequentialist perspective that might assume an even greater prominence in a deterministic world. This is because consequentialism doesn't concern itself with an individual's freedom to choose their actions. Instead, it focuses on the outcomes of actions. If every event in the universe, including human actions, is a result of causal chains stretching back to the dawn of time, then evaluating the ethical nature of these actions based on their outcomes seems more feasible.

But this raises another conundrum. How can a deterministic world have variable outcomes? If the universe is deterministic, then every action and its corresponding result are fixed, with no room for alternates. In such a scenario, how can one decide the moral value of an action when the result was already preordained? This is an issue that consequentialist theory might struggle with in a deterministic context.

Moreover, the concept of 'optimality' becomes murky in a deterministic universe. Consequentialists must evaluate the ethical nature of an action based on the 'goodness' of its result. But in a deterministic world, there are no alternatives to compare – every event unfolds as it was always going to. The idea of optimality becomes redundant since there are no other potential outcomes to consider.

Let's now turn our focus to deontology. Deontological ethics are often framed in opposition to consequentialism. Rather than looking at the outcomes of an action, deontology evaluates the inherent morality of the action itself. Kant, one of the foremost proponents of deontological ethics, proposed the concept of duty or moral obligation. According to Kant, moral actions are ones done out of respect for moral law, not because of the expected results. The emphasis is on the individual's intention, their choice to do what they perceive as right.

A deterministic universe might appear to create an existential crisis for deontology. If all actions and choices are pre-determined, how can we talk about moral duty or obligation? After all, duty implies the freedom to choose one's actions. If every action, choice, and decision is predetermined, then the individual cannot be said to have 'chosen' to do their duty. They are simply following a causal chain that was set in motion long before they were born.

However, one might argue that deontology still has a place in a deterministic universe. Kant's deontology is grounded not in the freedom to choose but in the nature of the moral law itself. Even if our choices are pre-determined, we can still evaluate whether those choices align with the moral law. If the moral law is considered universally valid and binding, then it remains so regardless of whether our actions are freely chosen or not.

Yet, this perspective still leaves us with the paradox of moral responsibility. If our actions are predetermined, can we be held morally accountable for them? This is a question that neither consequentialism or deontology can satisfactorily answer in a deterministic context.

The question of moral responsibility is indeed a thorny one, made even more so when viewed through the lens of determinism. The principle of "ought implies can" is a cornerstone of much ethical and moral philosophy. It posits that one can only be obligated to do what one is capable of doing. Applied to ethics, it implies that moral responsibility requires the ability to choose between right and wrong. In a deterministic universe, where all events are the inevitable result of preceding ones, this ability to choose seems to be fundamentally compromised.

However, this does not necessarily mean that moral accountability disappears entirely. What it does demand is a redefinition or reimagining of what accountability entails. Rather than viewing moral responsibility as tied to free will, we might instead see it as linked to the nature of human beings as rational, conscious entities. Even if our actions are determined, we remain capable of understanding and following moral laws or principles. Moreover, we can experience remorse or guilt when we violate those principles, and these emotions can, in turn, influence our future behavior. In this sense, moral responsibility could be reconceptualized as a kind of psychological or emotional response to our actions and their alignment (or lack thereof) with our understanding of morality.

Further, we could reconsider the role of punishment within this deterministic framework. If we accept that individuals cannot choose otherwise, it makes little sense to punish them as a form of retribution. However, punishment could be reconceptualized as a means of deterrence or rehabilitation, rather than retribution. From a consequentialist perspective, the 'good' of punishment is in its ability to deter future harmful actions or rehabilitate the offender.

In the end, consequentialist and deontological ethics both encounter significant challenges when confronted with determinism. Yet, these challenges may also provide us with an opportunity to reconsider and perhaps even enhance our understanding of morality. For consequentialism, it allows for a focus on broader societal outcomes rather than individual actions. For deontology, it forces us to grapple with the inherent value of the moral law, divorced from individual choice.

Taking a more abstract approach, it's worthwhile to note that determinism's impact on ethics is not inherently negative or destructive. As we have seen, it forces us to reconsider our fundamental assumptions about morality and human agency. In doing so, it allows us to explore new perspectives and possibilities.

To conclude, both consequentialism and deontology have room to adjust their theories in light of determinism. Though determinism initially seems to upend traditional notions of morality, upon closer inspection, it doesn't completely undo the moral fabric. Instead, it challenges us to reevaluate, redefine, and in some instances, reaffirm our ethical views. The deterministic viewpoint is like a litmus test for our ethical theories: it forces them to prove their worth even when the seemingly essential component of free will is absent.

Determinism's challenges do not demolish the significance of ethical frameworks such as consequentialism and deontology but instead emphasize the role of reason, understanding, and empathy in moral judgements. Free will or not, we remain thinking, feeling beings who live together in societies, and our interactions will always require some form of moral framework to function smoothly. In a deterministic universe, consequentialism and deontology, among other ethical theories, remain not only relevant but crucial to maintaining moral order.

In the next section, we will explore this idea further, focusing specifically on the notions of blame, punishment, and accountability in a deterministic universe. We will examine how these concepts might be reimagined in a way that retains their essential functions while fitting within a deterministic framework.

15.2 ACCOUNTABILITY: REIMAGINING BLAME AND PUNISHMENT

Accountability, blame, and punishment have long been intertwined with our conceptions of free will. As per traditional views, if a person has the freedom to make choices, then they should be held accountable for their actions, deserving blame and punishment when they err. However, in a deterministic world where every event, including human actions, is the consequence of preceding events, the concepts of blame and punishment necessitate reimagining.

First, let's discuss the conventional understanding of accountability. To hold someone accountable for their actions, we usually require that the person acted voluntarily and was aware of the potential consequences. When we blame someone, we are attributing the cause of an undesirable outcome to their choices or actions. Punishment, in turn, is the infliction of some type of pain or loss in response to an action that is perceived to be wrong or unjust. Collectively, these mechanisms play significant roles in society, serving to maintain order, provide justice, and discourage harmful behavior.

However, determinism presents a challenging perspective. If our actions are predetermined, can we justly hold people accountable for their actions? Can we blame them? Is punishment justified? Or do these concepts lose their significance entirely in a deterministic world?

To understand the implications of determinism on accountability, we need to take a detour through the landscape of moral and legal responsibility. Traditionally, the "ought implies can" principle has been at the center of our notions of accountability. According to this principle, a person should only be held accountable for what they could have controlled or affected. In deterministic terms, the principle might be translated as, "if all actions are the product of preceding events, then we ought not to hold individuals accountable for actions they couldn't control."

Nonetheless, it's important to bear in mind that determinism doesn't mean that our actions are independent of our decisions, desires, and intentions. Instead, these psychological states themselves are determined by prior factors. The crucial point here is that determinism doesn't strip us of the capacities that ground our basic deserts – the capacity to reason, the ability to respond to reasons, and the capability to control our actions based on our reasons. For these reasons, it's plausible to hold people accountable for their actions in a deterministic world, albeit with an adjusted perspective.

A deterministic world does not excuse or eradicate accountability; rather, it reframes it. On a personal level, blame or commendation becomes a deterministic outcome of an individual's actions and personal history. In a social context, punishment or reward becomes a mechanism for deterrence, rehabilitation, or public protection rather than retribution.

The reframing of blame and punishment under determinism aligns closely with consequentialist ethical theories, which assess the rightness or wrongness of an action based on its outcomes. In this light, punishment is justified if it results in greater overall utility – whether through deterring others from wrongdoing, rehabilitating the wrongdoer, or protecting society from harmful individuals. In stark contrast, retributive justice, which argues that punishment is justified as a deserved response to wrongdoing, is fundamentally at odds with determinism, as it requires a level of free will that determinism disputes.

Nevertheless, it's important to recognize the potential abuses of a purely consequentialist approach to punishment. Without the balancing act of desert – the idea that individuals should get what they deserve – there is a risk of justifying punishment in cases where it might achieve greater overall utility but where the individual has not committed any wrongdoing. This is the classic critique against utilitarianism – the most famous form of consequentialism – that it might, in theory, permit the scapegoating of an innocent person if it could prevent a riot, for example. As such, a blend of consequentialist and deontological considerations seems necessary, with an emphasis on respecting individual rights and ensuring proportionality in punishment.

The shift in perspective on accountability also has profound implications for criminal justice reform. The deterministic viewpoint challenges the traditional notion of retributive justice that underpins many legal systems. The prevailing view, characterized by "an eye for an eye" mentality, becomes questionable under determinism, as the element of desert – the notion that a person deserves to be punished for their wrongdoing – comes under scrutiny. After all, if an individual's actions are the result of a series of deterministic events, can we truly say they deserve punishment?

Here, the focus shifts towards restorative justice, an approach that prioritizes repairing the harm caused by criminal behavior. It views crime as more than breaking the law – it also causes harm to people, relationships, and the community. So a just response needs to address those harms as well as the wrongdoing. If the actions of a criminal are not freely chosen in the traditional sense, it becomes essential to focus on addressing the underlying issues that led to the crime in the first place.

Restorative justice aligns more closely with a deterministic worldview. It prioritizes healing, learning, and growth over mere punishment. It promotes dialogue, mutual understanding, and problem-solving. This approach seeks to reintegrate offenders back into society and to rebuild broken relationships and communities.

However, we must be cautious. A deterministic perspective should not equate to absolving individuals of their actions or dismissing the emotional responses of those affected. Feelings of anger, betrayal, and the desire for justice are natural human responses to harm and injustice. These feelings must be acknowledged and addressed, even within a deterministic framework.

This reimagined view of blame and punishment could revolutionize the field of criminal justice and how society addresses wrongdoing. Instead of a system predicated on punishment and blame, we may see a shift towards rehabilitation and restoration. In this model, the goals are to help the offender understand the impact of their actions, address the harms they've caused, and provide them with the resources they need to avoid future offenses.

Moreover, it would promote societal change in attitudes toward wrongdoers. Instead of viewing them as deserving of punishment, we may come to view them as individuals who need help. This could lead to broader societal changes, reducing stigmatization and discrimination against individuals who have made wrong choices in their past.

In the end, it's important to note that while determinism has profound implications for our understanding of accountability, blame, and punishment, it doesn't provide all the answers. Many questions and dilemmas remain. For instance, how do we balance the need for societal protection against the determinist notion that individuals are not wholly at fault for their actions? How do we ensure justice for victims while acknowledging the complex web of factors that lead to criminal behavior?

Addressing these questions will be a difficult but necessary part of our society's philosophical evolution as we continue to grapple with the implications of determinism. This shift in perspective will require ongoing conversations, research, and philosophical inquiry. And while the path forward may be challenging, it also holds the promise of leading us towards a more compassionate, understanding, and fair society.

15.3 THE WEIGHT OF RESPONSIBILITY: HOW DETERMINISM SHIFTS THE BALANCE

When we think of the bedrock of modern societies, a few key concepts come to mind: democracy, equality, freedom, and justice, among others. However, one fundamental principle underlies all of these: the notion of the social contract. Broadly speaking, the social contract is an implicit agreement among individuals of a society to cooperate for social benefits. Each person surrenders individual freedoms, abiding by certain rules and laws, in exchange for protection from the state and access to a system that promises fair opportunity and justice.

Responsibility is deeply interwoven into the social contract. As members of a society, we are not just beneficiaries but active contributors as well. We take on responsibilities to uphold the values and norms of our society, and in doing so, we enable the system to function smoothly.

However, when we cast these responsibilities under the deterministic lens, things start to look different. If we have no free will, if our actions are predetermined, where does that leave our responsibilities? How does determinism impact our societal contract?

Determinism does not mean absolution from responsibilities. Instead, it offers a nuanced perspective to understand them better. In a deterministic worldview, even if our actions are a consequence of a long chain of events and conditions outside our control, it does not invalidate the concept of responsibility.

Just because our actions can be traced back to previous events does not mean we are not acting. We are the instruments of these actions, and in that sense, we bear a type of responsibility. This is not to say that deterministic responsibility and the commonly understood notion of responsibility are the same. They differ in essence but serve similar functions within the framework of a societal contract.

In a deterministic society, the focus is not on blaming the individual but on understanding the sequence of events leading to the particular action. The aim shifts from retribution to mitigation, prevention, and if possible, rectification. The goal becomes creating conditions that reduce the likelihood of the repetition of undesired actions.

To understand the concept of responsibility in a deterministic worldview, consider the analogy of a river. In this metaphor, a person's life is like a river that flows from its source (birth) to its mouth (death). The river's course is determined by a variety of factors: the geography of the land it traverses, the climate of the region, the interplay of ecological factors, and so on. Similarly, the trajectory of a person's life is shaped by an intricate network of factors: genetics, upbringing, socio-economic conditions, education, and countless other elements.

In this context, imagine responsibility as the riverbank. It does not alter the course of the river but guides it, prevents it from flooding, and gives it a definite shape. In a deterministic framework, responsibility acts in a similar way. It does not grant individuals control over the factors that shape their actions but provides a social and moral framework to guide them.

A person is still held accountable for their actions. The deterministic perspective, however, shifts the focus from punitive measures to rehabilitation and systemic change. The objective becomes less about punishment for the sake of retribution and more about understanding the factors that led to the action and addressing them to prevent future occurrences.

This perspective calls for a profound transformation in societal attitudes and legal systems. It challenges us to rethink our traditional notions of blame, punishment, and justice. It urges us to acknowledge the complex interplay of factors that shape an individual's actions and to factor them into our assessment of responsibility.

An immediate repercussion of this viewpoint, especially pertinent, is the reorientation of our justice systems. It throws a gauntlet down to punitive, retributive justice models that focus primarily on punishment, in favor of a more rehabilitative and restorative approach. The latter attempts to understand the underlying factors and conditions that led to the crime, working towards reformation and reintegration of the offender into society.

Our societies have already begun this journey of transformation, albeit slowly. The growing awareness and understanding of the impact of mental health, socio-economic conditions, and other factors on criminal behavior have started to reshape our approach to justice. However, fully integrating a deterministic view would necessitate a radical transformation, a shift that is bound to encounter significant resistance, rooted in our instinctual, emotional responses and age-old practices.

Another vital aspect of responsibility, under the lens of determinism, is its redistribution from being solely an individual's burden to a collective endeavor. If our actions are the result of an intricate web of influencing factors, it implies that responsibility is also shared among these elements. Parents, educators, communities, and societies at large play a role in shaping an individual and, consequently, share in the responsibility of their actions.

This doesn't dilute personal accountability but rather situates it within a broader, more holistic context. It nudges societies towards empathy, understanding, and collective action to address systemic and structural issues. The deterministic perspective reinforces that our fates are interconnected. It pushes for solidarity, mutual aid, and social justice.

The deterministic viewpoint also challenges the 'just-world' fallacy, which posits that we live in a world where everyone gets what they deserve. This fallacy supports the idea that the successful merit their success purely through their own virtues, and the failures are a result of their own faults. It's a comforting belief, offering a sense of control and predictability, but also a breeding ground for victim-blaming and gross inequalities.

By acknowledging the role of external factors, determinism dismantles this oversimplified view of the world. It encourages us to recognize the role of privilege, circumstances, and systemic factors in shaping our lives, pushing for a more empathetic and egalitarian society.

One potential pitfall of the deterministic viewpoint is its impact on personal motivation. If we are not the true authors of our actions, and our achievements and failures are the result of factors beyond our control, it might seem like striving for personal growth and change is futile.

However, determinism doesn't equate to fatalism. It doesn't suggest a passive resignation to our circumstances, but rather a nuanced understanding of our agency within those constraints. This perspective can potentially alleviate the self-blame and guilt often associated with failures, while fostering humility in the face of success.

Determinism also underscores the importance of cultivating the right conditions and environments for positive change, both at individual and societal levels. Understanding that our behavior is shaped by our circumstances pushes us to create environments conducive to growth, learning, and wellbeing.

With determinism also comes a potential shift in our understanding and treatment of mental health. Too often, mental health issues are stigmatized, seen as personal failings rather than the result of a complex interplay of genetic, environmental, and psychological factors. Recognizing that our mental states are not entirely within our control can promote empathy and understanding, challenging the stigmatization and trivialization of mental health issues.

Moreover, determinism can inform therapeutic approaches in psychology. For instance, Cognitive Behavioral Therapy (CBT) acknowledges the impact of past experiences and current circumstances on our thoughts, feelings, and behaviors. It doesn't deem the individual as weak or defective but tries to provide tools to reshape their thinking and responses within the deterministic framework of their life.

The deterministic perspective has significant implications for education. If we consider that each child's behavior, learning style, and educational outcomes are shaped by a multitude of factors — including genetics, socio-economic background, upbringing, and school environment — then it challenges the 'one size fits all' approach to education.

Determinism encourages us to create educational environments that acknowledge individual differences, cater to diverse learning styles, and provide the support needed to bridge the gap between different starting points. It pushes us to question practices that perpetuate educational inequality, such as standardized testing and strict academic tracking based on age rather than individual learning pace and style.

While determinism can fundamentally change our perspectives on responsibility and judgment, it doesn't necessitate the eradication of personal responsibility altogether. The deterministic view of life doesn't assert that we are mere puppets controlled by the strings of causality. We still feel, think, and make choices - albeit within the constraints of our biology, environment, and experiences.

This perspective can help us strike a balance between understanding the forces that shape us and holding onto the concept of personal responsibility, which is crucial for maintaining social order and promoting personal growth. It encourages us to take control where we can, while being compassionate towards ourselves and others when things are beyond our control.

Acknowledging the weight of responsibility in a deterministic framework entails a significant shift in our perspectives on judgment, morality, mental health, education, and personal growth. While it may feel uncomfortable to relinquish the idea of ultimate free will, doing so can usher in a more compassionate, equitable, and understanding society. It can help us appreciate the joints of causality that shape who we are, encouraging us to be kinder to ourselves and others, promoting mental wellbeing, and pushing for social systems that reflect these insights.

15.4 Case Studies: Ethical Dilemmas in a Deterministic World

Our journey in Part IV: The Philosophy of Free Will continues to unravel intriguing perspectives. As we progress towards an in-depth analysis of ethical repercussions in a world devoid of free will, we now turn our focus towards the real world. We have theorized and philosophized, deliberated and contemplated the theories of free will, determinism, and the delicate equilibrium that resides within them. However, the essence of these discussions remains hollow unless we tether them to the ground realities of our world. Therefore, the purpose of this section is to traverse the bridge between the realm of theoretical abstractions to the gritty realism of everyday life.

Our first destination within this realism is the complex landscape of the criminal justice system. In our society, blame and punishment have long been attached to the idea that individuals freely choose their actions. Criminals are punished because they are perceived as having chosen to commit crimes. However, in a deterministic framework, this traditional view stands challenged.

Let's look at a hypothetical case of a man named John, who was born into a family plagued with issues of addiction, violence, and neglect. From early childhood, John's environment was one of chaos, and the only role models he had were individuals who were in and out of jail. Education took a backseat as survival became a priority. From petty theft to drug peddling, his offenses gradually escalated, ultimately leading him to murder. The deterministic perspective would argue that every aspect of John's life, from his genetics to his environment, contributed to this tragic outcome.

In light of this deterministic viewpoint, how does our approach to blame, punishment, and rehabilitation in the criminal justice system change? And, more importantly, how should it change?

Our second case study takes us to the realm of education. The modern education system largely operates under the assumption that individuals have the free will to succeed or fail. It's perceived that a student's academic achievement primarily hinges on their effort, commitment, and discipline.

Consider the case of Mary, an extraordinarily bright and hardworking student from a lower-income family. Mary's parents work multiple jobs, leaving little time to provide her with academic support. She lives in an area where her public school is underfunded and overcrowded. Despite her diligence and ambition, her learning environment poses a significant impediment to her success. From the determinist point of view, her environment and circumstances play a crucial role in her academic outcomes, regardless of her personal will and determination. The deterministic viewpoint challenges the meritocracy of the education system and prompts us to think about systemic changes necessary to ensure equality of opportunities.

The next area we will explore is mental health, another field that is closely intertwined with questions of free will and determinism. Individuals struggling with mental illnesses often face the stigma that their conditions are somehow a choice or a result of weak willpower.

Consider the case of Alex, who struggles with severe clinical depression. Despite his best efforts and desire to feel better, his mental health condition continues to affect his life profoundly. Is it fair to say that Alex chooses to be depressed? From a deterministic perspective, various factors, including genetics, biochemistry, environment, and personal experience, contribute to mental health conditions, far beyond the scope of individual free will.

Similarly, let us explore the ethical dilemmas that exist in criminal justice and rehabilitation programs. Consider Tom, who was born into a crime-ridden neighborhood, was abused during his childhood, and as an adult, ended up in prison for a series of thefts. Determinism would argue that the crime Tom committed was a result of a series of determinants that he had no control over, such as his upbringing and environmental influences. If we adhere to a deterministic view, it brings about the question of whether punishing individuals for their actions is ethical or not. It also encourages us to consider more compassionate approaches towards rehabilitation, acknowledging the various determinants that led individuals down such paths.

The same principles apply when we look at substance abuse. Consider Lisa, who has been struggling with alcoholism for the last decade. The stigma attached to addiction often blames the individual, viewing the condition as a result of moral failing or lack of willpower. However, the deterministic approach emphasizes the impact of genetics, environment, and psychological factors in developing an addiction, removing the blame from the individual and highlighting the role of various uncontrollable factors.

Understanding these determinants not only shifts our perspective towards empathy but also guides us in developing more effective treatment and prevention strategies. For instance, if we understand that genetic factors contribute significantly to the risk of addiction, preventive measures can be taken early for individuals who have a family history of substance abuse. The same principle applies to mental health issues, where a deterministic understanding could facilitate better diagnostic tools, personalized treatments, and greater societal acceptance and support.

Shifting from individuals to societies, a deterministic view could also impact the way we perceive socioeconomic inequalities. If we accept that individuals are largely shaped by their environment, it becomes harder to justify the massive wealth disparities that exist globally. For instance, if a person is born into poverty and ends up living a life of poverty, can we blame them for not 'working hard enough'? Or should we, as a society, recognize the limitations and barriers that these determinants impose and work towards creating equal opportunities for everyone?

On a grander scale, accepting determinism has implications for how we view human achievement and progress. Often, individuals are praised or rewarded for their success, as though it were solely a result of their efforts. However, in a deterministic view, this success would also be the product of numerous other factors outside the individual's control. Should we therefore rethink our attitudes towards success and failure? Should we be working to create societies that account for these determinants and aim for equal opportunities rather than equal outcomes?

To wrap up, we've seen how determinism can transform our perceptions of ethics, responsibility, and fairness, leading to profound shifts in society's structures and systems. These transformations wouldn't come easily, of course, and we must be prepared to grapple with the complexities and nuances of these issues. But if we believe in creating a fairer, more empathetic, and understanding world, these are challenges worth tackling.

Yet, these are just a few examples of how determinism might alter our ethical landscape. There are countless other contexts and scenarios where these ideas could be applied, and I invite you, dear readers, to ponder on these and explore the implications further.

Concluding Part IV

As we bring our philosophical exploration of free will to a close, we reflect on the journey we've undertaken. From the ancient thinkers who set the foundations of free will, through the turbulent shifts during the Renaissance and Enlightenment, and finally, to the contemporary debates around free will and determinism, we've explored diverse perspectives and wrestled with their implications.

Through Descartes' influential mind-body dualism and Augustine's profound theological insights, we traced the evolution of thought on human volition. Moving into the modern era, we delved into the competing philosophical stances of compatibilism, incompatibilism, and libertarianism, each offering unique perspectives on the enigma of free will. The existentialist claim of individual freedom and the counterarguments challenging the very existence of free will further enriched our dialogue.

Our exploration took a pivotal turn as we ventured into the ethical landscape of a world sans free will, investigating the consequentialist and deontological impacts of determinism. The reimagining of blame and punishment and the shifts in our understanding of responsibility under determinism were significant revelations.

However, the philosophical debates around free will are not solely abstract musings; they touch on the profound question of the meaning of our lives. As we move into Part V of our journey, we will look at how we might navigate our lives within the constraints of determinism. We'll consider if a life without free will can still hold purpose and meaning and explore the psychological and existential challenges such a life might entail. The underpinnings of free will and determinism provide more than just intellectual stimulation; they may profoundly impact how we live our lives and shape our understanding of self and others.

PART V: Navigating a Life Without Choices

Welcome, dear reader, to the culmination of our journey. This is where we dive into the deep end, where we take the abstract theories and academic dialogues of the preceding pages and plunge into the vivid reality of life itself. This is where philosophy meets the pavement, where we make sense of determinism in the practical, emotional, and existential dimensions of everyday life.

Our voyage through the realms of free will and determinism has challenged us, perhaps even transformed our outlook on life. It has led us to question fundamental notions of freedom and responsibility and to grapple with our place in the grand scheme of things. Now, we stand at the edge of an even more profound exploration - of our lives, ourselves, and our potential for meaning and purpose within the deterministic framework.

Here, we will delve into the heart of our existential quest. Can there be purpose and significance in a deterministic world? What role does existentialism play in carving out our path? Can we genuinely flourish and thrive within determinism's constraints? And what might personal reflections reveal about navigating life without free will?

We will strive to redefine what freedom might look like within determinism. We'll explore fresh perspectives on freedom, the role of self-actualization and self-determination, and the potential for freedom within constraints. Here, through illustrative stories, we will paint a picture of what this redefined freedom could look like in real-world contexts.

Finally, we touch practical wisdom and tools to help us navigate our lives without the concept of traditional free will. We will explore coping strategies, the power of self-awareness and mindfulness, and the strength that can be found in embracing uncertainty. By integrating these insights into our daily lives, we can learn to live meaningfully and purposefully within a deterministic world.

Part V represents the heart and soul of our journey. It is a deeply personal exploration and one that I hope will resonate with your own experiences, hopes, and challenges. As we embark on this final leg of our journey, I invite you to approach with an open heart and mind, a willingness to question, and, most importantly, the courage to redefine your understanding of life itself. This is where we take theory and apply it to life, where we take philosophy and make it personal. I hope that it will not just be an intellectual exercise but a profound exploration of the human condition within the boundaries of determinism.

CHAPTER 16: DETERMINISM AND PURPOSE

As we begin the end of this exploration, it is time to address one of the most profound philosophical questions we humans ever grapple with: the search for meaning. How do we find purpose and meaning in a world possibly governed by deterministic laws? Are our life paths merely sequences of causes and effects, or can we find a more profound existential purpose?

This chapter will delve into these questions. We will investigate the possible meanings within a deterministic framework and explore whether and how we can flourish in such a world. We will also reflect on existentialism and its views on purpose, as well as various philosophical stances on these issues.

Through careful scrutiny of these topics, we aim to bring our readers into a deeper understanding of these complex concepts and their impacts on our daily lives, ethics, decision-making, and our very understanding of ourselves as conscious beings.

With the wisdom gathered from the previous chapters and a firm grasp of the nuances of determinism, we step forward into these intriguing inquiries, ready to confront and understand the impacts of determinism on our pursuit of purpose and meaning. Let us embark on this journey, shall we?

16.1 MEANING IN A DETERMINISTIC FRAMEWORK: IS IT POSSIBLE?

A life without free will. To many, the concept seems to deny the very essence of our humanity. The freedom to choose, to direct our lives as we wish, and to be the authors of our own stories is often viewed as the bedrock of human experience. If determinism holds true and all our actions and decisions are the inevitable outcomes of prior events, does that not strip life of its meaning? The thought of being mere pawns in the cosmic game, with our lives unfolding according to a predetermined script, can indeed appear grim and disheartening. In the face of such existential dread, one might question: is it possible to find meaning in a deterministic framework? Can life still hold purpose and significance if we are devoid of free will?

The first step to navigating this quandary is to delve deep into what we mean by "meaning". In its most basic sense, meaning is about significance or importance. It's about mattering, about making a difference. It's about feeling that our existence counts for something in the grand scheme of things. This sense of meaning and purpose is often tied to our ability to make choices and influence outcomes. But is the connection absolute? Is our capacity for choice the only conduit to a meaningful life, or could there be alternative paths to significance in a deterministic universe?

A closer examination reveals that our instinctual equating of free will with meaning stems from certain deeply ingrained assumptions. The most notable among these is the idea that value and worth can only be derived from independent action—that only through free choice can we truly make a difference. But why should this be the case? Is it not possible that there could be intrinsic worth and dignity in simply being part of the cosmic tapestry, irrespective of whether our threads are self-spun or dictated by the loom of causality?

Even within a deterministic framework, our lives can hold immense significance. Consider, for instance, the interconnectedness and interdependence of all phenomena in the universe. Each event, no matter how seemingly insignificant, is part of the grand causal chain that shapes the course of reality. Our thoughts, feelings, and actions—deterministic as they may be—are thus integral to the unfolding of the universe. They matter, not because they are freely chosen, but because they are part of the grand cosmic narrative.

The search for meaning and purpose can still be a vibrant, fulfilling journey in a deterministic world. Such a journey would not be about carving our own destiny, but about discovering and embracing our place in the causal tapestry. It would involve a profound acceptance of the fact that we are part of something bigger than ourselves—a grand cosmic play that has been unfolding since the dawn of time. It would entail finding joy and significance in the mere act of being, of existing as part of the cosmos, and of contributing to the universe's ceaseless dance of cause and effect.

Even if our paths are predestined, the journey itself can be fulfilling and meaningful. Think of it as reading a riveting novel or watching a gripping movie. Even though the plot is fixed and the ending is known, the narrative can still captivate us, elicit strong emotions, and provide valuable insights. Similarly, our deterministic lives can be filled with wonder, discovery, growth, joy, sorrow, and a myriad of other experiences that imbue existence with richness and depth.

Finding meaning in a deterministic framework requires a paradigm shift—a radical redefinition of what constitutes purpose and significance. It calls for a move from a 'creator' mindset, where meaning is derived from crafting our own narrative, to a 'discovery' mindset, where meaning comes from uncovering and embracing our place in the predetermined cosmic narrative. It's about finding fulfillment, not in controlling the flow of the river, but in skillfully navigating its currents and appreciating the unique journey it offers.

This new perspective does not belittle or negate the human experience but enhances it by inviting acceptance and appreciation. Acceptance of the fact that we are part of a deterministic cosmos, and appreciation of the beauty and wonder of this cosmic dance. By embracing our deterministic nature, we can free ourselves from the illusion of control and the anxiety that often comes with it. This can pave the way for a profound sense of peace, equanimity, and connectedness with the universe.

A deterministic framework doesn't necessarily diminish our sense of individuality or uniqueness. Every event in the universe's history has led to each of us being exactly who we are - with our unique constellation of experiences, traits, thoughts, and feelings. While our paths may be predetermined, they are uniquely ours - unparalleled and unprecedented. Recognizing and embracing this can add a deep sense of significance and richness to our existence.

We may not be independent agents freely scripting our stories, but we are still integral to the unfolding of the cosmic narrative. Each of us plays a unique role, contributing to the evolution of the universe in our own ways. Our thoughts, actions, and experiences - all products of deterministic processes - matter because they are part of the greater whole. Recognizing this can lead to a sense of fulfillment and purpose, a feeling of being at home in the universe.

Meaning and purpose can also be found in our connections with others and our contributions to the world. Even if our actions are determined, they can still have a significant impact on those around us and on the world at large. Our deterministic nature doesn't negate the love we share, the joy we bring, or the positive changes we can engender. Indeed, our ability to connect, to contribute, to touch lives, and to make a difference - all of these can infuse life with deep meaning and purpose, irrespective of their deterministic origins.

Even within a deterministic framework, our perception and interpretation of our experiences can play a crucial role in the search for meaning. Even if our responses to events are predetermined, our subjective experience of those events - our thoughts, feelings, and interpretations - can still be incredibly diverse and nuanced. This subjective realm can be a rich source of insight, growth, and meaning. The quest for understanding, the joy of discovery, the thrill of insight, the comfort of empathy - these and many other aspects of our subjective experience can imbue life with a sense of purpose.

There is also an aesthetic dimension to life that can provide a deep sense of meaning. The beauty of nature, the magic of music, the elegance of mathematics, the narrative of history, the mystery of the cosmos - all of these can inspire awe, wonder, and a profound sense of the sublime. In our ability to appreciate such beauty and elegance - even if that ability is a product of deterministic processes - we can find a deep sense of satisfaction and fulfillment.

For many, the search for meaning involves a sense of spirituality or transcendence. Even within a deterministic framework, one can experience a sense of the sacred or the divine, a feeling of being part of something larger than oneself. This sense of transcendence can provide a deep sense of peace and fulfillment. The universe, in all its deterministic glory, can be seen as a grand, sacred tapestry - an interconnected dance of cause and effect, unfolding with mathematical precision and cosmic elegance. Our lives, as part of this grand narrative, can be imbued with a profound sense of meaning and purpose.

Finally, even within a deterministic universe, there is room for mystery, for the unknown, for the inexplicable. There is much about the universe and our existence that we do not yet understand, and perhaps never will. Embracing this mystery, savoring the enigmatic and the elusive, can add a sense of adventure and wonder to life. The journey of life, even if its path is predetermined, can be a grand adventure of discovery and exploration, a treasure hunt of sorts, teeming with awe-inspiring revelations and profound insights.

At the end, even within a deterministic framework, it is possible to find a deep sense of meaning and purpose. While determinism may challenge some traditional conceptions of free will, it opens up new avenues for finding significance in our existence. From embracing our unique roles in the cosmic narrative to celebrating our connections and contributions, from delving into the rich realm of subjective experience to savoring the aesthetic and spiritual dimensions of life, from relishing the thrill of discovery to embracing the enigma of existence - there are myriad ways in which life can be infused with profound meaning and purpose.

These pathways to meaning are not exhaustive, of course. They merely serve to illustrate the myriad ways in which we can find deep significance and satisfaction in our lives, even if we do not possess libertarian free will. We need not succumb to existential despair or nihilistic apathy in the face of determinism. Instead, we can choose to see determinism as a clarion call to delve deeper, to seek harder, to explore further, to understand better.

A deterministic worldview does not need to be a barrier to finding meaning in life. On the contrary, it can actually be a catalyst for deeper exploration and understanding. It forces us to confront the reality of our existence and to grapple with profound questions about meaning, purpose, and significance. It challenges us to not take life for granted, but to delve into its depths, to unravel its mysteries, and to seek its treasures.

In the grand scheme of things, whether the universe is deterministic or nondeterministic may not really matter. What matters is how we choose to perceive our existence and how we decide to live our lives. It is not the external reality of the universe that gives our lives meaning, but our internal perceptions, experiences, and responses. It is not the mechanistic unfolding of physical laws that define our lives, but our conscious engagement with the world, our creative interactions with reality, our dynamic interplay with existence.

Determinism or indeterminism, free will or fate, chance or necessity - these are metaphysical concepts, abstract ideas, philosophical constructs. They can provide a framework for understanding reality, for interpreting the world, for making sense of existence. But ultimately, life is not about understanding reality, but about experiencing it. It is not about interpreting the world, but about engaging with it. It is not about making sense of existence, but about living it.

Whether our actions are determined by preceding events or are the result of random quantum fluctuations, whether we are driven by inexorable destiny or are the authors of our own stories, whether we are puppets of fate or masters of our own destiny - these are profound and intriguing questions. But ultimately, they may be less important than how we choose to live our lives, how we decide to face the world, how we opt to navigate existence.

In the final analysis, determinism does not negate the possibility of a meaningful life. On the contrary, it can enhance it, enrich it, and illuminate it. It can inspire us to delve deeper, to seek further, to explore wider, to understand better. It can motivate us to appreciate the intricacies of existence, to savor the complexities of life, to celebrate the grandeur of the universe.

So, is meaning possible in a deterministic framework? The answer, unequivocally, is yes. Not only is it possible, but it can also be profound, enriching, enlightening, and fulfilling. Determinism does not diminish the significance of life, but amplifies it, enhances it, and accentuates it.

And thus we step into the next section, armed with a newfound appreciation for our place in the deterministic framework, we explore how existentialism and purpose find their way.

16.2 Existentialism and Purpose: Finding a Way

We now embark on a journey through existentialism, a philosophical lens that places the individual experience at the center of inquiry. The theme here is to explore how existentialism can offer a way to find purpose and meaning within a deterministic framework.

Existentialism is a philosophy that arose in the 19th and 20th centuries as a response to the disorientation and despair that many felt in the face of an increasingly complex, industrialized, and seemingly meaningless world. Its roots can be traced back to the works of Søren Kierkegaard and Friedrich Nietzsche, philosophers who grappled with the angst and despair arising from the recognition of life's apparent meaninglessness.

Kierkegaard, often considered the father of existentialism, emphasized individual existence, subjectivity, and the importance of personal choice. He posited that each individual is solely responsible for giving meaning to life and living it passionately and sincerely, despite the many existential obstacles, including despair, angst, absurdity, alienation, and death.

Nietzsche, meanwhile, propagated the idea of "life affirmation," urging individuals to embrace all aspects of life, including suffering and hardship, without resorting to metaphysical or afterlife comforts. He coined the term "will to power" to describe the driving force of human character, which can be seen as a precursor to the existentialist focus on individual freedom and responsibility.

This brief historical overview sets the stage for our exploration of how existentialism tackles the question of determinism and the quest for meaning in life.

The essence of existentialism is the belief that life is a series of choices, creating stress and confusion, but ultimately leading to the individual's unique and authentic existence. This is a philosophy not of despair but rather of hope: the existential courage to face these seemingly insurmountable challenges and continue living.

Existentialism highlights the importance of personal responsibility in creating one's own purpose and meaning. Instead of viewing humans as subjects in a deterministic universe, it emphasizes their role as active participants shaping their own lives. Even in the face of a deterministic framework, existentialism posits that individuals can still exert their will and make conscious decisions, thus imbuing their lives with purpose and meaning.

Take the existentialist concept of "bad faith" (mauvaise foi), proposed by Jean-Paul Sartre, for instance. It refers to the human tendency to allow societal pressures and conventions to determine our actions, rather than acting according to our authentic selves. For Sartre, this is a form of self-deception, where individuals blame circumstances or societal conventions for their actions, thus renouncing personal responsibility and freedom.

But Sartre, in essence, declares, "We are our choices." This statement encapsulates his assertion that humans, even under deterministic frameworks, have more agency than they might think. He argues that we are always free to choose, and that our existence is defined by these choices, thereby forming the essence of our being.

But how does existentialism provide a roadmap for finding a way amidst the constraints of determinism?

The existentialists' answer lies in personal responsibility and authenticity. Although we may not have control over the deterministic factors in our lives, we can still make choices that reflect our genuine selves. This means that rather than letting our lives be dictated by deterministic factors, we can instead consciously decide how we respond to them.

For instance, Viktor Frankl, an Austrian psychiatrist and Holocaust survivor, espoused a form of existentialism that focused on finding meaning in life, even in the direst of circumstances. In his seminal work, "Man's Search for Meaning," Frankl articulated his theory of logotherapy, which posits that life's primary motivational force is our search for meaning. He wrote, "We can discover this meaning in life in three different ways: (1) by creating a work or doing a deed; (2) by experiencing something or encountering someone; and (3) by the attitude we take toward unavoidable suffering." For Frankl, these three paths offer ways for individuals to construct meaning in their lives, even when facing seemingly insurmountable challenges.

Existentialists argue that we are free to choose our responses to the circumstances that life presents us with, and it is in these choices that we construct our own individual meaning and purpose. This perspective doesn't deny the presence of deterministic factors in our lives, but it does contest the idea that these factors solely define our existence. Instead, existentialism proposes that it is our responses to these factors and our conscious decisions that truly shape our lives.

Yet existentialism isn't without its challenges. A life of personal responsibility and authenticity requires courage. It's not always easy to stand against societal pressures, face up to our own existential angst, and make choices that are true to who we are. It's a constant battle against the easier route of living in "bad faith," as Sartre would put it.

Despite this, existentialism provides a beacon of hope for those feeling trapped in a deterministic world. It opens up a space for personal agency, even amidst the constraining factors of our existence, offering a way for us to navigate our lives with a sense of purpose and meaning. So even though determinism may limit our choices in some respects, existentialism highlights the choices we do have - the choices that ultimately shape our existence.

Revisiting Sartre's assertion, "existence precedes essence," we can see a guiding principle for our endeavor. In a deterministic universe, it can be easy to fall into the trap of defining our essence, our core being, by external circumstances and causal chains that are beyond our control. Yet, Sartre's assertion flips this idea on its head. Existentialism posits that we first exist, and then through our actions, choices, and decisions, we create our own essence.

This concept is intrinsically empowering. It doesn't negate the realities of determinism but instead reframes our perspective on it. It allows us to reassert control over our lives by emphasizing the importance of how we react to deterministic circumstances.

An individual's essence, therefore, is not predetermined but is a continually evolving product of their decisions and actions. In a deterministic world, this is an immensely liberating idea as it breaks the chain of predestination and reveals an avenue through which individuals can exercise personal freedom and agency.

Albert Camus, another existentialist, introduced the notion of the 'absurd' as a clash between our human desire for meaning and the indifferent, silent universe we find ourselves in. For Camus, acknowledging the absurdity of existence does not lead to despair or nihilism, but instead to a life of rebellion and passion. He proposes that we should accept the absurd condition without resorting to illusions or faith, and create our own meaning and value in life. For him, the greatest act of freedom is to face absurdity and keep living passionately.

Applying this to determinism, we can draw parallels between Camus's 'absurd' universe and a deterministic world. They both represent environments where external factors seem overwhelmingly beyond individual control. Yet, just as Camus suggested, we can choose to embrace this reality, not with resignation but with defiant passion. By doing so, we reclaim our power and carve out a meaningful existence within a deterministic framework.

The existentialist perspective thus provides a philosophical model through which we can navigate a deterministic world. It empowers individuals to take control of their responses to deterministic circumstances, thereby actively participating in the creation of their own life's meaning and purpose. It's about continually choosing to create ourselves, to evolve, to engage with the world passionately, and to keep moving forward despite external circumstances.

Delving further into the existentialist thought, we come across the philosophy of Friedrich Nietzsche. Nietzsche's assertion of the "will to power" aligns with the existentialist tradition of finding individual meaning in life. According to Nietzsche, the will to power is the main driving force in humans - a fundamental part of our nature. It is our basic drive for self-assertion, achievement, and overcoming challenges.

In a deterministic universe, the will to power can be interpreted as the ability to exercise influence within the constraints of our circumstances. It's not about changing the deterministic laws of the universe, but rather, leveraging them to make the most of our situation. It's the will to exercise control over one's own mind, reactions, interpretations, and emotional responses, regardless of the deterministic universe outside.

This approach is particularly helpful in a deterministic framework as it encourages individuals to focus on the elements they can control. When we consider determinism as a given and focus our efforts on asserting our will to power within this framework, we create a space for personal growth and self-improvement.

Simone de Beauvoir, another prominent existentialist, adds to this by emphasizing the importance of freedom and responsibility. For Beauvoir, we are free to make our own choices, but this freedom comes with immense responsibility. Even in a deterministic universe, the choice of how we respond to our circumstances is ours, and we must bear the responsibility for these choices.

In Beauvoir's perspective, we can find another helpful tool for navigating a deterministic universe. By acknowledging and embracing our responsibility for our responses to deterministic circumstances, we claim a significant measure of control over our lives. We cannot control the deterministic universe, but we can control our reactions, our choices, and by extension, our essence.

Thus, existentialism, in various interpretations, offers us a framework to approach determinism not as a confining doctrine but as a platform on which we exercise our freedom and responsibility. It suggests that even within a deterministic framework, we can live lives rich with purpose, intent, and personal meaning.

The Danish philosopher Søren Kierkegaard, often regarded as the first existentialist philosopher, too offers a unique perspective on finding meaning in a deterministic world. Kierkegaard's philosophy places individual experience and emotion at the center. He argues that truth is subjective, meaning that individual experiences and emotions determine our personal truths. This focus on individuality and personal experience, again, fits well within the deterministic framework. In a world where external events and circumstances are predetermined, the internal realm of thoughts, emotions, and experiences becomes our primary sphere of influence.

One of Kierkegaard's most potent concepts in this regard is that of "despair." For Kierkegaard, despair is not merely a negative emotional state; instead, it is the condition of not being true to oneself, not realizing one's potential, or not living authentically. From this perspective, even in a deterministic universe, despair can be avoided by living authentically, embracing our individuality, and taking ownership of our personal experiences and emotional responses.

Another important contribution of existentialism towards navigating a deterministic world comes from Martin Heidegger. Heidegger introduced the concept of "thrownness" (Geworfenheit), representing the fact that we are "thrown" into a world and a reality that we did not choose, and in which we must nonetheless find our path. This concept aligns neatly with determinism, which asserts that our circumstances are not of our own choosing but predetermined.

However, Heidegger suggests that despite this thrownness, we can still find a sense of purpose and direction. We do this by embracing our "being-in-the-world" and our interactions with the world and others around us. In this perspective, even in a deterministic framework, our lives are not devoid of meaning or purpose. Instead, the meaning arises from our authentic engagement with our circumstances and our active participation in the world, however predetermined it may be.

Therefore, existentialism offers us a framework for finding personal meaning and purpose even in a deterministic universe. It suggests that even if we cannot control the macrocosm of the universe, we can still find meaning in the microcosm of our individual experiences, emotions, and responses. And in doing so, it opens a new way of understanding and navigating determinism – not as a doctrine of predetermination and fatalism but as a backdrop against which we paint our own, unique story.

With its emphasis on personal choice, existentialism also challenges the traditional notion of destiny, which could be a core tenet of a deterministic worldview. Many existentialists argue that we create our destiny through our actions and decisions, effectively making us the "authors" of our lives. This stance seems antithetical to determinism at first, but upon closer inspection, it is not necessarily so.

The deterministic perspective does not deny that we make choices. Instead, it posits that these choices are the result of previous causes – our genetic makeup, upbringing, experiences, environment, and so on. Therefore, when existentialists say we create our destiny, this could be seen as consistent with determinism if we understand "creating" not as initiating a completely free and uncaused act, but as participating in a chain of cause-and-effect where our decisions are the effects of previous causes.

Existentialism, in essence, encourages us to take an active role in life, to make choices and bear their consequences, and to strive for authenticity. Even within a deterministic universe, these remain valid and vital endeavors. Existentialists like Jean-Paul Sartre emphasize the importance of authenticity – living according to our true nature and values, irrespective of external circumstances.

Sartre's philosophy, especially his concept of "bad faith," has a crucial role in understanding how to find meaning and purpose in a deterministic world. "Bad faith," for Sartre, is the act of self-deception, where individuals deny their freedom and authenticity and instead blame their circumstances or other external factors for their condition. Sartre saw this as a way for individuals to evade responsibility for their actions.

While determinism posits that external factors play a role in shaping our actions, it does not absolve us of responsibility. Our understanding of our actions' causes can guide our future behavior, leading to personal growth and transformation. So, living authentically, according to Sartre, means acknowledging and embracing our deterministic nature, and striving to act responsibly within that framework.

In essence, existentialism offers a means to carve out personal purpose and meaning within the confines of a deterministic world. It encourages us to grapple with our existence's realities, to question, to probe, and to strive for an authentic life, despite – or perhaps because of – the constraints imposed by determinism.

Existentialists also engage with the idea of the "absurd," a concept famously associated with Albert Camus. The "absurd" arises out of the confrontation between our human desire for order, meaning, and clarity, and the silence and indifference of the universe. In a deterministic view, the universe operates according to laws of cause and effect, without any inherent purpose or meaning. The deterministic universe is indifferent to our human quest for purpose, thus mirroring the existentialist notion of the absurd.

Yet, for Camus, the realization of the absurd should not lead to despair, but rather to a radical form of freedom. Even though the universe may be indifferent, we can still create our own sense of meaning and purpose. This creation of personal meaning mirrors the previously discussed theme of finding purpose within a deterministic framework. For Camus, we can heroically accept the absurd and continue to strive for personal meaning. This, according to him, makes life worth living.

Interestingly, some existentialists propose that the realization of our existential freedom can lead to feelings of anxiety and dread, often termed as "existential angst". This angst arises from the profound realization that we are the sole authors of our life, that the onus of decision making, and by extension, the responsibility of our actions, falls on us. In a deterministic framework, existential angst can arise from the realization that our choices, though seemingly free, are conditioned by a myriad of factors beyond our conscious control.

Despite this, existentialism does not advocate for a passive resignation to these feelings of dread. Instead, it suggests that we confront these feelings, embracing them as a part of our human condition, and then use them as a catalyst to propel us forward. We find our own way in the face of these overwhelming odds, thus carving out a path that is unique to us, and in doing so, we find our purpose.

In a deterministic world, existentialism provides a roadmap to finding our unique path. It stresses the importance of authenticity, personal responsibility, acceptance of the absurd, and the active creation of meaning as avenues for deriving purpose. These concepts can be of great assistance to individuals grappling with the philosophical implications of determinism and seeking to find a sense of direction and purpose in their lives.

Simone de Beauvoir, a prominent existentialist, provides another unique perspective on navigating life under determinism. According to Beauvoir, while it's true that our circumstances may limit us, it is also true that we are always free to interpret our situation and make choices within it. In her book, "The Ethics of Ambiguity," Beauvoir argues that our freedom is always situated within our circumstances and that we have the responsibility to navigate our choices within those bounds.

In a deterministic framework, we could interpret Beauvoir's perspective as an acknowledgment that while our choices may be conditioned by a multitude of factors, we still retain a measure of freedom in how we interpret and react to our circumstances. We are not just passively subjected to deterministic forces; instead, we can actively engage with them, carve out our individual paths, and in the process, find our purpose.

Beauvoir's partner, the famous existentialist Jean-Paul Sartre, echoes a similar sentiment. Sartre posits that "Man is condemned to be free," which means that even in the face of determinism, we cannot escape the responsibility that comes with our freedom. To Sartre, regardless of the constraints we face, we are always free to choose our actions, and we must bear the weight of the outcomes of those choices.

In a deterministic framework, this translates to taking ownership of our actions, even when they're conditioned by factors beyond our conscious control. We must confront and accept the reality of our conditioned choices, and we bear the responsibility for their outcomes. This sense of radical responsibility can be overwhelming, but it is also empowering. It urges us to take an active role in our lives and not resign ourselves to a passive existence determined by external forces.

In essence, existentialism can offer valuable insights on navigating life within a deterministic framework. It encourages us to take ownership of our lives, confront the reality of our conditioned choices, accept the absurd, and actively create our own sense of meaning. It argues that even within the confines of determinism, we can find a sense of purpose by actively participating in our lives and making the best choices we can within our circumstances.

Existentialism suggests that purpose is not something to be found or discovered, but something to be actively created by us, within the constraints of our human condition. Even in a deterministic world, there is room for the creation of personal meaning, authenticity, and purpose. The existentialist outlook could serve as a valuable perspective for individuals seeking to navigate a life without free will.

Friedrich Nietzsche, another important existentialist thinker, contributes a noteworthy concept that could resonate with our exploration: the "Will to Power." Nietzsche's Will to Power posits that all beings strive for a fundamental drive for power, and this drive is the primary force that motivates all human action. In a deterministic world, this might translate to a drive to exert control over our circumstances, even if such control is ultimately an illusion.

What's fascinating about Nietzsche's Will to Power in the context of determinism is how it might compel us to confront our deterministic reality rather than shy away from it. It could encourage us to face the deterministic forces that condition our choices and take proactive steps to understand and engage with them. This proactive stance could lead us to a sense of empowerment and purpose within a deterministic framework.

Nietzsche's infamous declaration of "God is dead" isn't just a provocative assertion—it's a challenge for humanity to reinterpret their place in the universe. In a world without God—a deterministic world where our choices are conditioned by laws of nature, genetics, and environment—we are left with the profound responsibility to create our own values and purpose.

Embracing Nietzsche's ideas, we can understand that even in the face of determinism, we're not just helpless victims of fate. We are active participants in the process of life, and we have the power to create our own purpose and meaning, even if our choices are conditioned.

Existentialism provides an enriching framework for making sense of a deterministic world and carving out a sense of purpose within it. The existentialist thinkers we've examined—Kierkegaard, Heidegger, Sartre, Beauvoir, and Nietzsche—each offer unique insights that collectively shed light on the human condition within a deterministic framework.

Despite the deterministic forces that condition our choices, existentialism encourages us to take active control of our lives, confront our realities, and create our own sense of purpose. Even in a world without free will, there is room for autonomy, authenticity, and the creation of personal meaning.

Essentially, existentialism presents a compelling perspective for those navigating life without free will. It's an approach that doesn't shy away from the harsh realities of our existence, but rather confronts them head-on, fostering resilience, strength, and a sense of personal agency.

Jean-Paul Sartre's proclamation that "existence precedes essence" signifies an important distinction in the existentialist perspective. He proposes that we exist first, and it is through our actions and choices (even those conditioned by deterministic forces) that we define our essence or nature. We're not born with a predetermined essence or purpose. Instead, we are thrown into existence, and it's up to us to navigate it and define ourselves.

This tenet provides a substantial challenge to determinism. If existence truly precedes essence, then our essence—our self-definition, values, and purpose—is not predestined. While determinism might shape the range of our choices, it does not predetermine our essence. We are the authors of our life narratives.

Interestingly, Sartre's ideas do not contradict determinism. They invite us to look beyond the limitations that determinism places on our choices and focus on the choices that are still within our control. Even in a deterministic world, there's room for self-definition, personal values, and a sense of purpose.

Søren Kierkegaard, another foundational existentialist, also provides valuable insights for navigating a deterministic framework. He posits that individuals are always in a state of becoming and that it's in this process of becoming that we find purpose and meaning. Determinism does not negate the process of becoming, nor does it strip it of its meaning or value.

If we accept that we're always in a state of becoming and that our essence is not fixed but is continually evolving, then a deterministic framework can be viewed as another layer of the human experience, another aspect of our becoming. It doesn't take away our ability to grow, learn, and evolve. Instead, it adds complexity to the process.

Furthermore, Kierkegaard suggests that our deepest source of despair is not in being determined but in failing to become who we truly are. In a deterministic world, this might translate to a failure to fully engage with and understand the deterministic forces that condition our choices, thereby failing to actualize our potential within the constraints of determinism.

The philosophy of existentialism, as proposed by Kierkegaard and Sartre, offers us a powerful tool for finding purpose in a deterministic world. By focusing on the process of becoming and recognizing the importance of personal agency in self-definition, existentialism invites us to create our own purpose within the constraints of determinism.

As we wrap up this exploration of existentialism and purpose, we can conclude that existentialist philosophy provides a compelling framework for making sense of our place in a deterministic world. It offers valuable insights for those seeking to carve out a sense of purpose in life without free will, encouraging us to focus on the process of becoming, self-definition, and personal agency.

Existentialism urges us not to despair in the face of determinism but to embrace the complexity of our existence and create our own values and purpose within it.

Existentialism's dialogue with determinism extends beyond Sartre and Kierkegaard. Friedrich Nietzsche's concept of "eternal recurrence" is another existentialist thought that could lend itself to navigating life within determinism.

The eternal recurrence posits the idea that all events in the universe repeat themselves over and over again, infinitely. Nietzsche invites us to imagine how we would react if a demon came to us and told us that we would have to live this life, as it is now, again and again, forever. Would this thought be a heavy burden, or would it give our life tremendous value?

In a deterministic framework, the eternal recurrence can serve as a metaphor. If our choices and actions are the products of deterministic processes, and if, hypothetically, these processes were to recur infinitely, would we be content with the life we've lived? Are we making the most of the choices and opportunities available to us, even within the constraints of determinism?

This thought experiment encourages us to live in a way that we'd be willing to repeat – to strive to make each moment worthy of recurrence. It suggests that even in a deterministic world, our lives can hold significant value, and that we can find satisfaction and meaning within the parameters set by determinism.

Another existentialist philosopher, Albert Camus, offers a metaphor that might help us make sense of purpose in a deterministic world. Camus presents the myth of Sisyphus, a figure from Greek mythology condemned to roll a boulder up a mountain for eternity, only to watch it roll back down each time he nears the top.

Camus uses this myth to explore the absurdity of life. But in the context of our discussion, the myth of Sisyphus can serve as a metaphor for deterministic existence. Like Sisyphus with his boulder, we find ourselves in a world where our choices are conditioned by deterministic forces beyond our control.

However, Camus imagines Sisyphus as happy. Despite his eternal, fruitless toil, Sisyphus finds joy in his struggle. This suggests that even in the face of seemingly futile circumstances, we can find meaning and satisfaction. It's the struggle itself, the process of living and engaging with our deterministic conditions, that can give our lives purpose.

It's essential to note that finding a way in a deterministic world doesn't mean passively accepting the deterministic conditions.

Existentialism encourages us to actively engage with our circumstances, to constantly define and redefine our values, and to strive for authentic existence – even within the constraints of determinism.

In conclusion, existentialism provides several pathways for finding purpose in a deterministic framework. From Sartre's emphasis on existence preceding essence to Nietzsche's eternal recurrence and Camus's happy Sisyphus, existentialist thought offers a variety of perspectives that allow us to find purpose and meaning, even when our choices are conditioned by deterministic forces.

Existentialism invites us to take an active role in defining our lives, to embrace the process of becoming, and to live authentically within the boundaries of our circumstances. In this way, we can carve out a meaningful existence in a deterministic world.

In addition to these existentialist perspectives, the works of Victor Frankl, a renowned psychiatrist and Holocaust survivor, also offer profound insights into finding purpose in difficult circumstances. While Frankl was not strictly an existentialist, his philosophy, known as logotherapy, is closely aligned with existentialist ideas about the importance of finding meaning in life.

Frankl argues that the primary motivational force in humans is not pleasure, as posited by Freud, but the pursuit of what we find meaningful. In his seminal book, "Man's Search for Meaning," Frankl details his experiences in Nazi concentration camps and how the search for meaning played a crucial role in survival. He argues that even in the most adverse conditions, individuals can find meaning in life, and this meaning provides a reason to continue living.

Frankl's ideas can provide a powerful lens through which to view a deterministic world. Even in a world where our choices may be constrained by deterministic forces, we can find purpose and meaning. According to Frankl, meaning can be found in three ways: by creating a work or doing a deed, by experiencing something or encountering someone, and by the attitude we take toward unavoidable suffering.

The first pathway to meaning aligns with the active engagement encouraged by existentialism. We can find purpose in the things we do and the impact we make on the world, even within deterministic constraints. The second pathway suggests that we can derive meaning from our experiences and relationships, again, notwithstanding deterministic influences.

The third pathway is especially pertinent when considering the limits imposed by determinism. In circumstances where we cannot change our situation, we can still choose our attitude towards it. This is a form of freedom – the freedom to choose our perspective, even when we cannot choose our circumstances.

Through this lens, determinism doesn't preclude meaning but provides a context within which we search for it. The constraints of determinism can even heighten our sense of purpose by challenging us to find meaning within these constraints.

This discussion of existentialist thought and Frankl's logotherapy reveals how we can find purpose in a deterministic framework. Despite the deterministic forces at play, our lives are not devoid of meaning. On the contrary, these philosophies argue that meaning and purpose can be found within our circumstances, shaped by our active engagement with the world and the attitudes we adopt.

While determinism may limit our choices in some respects, it does not limit our ability to create, experience, and define our own meaning. Thus, existentialism and logotherapy provide robust tools for finding a way – for carving out a meaningful existence within a deterministic world.

In the next section, we will further explore how this understanding of purpose in a deterministic framework impacts our psychological well-being. Can we flourish in a deterministic world? Let's delve into this question.

16.3 PSYCHOLOGICAL WELL-BEING: CAN WE FLOURISH IN A DETERMINISTIC WORLD?

To commence this significant exploration of our potential to flourish within a deterministic world, it is worth noting that our perception of free will, or the lack thereof, has profound implications for our psychological well-being. The way we view our place in the world, our interactions with others, and our personal identity are shaped, in no small measure, by our beliefs concerning determinism and free will.

In this section, we will delve into the complex relationship between determinism, psychological well-being, and the possibility of flourishing within the constraints of a deterministic worldview.

Determinism presents us with a paradox of sorts when it comes to psychological well-being. On one hand, the notion that every event, including our thoughts, feelings, and actions, is determined by an unbroken chain of prior occurrences might provoke feelings of unease and anxiety. On the other hand, it might offer a certain sense of relief, alleviating the weight of responsibility that comes with absolute freedom.

The initial transition from a belief in free will to a deterministic perspective can trigger cognitive dissonance – a mental
360

conflict resulting from inconsistencies between two held beliefs or a belief and a behavior. This dissonance can lead to psychological discomfort, even distress, as we grapple to reconcile our deeply ingrained belief in personal agency and the deterministic view of the world.

A fundamental element of human psychology is the belief in personal agency, the feeling that we are the masters of our own destinies. This belief confers a sense of control and purpose, acting as a buffer against feelings of helplessness and despair. Agency, thus, plays a crucial role in our psychological well-being.

From a deterministic standpoint, however, this agency is largely illusory. Every action we take, every decision we make, is predestined by a sequence of prior events, effectively nullifying the notion of free will. This apparent loss of agency can lead to existential anxiety and a perceived lack of control, potentially impairing our psychological well-being.

Yet, it is essential to clarify that determinism does not negate the experience of making choices. Even if these choices are the result of deterministic processes, they still constitute our lived experiences. Recognizing and accepting this can aid in mitigating the negative psychological effects associated with a deterministic worldview.

The belief in free will has traditionally been linked with the perception of life as meaningful. The ability to exercise free will, to make autonomous choices, lends a sense of purpose to our existence. However, determinism challenges this perception, inviting questions regarding the meaningfulness of life in a predetermined world.

But, does determinism necessarily equate to a life devoid of meaning and purpose? Not necessarily. Determinism does not preclude the existence of subjective experiences, emotions, goals, and values – elements that contribute to a sense of meaning and purpose in life. It merely re-contextualizes them within a deterministic framework.

The concept of psychological flourishing, often discussed within the framework of positive psychology, refers to a state of thriving characterized by a sense of purpose, engagement, positive relationships, accomplishment, and personal growth. It is, in essence, the pursuit and actualization of one's potential.

In a deterministic universe, psychological flourishing can still be pursued and attained. In fact, acknowledging determinism can even add a layer of profundity to our pursuit of a meaningful life.

If every action and choice is determined by a complex interplay of genetic, environmental, and historical factors, then our unique trajectories – our personal narratives – are also the products of these deterministic processes. This realization, far from diminishing our sense of self, can lead to a profound appreciation for the beauty of existence that led to our being.

Moreover, even within a deterministic framework, we can still strive towards personal growth, pursue our interests, cultivate positive relationships, and contribute to our communities. These activities, which form the bedrock of psychological flourishing, remain unaffected by whether the universe is deterministic or not.

In essence, life in a deterministic universe need not be devoid of meaning or purpose. Instead, it invites a redefinition of these concepts, a reassessment of what constitutes a fulfilling life.

Accepting determinism may involve a shift in perspective, an existential adjustment. It necessitates recognizing that while our lives might be determined by factors beyond our control, they are still lived in the first-person perspective. Our experiences, emotions, aspirations, relationships, and actions continue to hold significance for us.

Furthermore, determinism underscores the interconnectedness of all things, of our lives being woven into the vast cosmic tapestry. It allows for a sense of awe and wonder at the complexity of existence, fostering a deep sense of humility and gratitude.

Ultimately, the question of whether life in a deterministic framework can be meaningful hinges on how we choose to perceive and navigate our existence. By embracing a deterministic worldview, we are not resigning ourselves to a life devoid of purpose or meaning. Instead, we are recognizing the incredible complexity and interconnectedness of the universe and finding our place within it.

One significant concept within the context of psychological well-being and flourishing is eudaimonic happiness. This term, derived from Aristotle's philosophy, refers to the highest form of happiness achieved through living a virtuous life, fulfilling one's potential, and actualizing one's true self. It's not about fleeting pleasures or instant gratification but a deep, enduring sense of fulfillment and purpose.

Even in a deterministic world, individuals can strive for eudaimonic happiness. The fulfillment of personal potential, the development of virtues, and the pursuit of a life aligned with one's true self can all occur within the bounds of determinism. Each individual, being a unique product of a specific set of determinants, has a unique potential to fulfill and a unique path to tread. The journey towards self-actualization, then, remains a personal and profound one, regardless of determinism.

Furthermore, determinism doesn't negate the importance of authenticity, a key component of existential thought and psychological well-being. Authenticity involves living in accordance with one's true self, holding true to one's values, and maintaining integrity in the face of societal pressures. While the "true self" is influenced by deterministic factors, living authentically is still a viable and worthwhile pursuit.

This authenticity isn't diminished by determinism. Instead, it involves recognizing, understanding, and accepting the factors that have shaped us, and then living in a manner that aligns with our authentic selves. Far from undermining authenticity, determinism can deepen it, fostering a greater understanding of oneself and one's place in the world.

Finally, determinism and psychological well-being intersect in the practice of mindfulness. Mindfulness, defined as the non-judgmental awareness of the present moment, can flourish within a deterministic framework. In mindfulness practice, the focus isn't on controlling or changing the deterministic processes of the mind, but rather on observing them with kindness and curiosity.

By cultivating mindfulness, individuals can develop a more nuanced understanding of their thoughts, feelings, and reactions, all of which are influenced by deterministic factors. Mindfulness can foster acceptance of the deterministic nature of our minds, reduce suffering, and enhance psychological well-being.

Psychological well-being isn't incompatible with a deterministic worldview. Instead, acknowledging determinism can deepen our understanding of ourselves and our place in the universe, leading to greater self-awareness, authenticity, and, ultimately, a fulfilling life. As such, even in a deterministic universe, we can indeed flourish.

Furthermore, resilience, the capacity to cope with stress and adversity, also plays a vital role in psychological well-being. In the face of determinism, resilience can still thrive. Understanding that our responses and reactions to external circumstances are influenced by a range of factors beyond our control can, paradoxically, encourage resilience.

Resilience involves adaptability, flexibility, and the ability to bounce back from difficult experiences. Even in a deterministic world, these qualities can be fostered. For example, understanding the deterministic factors that have shaped one's life can lead to acceptance, and acceptance is a significant aspect of resilience. It empowers us to move forward, not by denying or fighting against the determinism of our lives, but by acknowledging and adapting to it.

Self-compassion, another essential aspect of psychological well-being, involves treating oneself with kindness and understanding during times of failure or suffering, recognizing the shared human experience, and maintaining a balanced awareness of negative emotions. Self-compassion can be fostered within a deterministic framework. Understanding and acknowledging the deterministic influences on our behavior can promote forgiveness and self-kindness, key components of self-compassion.

Instead of blaming ourselves for perceived failures or shortcomings, we can recognize that a complex interplay of factors has shaped our lives. By acknowledging these factors, we can foster self-compassion, and this can have a profoundly positive impact on our psychological well-being.

Even within the deterministic framework, psychological well-being can be cultivated. Meaning and purpose can still be derived from our life experiences, whether they're perceived as freely chosen or not. The key lies in understanding and acknowledging the deterministic nature of our existence and learning to navigate within it to achieve a state of fulfillment, self-actualization, and overall psychological well-being.

16.4 PERSONAL REFLECTIONS: NAVIGATING A LIFE WITHOUT FREE WILL

Embracing determinism and living without free will is a deeply personal journey. Each person navigates their way through this path differently, armed with their unique set of experiences, beliefs, and coping mechanisms. This chapter seeks to explore and share a variety of personal reflections, not only as a means of humanizing the theory of determinism but also as a tool to navigate a life without free will.

Let's start with Lisa, a middle-aged professional. Lisa was always a firm believer in the idea that we are masters of our destiny. Her firm belief in free will gave her the conviction that she could shape her life just the way she wanted. This belief was what drove her through college, pushed her to work late nights, and fueled her ambition to rise in her career.

Then, Lisa discovered determinism.

The impact was profound. Lisa recalls, "It felt like my whole world had shifted. I went from believing that I was the pilot of my life to realizing that I was a passenger." She grappled with the idea, trying to reconcile her deeply ingrained beliefs about free will with the scientific evidence supporting determinism. It was a struggle, but Lisa pushed through. She read more, researched, and sought to understand.

"It wasn't easy," Lisa admits. "There were times when I felt like I was losing myself. But I wasn't. I was just losing a part of myself that I had outgrown."

Lisa's narrative is filled with emotional turmoil, introspection, and growth. But there's one thing she emphasizes:

acceptance. Acceptance, for Lisa, was the key to navigating a life without free will.

Then we have John, a retired engineer. John's journey into determinism began later in life. "I was always a science guy," John says, "I believed in laws and rules. The notion of free will seemed out of place in a world governed by physics and mathematics." When John stumbled upon determinism, it made sense to him. "It was as if I found the missing piece of the puzzle," John recalls.

In contrast to Lisa's story, John's transition to determinism was smooth. But it wasn't without challenges. "The hardest part was communicating it to others," John shares. He struggled to explain his new beliefs to his family and friends. He faced opposition, confusion, and even ridicule. But John persevered.

John's story is a testament to the resilience we possess. It shows that while our beliefs can shape our worldview, they can also adapt to accommodate new knowledge. It underscores the fact that change, while difficult, is also an inherent part of being human.

These stories illustrate the struggles and triumphs, the highs and lows, the challenges and victories of individuals grappling with determinism. They provide a rich tapestry of experiences, each narrative adding a new thread, contributing to a more comprehensive understanding of what it means to live without free will.

Now we look at the reflections of Sarah, a university student.

Sarah was first introduced to determinism in a philosophy class. She recalls feeling a sense of disquiet. "It felt like my autonomy was being questioned. The notion that I was not entirely in control of my actions was discomforting." Yet, curiosity drove Sarah to delve deeper into determinism.

Sarah's reflections reveal a fascinating aspect of the journey towards understanding determinism: the oscillation between fear and curiosity. "There were nights when I'd lose sleep over the thought that I wasn't in control," Sarah shares. "But there was also this need to understand, to probe, to see if I could live with this idea."

Her journey wasn't linear. There were moments of acceptance, followed by periods of intense resistance. There were instances of clarity, followed by bouts of confusion. But in every step, every stumble, Sarah's narrative underscored one crucial element: the human capacity to question, to learn, and to adapt.

Next, we delve into the reflections of Tom, a psychiatrist. Tom's encounter with determinism was through his patients. He observed patterns in his patients' behavior that seemed less about conscious decisions and more about unconscious influences.

"I began to see that our actions weren't always a result of conscious, deliberate decisions," Tom notes. "Our past, our environment, our biology—all these seemed to have a more significant role than we thought." This realization was Tom's introduction to determinism.

Tom's reflections underscore a subtle, yet crucial aspect of determinism: its presence in our everyday lives. Even without the scientific jargon, without the philosophy, determinism is evident in our routines, in our habits, in our responses. And realizing this can be both unnerving and enlightening.

Each of these personal reflections highlights the journey of acceptance. It isn't linear, nor is it the same for everyone. It's filled with struggles and victories, doubts and realizations. But in each narrative, we see a similar thread of resilience and adaptation.

These personal reflections are more than just stories. They serve as guides, as markers, as reminders that while the journey towards navigating a life without free will may be challenging, it is also achievable. And while it may seem like we're losing control, we're also gaining insight, understanding, and perhaps, a sense of peace.

Let's now dive into the reflections of Maya, a professional artist. Art, for Maya, was always a free expression, an exercise of free will. To paint or not, to choose this color over that, to draw this line here and not there - these were decisions that she thought she consciously made. But the concept of determinism challenged this belief.

"I remember feeling lost," Maya confesses. "If my decisions were all predetermined, then was my art truly mine? Was I merely a puppet, following a script written by the universe?" These questions haunted Maya, driving her to explore determinism further.

Maya's journey with determinism was fraught with existential crises. There were moments when she felt disconnected from her art, questioning its authenticity. Yet, there were also times when determinism made her feel more connected to her work. "I realized that my art was a culmination of my past experiences, my current circumstances, and my biological wiring," Maya shares. "In a way, it made my art feel more... real. More honest."

The reflection of Maya shows us how determinism can shift our perspective on creativity. It challenges the conventional belief of art as a product of pure conscious decision-making, and presents it as a result of deterministic factors. This shift can be disconcerting, but also enlightening, providing a deeper understanding and appreciation of one's artistic expressions.

Lastly, we look at the reflections of Ben, a retired engineer. For Ben, the deterministic view seemed to fit comfortably with his scientific outlook on life. "As an engineer, I was trained to see the world in patterns and laws," Ben explains. "Determinism, to me, was simply an extension of this mindset."

However, the transition from understanding determinism intellectually to living it personally was not smooth for Ben. "I found it hard to reconcile determinism with my daily life," Ben confesses. "It was easy to see determinism in the patterns of weather or in the laws of physics. But seeing it in my actions, in my choices—that was hard."

Ben's reflection underlines the cognitive dissonance many of us may experience while grappling with determinism. It's easier to accept determinism in abstract concepts than to see it reflected in our daily lives. Yet, as Ben's narrative shows, it's this personal engagement with determinism that truly expands our understanding of it.

The stories of Sarah, Tom, Maya, and Ben reflect different facets of our collective journey with determinism. They underscore the diverse paths we take, the varied challenges we face, and the unique insights we gain. They remind us that while determinism may question our belief in free will, it also opens new avenues of understanding ourselves and the world we inhabit.

Despite the initial fear and apprehension, these individuals found that embracing a deterministic worldview didn't diminish their sense of self or the richness of their lives. If anything, it enhanced their understanding of themselves and their relationships with others.

In the absence of traditional free will, Sarah learned to value her strengths and vulnerabilities more deeply. Understanding that her personality traits and abilities were not her 'choice' allowed her to shed the guilt and self-blame she'd previously felt for her perceived shortcomings. Sarah found peace in accepting herself as she was—determined by a host of factors beyond her control.

Tom, who had struggled with feelings of resentment and bitterness towards his parents for his troubled childhood, found solace in determinism. Realizing that their behavior, like his own reactions, were predetermined, he was able to let go of his anger. It didn't absolve them of the harm they'd caused, but it helped him heal and move on.

For Maya, the deterministic perspective added depth to her artistic expression. Rather than diluting her creativity, it enhanced her artwork, making each stroke a testament of her experiences, her environment, and her genetic composition. The colors on her canvas told stories of an interplay of deterministic forces, making her art even more profound and beautiful.

In Ben's case, the deterministic outlook gave him a greater appreciation of the interconnectedness of life. Every decision he made, every step he took, was an outcome of a grand chain of causes and effects. It made him feel like a part of a bigger tapestry, delicately woven by the threads of determinism. This realization didn't belittle him; instead, it amplified his sense of wonder and curiosity about life.

These reflections demonstrate how a deterministic view doesn't necessarily rob us of our individuality or life's vibrancy. Instead, it offers a different lens to view and understand our existence. Each of these individuals, in their unique ways, found that their lives without traditional free will were not just bearable but also meaningful, fulfilling, and profoundly human.

Determinism doesn't dictate a life devoid of purpose, joy, or growth. We can still dream, strive, and make a difference. We can still feel pain, regret, and joy. We can still love, create, and explore. What determinism does is shift the focus from an individualistic, isolated perspective to one of interconnectedness and unity. It challenges us to reconsider the concepts of blame, guilt, pride, and achievement.

In doing so, determinism enriches our lives, empowering us with a deeper understanding of our place in the universe. It enables us to navigate life with more acceptance, compassion, and wisdom.

Chapter 17: Freedom in a Deterministic World

As we move deeper into the heart of our discourse, we transition from the exploration of purpose and personal reflections in a deterministic world to a re-examination of our understanding of 'freedom.' How can we redefine and reclaim freedom within a deterministic framework? This is the overarching question that Chapter 17 sets out to answer. We will traverse the pathways of alternative perspectives, exploring how freedom can still exist and flourish even when unbound from the notion of free will.

As always, our quest will be guided by a relentless pursuit of understanding, empathy, and a desire to harness the insights for navigating our existence meaningfully.

17.1 Alternative Conceptions: A Fresh Look at Freedom

As we traverse deeper into the landscapes of determinism and its implications, it becomes increasingly paramount to reevaluate our understanding of certain fundamental concepts. Freedom, in particular, demands a fresh examination in the light of determinism. As established previously, the traditional conception of freedom - as the ability to do otherwise in a given situation - is challenged by deterministic ideas. This naturally prompts the question: Can we envisage freedom in a different light that accommodates determinism? The purpose of this section is to venture into alternative conceptions of freedom that can coexist with determinism, thereby, giving us a more nuanced perspective on the nature of freedom.

We briefly touch upon the notion of compatibilism – the philosophical proposition that free will and determinism are not necessarily incompatible. We have delved into this concept in detail in earlier sections of this book. Compatibilism offers an initial template to reconcile freedom and determinism. It posits that we can be free even if our actions are causally determined, as long as we act according to our internal desires and motivations.

A step further from this premise takes us to the concept of freedom as autonomy. Here, freedom is not perceived merely as the ability to act as per one's wishes, but rather the capacity for self-governance and self-directed behavior. The essence of autonomy lies in the capacity to set personal rules and principles and guide one's actions accordingly. This perspective is compatible with determinism, as it does not inherently require the ability to do otherwise, but emphasizes the alignment of actions with self-generated principles.

A second alternative conception is freedom as flourishing. This view correlates freedom with personal development and the actualization of one's potential. The freedom here is not only about making choices or being autonomous; it's about growth, self-discovery, and self-improvement. From this perspective, a person is free when they can develop their skills, foster their talents, and cultivate virtues. Such an understanding of freedom sits comfortably with determinism, as deterministic factors (genes, upbringing, social environment) can contribute to the development and expression of one's potential.

Finally, we explore freedom as the power to act. This conception emphasizes the capacity to transform thoughts and desires into actions. It's not just about having choices (real or perceived) or being the originator of actions, but about the capability to put plans into motion. From this angle, freedom becomes a question of empowerment, regardless of whether one's actions are causally determined or not.

These alternative conceptions invite us to look beyond the traditional dichotomy of free will versus determinism and open up novel ways of thinking about freedom. This journey of redefining freedom will continue in the next sections as we delve deeper into each of these conceptions, their implications, and their relevance in a deterministic world.

With the foundation laid for alternative conceptions of freedom, we now delve into the first notion: freedom as autonomy. To truly appreciate this perspective, we need to disentangle it from our traditional understanding of freedom. Autonomy is not about choosing A over B in a given moment, nor about being able to do otherwise if we rewind time. It's about being the source of our actions in a sense that reflects our personal identity, our values, and our principles.

Autonomy, in the philosophical sense, is deeply intertwined with notions of authenticity and individuality. It speaks of leading a life that is truly one's own, a life not dictated by external pressures or conformities but steered by the compass of personal integrity. Even in a deterministic framework, a life lived authentically, aligned with one's deeply held values and beliefs, is a life lived autonomously.

This concept becomes all the more pertinent in a deterministic world where external factors, unbeknownst to us, shape our desires, motivations, and choices. Autonomy emerges as the ability to introspect, to critically evaluate these factors, and to align our actions with our authentic selves. For instance, consider a person who grows up in an environment that valorizes academic achievement. Their desire to excel academically may seem like a predetermined path. Yet, if they introspect, critically assess this inherited value, and still decide to pursue it because it aligns with their authentic self, they exercise autonomy. The deterministic factors remain, but they do not infringe on the individual's autonomy.

However, the relationship between autonomy and determinism is not without complexities. The critical evaluation of one's values and desires could also be a deterministic outcome of one's upbringing and experiences. While this might challenge the notion of autonomy at first glance, it does not necessarily negate it. After all, our ability to reason and introspect is part of who we are as individuals. Thus, even if our critical thinking is shaped by deterministic factors, it still constitutes a part of our authentic selves and can contribute to our autonomy.

Dovetailing into this is the question of whether autonomy can exist in the absence of absolute free will, and if so, how. A possible response to this can be found in the philosophy of existentialism, particularly in the ideas of philosophers like Jean-Paul Sartre and Albert Camus. For them, life might be absurd and devoid of inherent meaning, but this does not preclude the possibility of individual freedom – not freedom from causality, but freedom in the sense of creating one's own meaning and purpose. Thus, they champion the idea of subjective freedom: the freedom to define who we are, what we stand for, and how we wish to navigate life.

If we apply this existentialist view to the question of autonomy within determinism, we can argue that regardless of the deterministic chains binding us, we can still exercise autonomy by actively creating and defining our personal meaning and purpose. This act of self-creation and self-definition is, in and of itself, an assertion of autonomy – the autonomy to narrate our own story, even within a deterministic framework.

Even more empowering is the idea of personal transformation or growth under this concept of autonomy. You may begin your life with certain deterministic factors guiding your course. However, as you live, experience, introspect, and learn, you can reshape your perspectives, values, and aspirations. This journey of personal growth, of becoming more than what your initial circumstances might have determined, can be seen as a profound exercise of autonomy.

Such an exercise of autonomy is perhaps best represented by the metaphor of a skilled sailor navigating treacherous seas. The sailor cannot control the sea or the weather, both of which are deterministic factors. However, by using their knowledge, skills, and courage, they can navigate effectively, reaching their destination despite the challenges. They do not break the laws of nature; rather, they work within these laws to exercise their autonomy and achieve their goals.

While exploring the concept of freedom as autonomy, we should be cognizant of the potential objections and pitfalls. The most obvious one is the risk of falling into a state of cognitive dissonance or self-delusion, where we convince ourselves of our autonomy while being blind to the deterministic factors shaping us. This is a legitimate concern and navigating it requires sincerity, humility, and continuous introspection.

While determinism might challenge our traditional conceptions of freedom, it does not necessarily negate the possibility of autonomy. By understanding freedom as a reflection of our authenticity, individuality, and ability to self-direct our lives in line with our values, we can reclaim a sense of agency, even within a deterministic framework. This perspective not only enriches our understanding of freedom but also opens up avenues for personal empowerment and growth.

However, even within this more expansive understanding of freedom, there still exist paradoxes and tensions that must be acknowledged and navigated.

For instance, the very notion of subjective freedom – the freedom to create our own meaning and purpose – seems to hinge on some degree of free will. If our thoughts and desires are determined by external factors, how can we genuinely claim that the purpose we create is indeed ours and not just a product of deterministic forces? How do we disentangle the threads of self-directed purpose from the deterministic fabric into which it is woven?

The key to resolving these tensions lies in acknowledging and integrating the reality of determinism into our understanding of freedom. In other words, rather than seeing determinism and freedom as opposed, we can see them as interrelated facets of our existence. While our thoughts, desires, and actions are undoubtedly influenced by deterministic factors, they are not entirely reducible to these factors.

We are complex beings capable of reflection, creativity, and change. And while these capacities are influenced by deterministic factors, they also enable us to transcend these factors to some degree. Our ability to reflect allows us to understand our deterministic influences and how they shape us. Our ability to be creative allows us to imagine alternative ways of being and acting. And our ability to change allows us to actualize these alternatives, reshaping our deterministic influences in the process.

This is not to deny the reality of determinism or to fall into a state of self-delusion. Rather, it is to fully embrace the complex interplay between determinism and freedom that defines our human condition. It is to recognize that while we are shaped by deterministic factors, we are not defined by them. We have the capacity to reflect upon, understand, and reshape these factors through our thoughts and actions.

This perspective of freedom can be quite empowering. It allows us to claim agency and responsibility for our lives, despite our recognition of determinism. It allows us to see that while we might not be free from causality, we are free to engage with it, understand it, and navigate it in ways that align with our values and aspirations.

Ultimately, the goal is not to find a way to eliminate or bypass determinism – a task that would be both impossible and self-defeating – but to find a way to live meaningfully within it. This is the essence of redefined freedom – a form of freedom that acknowledges and incorporates determinism rather than denying or fighting against it.

17.2 SELF-ACTUALIZATION AND SELF-DETERMINATION: THE NEW FACE OF FREEDOM

Beginning our exploration of self-actualization and self-determination, it's necessary to establish a fundamental understanding of these concepts, ensuring that we navigate uncharted waters rather than retracing previously tread paths. The idea of self-actualization was famously brought to the fore by psychologist Abraham Maslow, who posited it as the pinnacle of human psychological development. It signifies a state where a person realizes and fulfills their potential, reaching the zenith of their capabilities. Rather than it being a concrete end point, self-actualization is often seen as a continuous journey of growth and personal evolution, a process of becoming the best version of oneself.

Conversely, self-determination relates to the ability of an individual to make choices and manage their life without external interference. It embodies autonomy and independence, with a focus on personal decisions leading one's life trajectory. Now, these concepts of self-actualization and self-determination might appear in stark contrast to the deterministic framework we've been exploring, but a deeper exploration reveals a fascinating interplay that redefines freedom within this seemingly restrictive paradigm.

The deterministic universe postulates a cause-and-effect relationship, an inexorable chain of events set into motion by preceding conditions. In such a context, how can one self-actualize? How can one exercise self-determination? To resolve this paradox, we must delve into the realm of subjective experiences and the manifestation of personal identity within the deterministic fabric.

While the deterministic universe lays the blueprint for our existence, it doesn't negate the subjective experiences and our inner realities. Even though our thoughts, choices, and actions might be the result of a long chain of causality, they are still real and still ours. In a deterministic perspective, these are not illusions but an integral part of our identity – the reality we perceive, experience, and live every day.

When we speak of self-actualization, we refer to the process of recognizing, accepting, and pursuing our innermost desires and aspirations. It's about living authentically, embracing our strengths and weaknesses, our quirks and eccentricities, and expressing our unique identity through our actions and interactions. It involves living congruently with our values and beliefs, nourishing our passions, and realizing our potential. But how is this possible in a deterministic universe?

Let's consider an analogy. Imagine life as a grand piece of music written by the deterministic forces of the universe. We are musicians, and our instrument is our brain. Even though the composition is predetermined, it is our unique interpretation and expression of the piece that gives it life. Each musician brings their personal touch, their emotions, their experiences to the performance. Despite the notes being set in stone, the music that fills the air is unique, vibrant, and deeply personal. Similarly, in a deterministic universe, we bring our unique flavor to the predetermined course of our lives.

Our aspirations, passions, values, and beliefs are a part of the unique configuration of our brains shaped by the deterministic forces. When we live in alignment with them, we self-actualize. Our unique configuration influences how we interpret and navigate the deterministic world, shaping our decisions, choices, and actions.

Maslow's hierarchy of needs, which outlines the progression from basic physiological needs to self-actualization, offers a valuable framework for understanding this process. However, it's essential to view this not as a sequence of stages that one must pass through sequentially but rather as an interconnected web of needs that shape our experience and understanding of the world.

In a deterministic framework, each stage in Maslow's hierarchy can be seen as a response to different types of determinants. For instance, physiological needs (food, shelter, warmth, rest) are primarily driven by biological determinants, while safety needs (security, safety) are influenced by environmental determinants. As we progress up the hierarchy, the determinants become more complex and multifaceted, involving social, cultural, and psychological determinants. The need for esteem (feeling of accomplishment) and love and belonging (intimate relationships, friends) reflect the influence of social and cultural determinants.

At the top of the hierarchy, self-actualization represents the pinnacle of human aspiration, where one strives to achieve their full potential, including creative activities. In a deterministic universe, it's the unique combination of all these determinants that shape an individual's path towards self-actualization.

Understanding self-actualization in this deterministic framework not only enriches our understanding of the concept but also provides us with practical tools to cultivate it. Acknowledging that our journey is shaped by multiple determinants can lead us to become more open-minded, empathetic, and understanding of ourselves and others. It encourages us to view life as a journey of discovery, where we continually uncover and explore the various determinants that have shaped us into who we are.

If self-actualization seems like a lofty and distant goal in a deterministic world, it's worthwhile to consider how self-determination theory can provide a practical and accessible pathway towards this aspirational peak. According to psychologists Edward Deci and Richard Ryan, self-determination theory is a macro theory of human motivation, personality development, and well-being, which suggests that people are motivated to grow and change by three innate and universal psychological needs. These needs are autonomy (the desire to control and regulate one's own life and actions), competence (the need to master tasks and learn different skills), and relatedness (the desire to feel connected to others, to care, and to be cared for).

In a deterministic framework, the emphasis on autonomy may seem paradoxical. How can one exert control and direction in a universe where every action and decision is preordained? The answer lies in the understanding of autonomy in a nuanced way. Autonomy, in this context, does not refer to the ability to act independently of causation or deterministic laws but to the ability to act in harmony with one's authentic self and values. It's the difference between being driven by external pressures and demands, and being guided by intrinsic values and aspirations.

It's worth noting that determinism does not imply that all behaviors and choices are equally determined. While we cannot step outside the causal chain that governs the universe, we can understand and work with it to shape our lives more effectively. Recognizing the deterministic factors that influence our behaviors and choices - from genetic predispositions to environmental influences - can empower us to steer our lives in directions that align with our authentic selves and values.

This notion of self-determined autonomy aligns closely with the Stoic philosophy's concept of living in accordance with nature. The Stoics, too, recognized the pervasive role of causation in shaping our lives and encouraged individuals to understand and embrace it rather than resist or deny it. In the words of Epictetus, "Do not seek to have events happen as you want them to, but instead, want them to happen as they do happen, and your life will go well."

Developing competence in a deterministic world, on the other hand, can be thought of as a process of discovery rather than creation. It's not so much about creating abilities and skills out of nothing, but about discovering, nurturing, and refining the abilities and skills that are already within us. In this sense, determinism does not stifle or limit the development of competence; rather, it guides and informs it.

For example, if we accept that our abilities and potentials are largely determined by our genetic makeup and early life experiences, then it makes sense to focus our efforts on areas where we have natural strengths or predispositions. Instead of trying to become something we're not, we can aim to become the best versions of who we already are. This approach to developing competence aligns with the strengths-based approach in positive psychology, which emphasizes the cultivation of individual strengths and virtues.

Moreover, recognizing that our abilities and potentials are not entirely within our control can cultivate a healthier attitude towards failure and setbacks. Instead of attributing failures to personal inadequacies, we can view them as inevitable outcomes of deterministic factors beyond our control. This perspective can foster resilience, perseverance, and a growth mindset – attributes that are crucial for competence and mastery.

Relatedness, the third psychological need identified by self-determination theory, is perhaps the most unaffected by a deterministic worldview. The human desire for connection and belonging is universal and innate, and determinism does not diminish or invalidate this desire in any way. In fact, acknowledging the deterministic factors that shape our thoughts, emotions, and behaviors can deepen our understanding and empathy for ourselves and others.

For instance, recognizing that a person's behaviors are influenced by their genetics and environment can foster a sense of compassion and understanding for individuals who might otherwise be judged harshly. This recognition can also foster a sense of humility and interconnectedness, as we realize that our successes and achievements are not entirely our own, but the products of numerous deterministic factors that have shaped our lives.

The deterministic worldview, far from fostering a sense of helplessness or fatalism, can empower individuals to navigate their lives with greater wisdom, compassion, and authenticity. By acknowledging and understanding the deterministic factors that shape our lives, we can guide our lives in directions that align with our true selves and values, cultivate our strengths and abilities, and foster deeper and more meaningful connections with others. In this way, determinism does not extinguish the flame of self-actualization and self-determination, but fuels it with a more nuanced and realistic understanding of human nature and existence.

Yet, as illuminating and empowering as this deterministic perspective may be, it is crucial to acknowledge that it may not resonate with everyone. There may be individuals who find the deterministic worldview disheartening, disempowering, or even terrifying. These individuals may resist or reject the deterministic worldview, clinging instead to the belief in radical free will as a source of hope, comfort, and agency. This resistance or rejection is itself an expression of self-determination, a demonstration of individuals exercising their autonomy and self-direction in the face of challenging and potentially disquieting information.

Furthermore, the deterministic perspective on self-actualization and self-determination is not a one-size-fits-all approach. The specific ways in which individuals interpret and apply this perspective may vary widely, reflecting the diverse and multifaceted nature of human beings. Some individuals may find solace and empowerment in the deterministic understanding of their lives, while others may derive a sense of purpose and meaning from resisting or transcending deterministic influences.

It is also worth noting that the deterministic worldview does not necessitate the rejection of spiritual or religious beliefs. Many spiritual and religious traditions espouse deterministic elements, such as the belief in karma in Hinduism and Buddhism, predestination in Calvinism, or the will of God in Islam. These religious deterministic views often coexist with notions of free will and moral responsibility, reflecting the nuanced and complex interplay between determinism, free will, and morality in human consciousness and culture.

Additionally, while the deterministic worldview may challenge certain traditional notions of morality and responsibility, it does not negate the value or importance of moral and ethical behavior. Even if our thoughts, emotions, and actions are determined by factors beyond our control, we can still strive to behave in ways that align with our moral and ethical values. Indeed, the deterministic worldview can foster a deeper understanding of the root causes of harmful or unethical behavior, enabling more effective and compassionate responses.

Part of self-actualization and self-determination in a deterministic world involves understanding the limitations and constraints that determinism imposes on us, yet choosing to operate within these boundaries in a manner that aligns with our values and aspirations. From a deterministic viewpoint, self-actualization is not about manifesting an unbound potential or creating oneself from nothing, but about acknowledging, embracing, and navigating the unique configuration of genetic, environmental, and experiential influences that shape who we are.

One could argue that this deterministic perspective on self-actualization and self-determination is more realistic, grounded, and empowering than the traditional view of free will. Rather than placing the burden of absolute responsibility on individuals and blaming them for failing to overcome insurmountable obstacles, it recognizes the significant role of external factors in shaping individuals' thoughts, emotions, and behaviors. This understanding can foster empathy and compassion for oneself and others, which can be instrumental in promoting mental health, interpersonal relationships, and social harmony.

A deterministic perspective can also inform our approach to personal growth and self-improvement. By highlighting the causal influences on our thoughts, emotions, and behaviors, determinism can help us identify the areas of our lives that are amenable to change and those that are not. This awareness can enable us to focus our energy and resources on the aspects of ourselves that we can realistically improve or alter, instead of struggling against immutable traits or circumstances.

For instance, if we recognize that our propensity for procrastination is partly influenced by our genetic makeup, we may stop berating ourselves for our lack of willpower and instead explore strategies that can help us manage this trait more effectively. These strategies might involve structuring our environment in ways that minimize distractions, breaking tasks into smaller, manageable chunks, and using rewards and punishments to motivate ourselves. In this way, determinism can inspire a more adaptive, targeted, and effective approach to self-improvement.

In summary, the deterministic understanding of self-actualization and self-determination provides a fresh, nuanced, and potentially empowering perspective on freedom. By acknowledging and embracing the constraints imposed by determinism, we can navigate our lives more wisely, compassionately, and effectively. This perspective invites us to redefine freedom, not as the ability to act without constraints, but as the capacity to operate optimally within the given constraints, to shape and direct our lives in ways that reflect our unique configuration of deterministic influences.

17.3 Freedom Within Constraints: The Expanded View

As we venture into this expanded view of freedom, we must recognize that determinism does not strip away our agency or our ability to make choices. On the contrary, it offers us a renewed perspective on our ability to operate within constraints, a perspective that empowers us to navigate our lives effectively and make the most of our deterministic influences.

When we talk about freedom within constraints, we are referring to a kind of freedom that is not absolute, but relative to our circumstances. We acknowledge that while we are constrained by various deterministic factors – our genes, upbringing, experiences, and current circumstances – we still have a degree of latitude within these constraints. This latitude allows us to influence the course of our lives, make meaningful choices, and strive towards our goals and aspirations.

For instance, if we accept that our genetic makeup predisposes us to certain behaviors, we might feel confined by these predispositions. However, if we understand these predispositions as tendencies rather than destinies, we can realize that while they influence our behavior, they do not dictate it. We have the freedom to choose how we respond to these tendencies. We can acknowledge them, learn to manage them, and strive to align our behaviors with our values and aspirations, despite these predispositions. This is the essence of freedom within constraints.

The concept of freedom within constraints also challenges the conventional view of freedom as an all-or-nothing concept. Instead, it invites us to see freedom as a continuum. On this continuum, absolute freedom, or the ability to act without any constraints, is an unrealistic and unattainable ideal.

Conversely, absolute determinism, or the complete absence of freedom, is a theoretical construct that does not reflect the complexity and dynamism of human behavior. The reality of our lives lies somewhere in between these extremes.

From a deterministic perspective, it might be argued that we are utterly constrained, that our lives are wholly pre-determined by forces beyond our control. However, such an extreme view of determinism overlooks the nuances of the human experience. It fails to account for the complex interplay of deterministic and probabilistic factors that shape our lives. It does not capture the agency that we exercise when we make choices, pursue our goals, and navigate the challenges of our lives.

In this regard, our understanding of freedom needs to be nuanced. It needs to reflect the realities of our lives – the realities of operating within constraints. We can never be entirely free of deterministic influences, but that does not mean that we are powerless. We have the power to choose, within the constraints that we face. We have the power to strive, to aspire, to evolve, and to make our mark on the world.

Consider, for instance, the creative process. When an artist creates a work of art, they operate within certain constraints – the materials they have at their disposal, the techniques they have mastered, the influences they have absorbed, and even their creative vision. These constraints shape their creative process and influence their work. Yet, it is within these constraints that the artist finds their freedom – the freedom to express themselves, to experiment, to innovate, and to create something unique and meaningful. This is a testament to the power of freedom within constraints.

Likewise, when we navigate our lives, we operate within certain constraints – our circumstances, our abilities, our resources, our influences, and even our aspirations. These constraints shape our lives and influence our choices. Yet, it is within these constraints that we find our freedom – the freedom to choose, to strive, to grow, and to make our lives meaningful.

This expanded view of freedom, which acknowledges the constraints we face, is not a surrender to determinism, but a bold and resilient affirmation of our agency. It is a recognition of our power to navigate the complexities and uncertainties of our lives, to make choices that reflect our values, and to pursue our aspirations with courage and tenacity. It is a celebration of our capacity for growth, adaptation, and resilience.

It is also a reminder that we are not passive recipients of our fate, but active participants in shaping our destiny. We may not control the deterministic forces that influence our lives, but we can control how we respond to them. We can choose to be proactive, to take initiative, to seize opportunities, and to create possibilities. We can choose to learn, to grow, to evolve, and to make our mark on the world.

In this regard, the expanded view of freedom is an empowering perspective. It invites us to rise above our constraints, to transcend our limitations, and to realize our potential. It encourages us to embrace the challenges of our lives, to engage with the world around us, and to make a meaningful contribution to society. It motivates us to strive for excellence, to pursue our passions, and to lead a fulfilling and rewarding life.

In sum, the expanded view of freedom is a call to action. It is a call to seize the day, to make the most of our lives, and to become the best version of ourselves. It is a call to celebrate our humanity, to honor our dignity, and to embrace our destiny. And it is a call to embark on the journey of self-discovery, self-actualization, and self-determination – a journey that is at once challenging and rewarding, demanding and fulfilling, and ultimately, deeply meaningful.

Finally, the expanded view of freedom demands our responsibility. If we are to claim our capacity for agency and initiative within the deterministic framework, we must also accept the obligations that come with it. We must take responsibility for our actions and their consequences. We must be accountable for our decisions and their outcomes. We must understand that our freedom to choose entails the duty to choose wisely and ethically.

This aspect of the expanded view of freedom can be challenging. It can be difficult to accept responsibility, to admit our mistakes, and to take the blame when things go wrong. But it is also an essential part of being human. It is part of our moral growth, our ethical development, and our personal maturation.

Moreover, responsibility is not just a burden or a duty, but a source of empowerment and fulfillment. It gives us a sense of control over our lives. It allows us to shape our identity and define our character. It helps us build relationships of trust and respect. It enables us to contribute to the well-being of others and the common good.

The expanded view of freedom - to be free within constraints - is a rich and multifaceted concept. It includes the capacity for agency, the potential for growth, the resilience to navigate obstacles, the commitment to responsibility, and the joy of self-actualization. This view of freedom might be different from the traditional notion of free will, but it provides a new and inspiring way to understand our place in the deterministic universe. It provides a new lens to appreciate our lives, not as a series of predetermined events, but as a journey of self-discovery, self-improvement, and self-fulfillment.

17.4 STORIES OF FREEDOM: ILLUSTRATIONS AND EXAMPLES

As we journey through this exploration of freedom in a deterministic world, it is essential to remember that the theories, principles, and concepts we discuss are not simply abstract ideas. They live and breathe in the world around us, reflected in the stories of individuals, societies, and nations. Stories possess a unique power to illuminate the human experience, to breathe life into ideas, and, most importantly, to make the abstract tangible. They offer us a means to contextualize and understand complex concepts in a relatable way. It is through stories that we learn, empathize, and ultimately, grow. In this section, we will delve into narratives that showcase the various forms of freedom we've discussed. We will explore the triumphs, struggles, and the profound moments of realization that punctuate the journey towards freedom, despite the deterministic forces at play.

Story 1: Overcoming Constraints - The Journey of Malala Yousafzai

Let's start with a tale of courage and resilience, a story that resoundingly demonstrates the power of an individual to overcome oppressive constraints and assert their freedom. We look at the life of Malala Yousafzai, the youngest Nobel laureate in history, who stood against the Taliban's oppressive regime in her home country of Pakistan to fight for girls' right to education.

Born into a modest family in the Swat Valley of Pakistan, Malala's life was bound by many constraints - social, economic, and political. The emergence of the Taliban, an extremist group enforcing a harsh interpretation of Islamic law, only added to these constraints. They banned music, controlled people's daily lives, and most shockingly for Malala and her peers, they forbade girls from attending school.

From a young age, Malala possessed a deep appreciation for education. Encouraged by her father, an educator and an advocate for girls' education, Malala viewed education as a tool of liberation - a means to break free from the chains of ignorance and to challenge the unjust structures of society. Her passion for learning made the Taliban's edict a direct affront to her values and her freedom. So, instead of succumbing to the oppressive constraints, she chose to resist.

Through her blog for the BBC, she narrated the struggles of living under the Taliban rule, painting a vivid picture of the human rights abuses that were taking place. She used her voice, her words, to claim her freedom - the freedom to learn, to grow, and to aspire. Her resistance did not come without a price. In 2012, she was shot by the Taliban but survived the assassination attempt. Instead of silencing her, the incident amplified her voice on the global stage, turning her into a symbol of peaceful resistance.

Malala's story is one of resilience and determination. It demonstrates that even when faced with the most significant constraints, individuals can find ways to assert their freedom. It is a powerful reminder that the human spirit, armed with conviction and courage, can challenge deterministic forces and carve its path.

Story 2: The Liberation of Choices - Viktor Frankl and the Last of Human Freedoms

The next story takes us to the gruesome landscapes of Nazi concentration camps, into the life and thoughts of a remarkable psychiatrist - Viktor Frankl. His story embodies the concept of 'freedom within constraints' and exemplifies how, even in the harshest of realities, humans can exercise a profound form of freedom.

Viktor Frankl, an Austrian psychiatrist, and a Jew, spent three years in Nazi concentration camps, including Auschwitz. The conditions were horrifying, dehumanizing - a chilling testament to the depths of human cruelty. His family perished in these camps, and Frankl himself was subjected to brutal physical labor, starvation, and constant threat of death. His external freedom was undeniably stripped away. Yet, Frankl found a form of freedom that transcended the physical and situational constraints - the freedom to choose one's attitude and responses in any given set of circumstances.

In his book 'Man's Search for Meaning,' Frankl wrote: "Everything can be taken from a man but one thing: the last of the human freedoms—to choose one's attitude in any given set of circumstances, to choose one's own way." He believed that even in the direst situations, humans could exercise their freedom to choose their attitude, find meaning in their suffering, and thereby preserve their dignity and identity.

Frankl's philosophy, known as logotherapy, posits that the primary motivational force in humans is the pursuit of meaning. He emphasized that this search for meaning is a choice available to every individual, irrespective of their circumstances. By consciously choosing to seek meaning, even in suffering, one can experience a sense of purpose and direction that can help them navigate through life's darkest hours. This profound form of freedom - the freedom to choose one's attitude and to find meaning - is a testament to the indomitable human spirit and its ability to transcend the deterministic forces of environment and circumstance.

Viktor Frankl's story and his philosophy are an affirmation of human freedom in its most profound form. They remind us that while our environment and circumstances may impose constraints on our physical realities, our mental and emotional worlds always retain the capacity for self-determination.

Story 3: The Choice of Non-Violence - Martin Luther King Jr.

Our third story brings us to the heart of the American Civil Rights Movement, where a young Baptist minister named Martin Luther King Jr. stood at the forefront. Driven by a profound sense of justice, equality, and human dignity, he championed nonviolent resistance as a potent force against racial segregation and social injustice. His story demonstrates how freedom is not just about the ability to make choices but also about the moral courage to make the right ones.

Born into an era of institutionalized racism and segregation, King faced systemic discrimination and prejudice that sought to limit his potential and dictate his life's path. His personal and professional experiences exposed him to the ugly realities of racial inequality, prompting a deep desire for social change. But instead of succumbing to bitterness, resentment, or violence, King chose a path of non-violence, inspired by the teachings of Mahatma Gandhi.

King's philosophy of nonviolent resistance became a defining feature of the Civil Rights Movement. He believed that nonviolence was not a strategy of passivity but a method of active resistance that challenged the status quo through moral strength and integrity. By choosing nonviolence, King and his followers took control over their responses to oppression, thus exercising their freedom in the face of systemic constraints.

King's "Letter from Birmingham Jail" is a powerful testament to his belief in freedom within constraints. Arrested for his part in nonviolent protests, King wrote this letter responding to critics who called his actions "unwise and untimely". In the letter, King emphasized that the oppressed cannot wait for a convenient time to demand their rights. They must create tension in society that forces people to confront the issue. This was a proactive choice, a demonstration of freedom within the constraints of a deeply unjust system.

King's life, his commitment to non-violence, and his leadership during the Civil Rights Movement underscore the concept of freedom within constraints. Even within a system that sought to limit his choices and control his destiny, King exercised his freedom in a profound and impactful way, making choices that not only transformed his life but also altered the course of history.

Story 4: Redefining Freedom - The Story of Stephen Hawking

Our final story is of Stephen Hawking, one of the most influential scientists in the history of physics. Diagnosed with a debilitating motor neurone disease at the age of 21 and given only two years to live, Hawking's life was bound by physical constraints that would seem unimaginable to most. Yet, within these constraints, Hawking redefined his personal concept of freedom, demonstrating that limitations could become catalysts for extraordinary accomplishments.

Faced with a life bound to a wheelchair and the progressive loss of most bodily functions, Hawking's physical world shrank dramatically. Yet, his intellectual universe expanded. He used his condition as a motivation to delve into the mysteries of the cosmos, driven by the desire to uncover the fundamental laws that govern the universe.

Hawking's exploration of the universe was not hindered by his physical constraints. Instead, it was liberated by them. His body may have been imprisoned by his disease, but his mind was unbounded. As he once said, "Although I cannot move and I have to speak through a computer, in my mind, I am free."

Hawking's life exemplifies freedom within constraints. His physical world was full of restrictions, but his intellectual world was limitless. Despite his disease, he made groundbreaking contributions to cosmology, particularly in the study of black holes and the nature of time.

Furthermore, Hawking's ability to communicate complex ideas to the public despite his severe speech impediment highlights another form of freedom within constraints. He was able to express his thoughts through a voice synthesizer, displaying his intellectual prowess to the world.

In conclusion, the stories of freedom, as exemplified by these individuals, illustrate that freedom can be conceptualized and experienced within deterministic and constrained realities. Freedom is not just about the ability to make unconstrained choices but involves the exercise of moral autonomy, the pursuit of self-actualization, and the resilience of the human spirit in the face of adversity. The understanding of freedom is incomplete without acknowledging the capacity for individuals to exercise freedom within constraints, highlighting the complexities, paradoxes, and richness of the human experience.

Chapter 18: Living a Life Without Freewill

Having traversed the landscape of determinism, explored its implications on our understanding of free will, and probed the depths of its impact on morality, ethics, and personal meaning, we arrive at our final destination: practical navigation. This concluding chapter is designed to serve as a compass for readers, offering strategies and tools to manage life in the shadow of determinism. The insights from the preceding chapters have prepared us for this moment, equipping us with a fresh perspective to confront the challenges and possibilities of a life without free will. Now, we turn our attention to concrete, actionable paths forward, providing a guide to not just surviving, but indeed thriving in a deterministic world.

18.1 Coping Strategies: Surviving Without Free Will

As we commence this final stage of our journey, we stand at the precipice of a seemingly daunting reality - the idea of a life in which our actions and decisions are not as free as we once thought. Accepting a deterministic view can be an emotionally arduous process, potentially leading to feelings of disorientation, fear, and even existential dread. However, it's important to remember that these feelings are natural responses to a significant paradigm shift. This section aims to guide you through these emotional landscapes, offering strategies that can help not just in surviving, but in thriving, within a deterministic framework.

Focus on What You Can Control

Our first step towards learning how to cope with a deterministic view is to focus on the aspects of life that we can control. This is a fundamental concept derived from Stoic philosophy, which holds that while we may not control external events, we can control our reactions and perspectives towards them. The Stoic philosopher Epictetus famously said, "We cannot choose our external circumstances, but we can always choose how we respond to them." Indeed, while we may not control the causal chain of events leading to our present moment, we can control how we interpret and respond to our circumstances.

In a deterministic universe, our actions might be determined by a chain of previous events, but that does not negate our capacity to engage in thought processes, make decisions, and exercise our abilities to reason and learn. By focusing on what we can control – our reactions, our mindset, our actions – we can navigate life more effectively, even within a deterministic framework.

Consider, for instance, a challenge you might be facing in your personal or professional life. You may not have had control over the circumstances that led to this situation, but you can control how you respond to it. You can choose to view it as an insurmountable problem or as an opportunity for growth. You can choose to be proactive and look for solutions, or you can succumb to frustration and inaction. By focusing on what you can control, you empower yourself, reclaiming agency within a deterministic world.

Finding New Meanings and Purposes

A deterministic worldview does not preclude the existence of meaning or purpose in our lives. Even if our actions are determined by factors beyond our control, that does not mean they are devoid of significance or value. The quest for personal meaning and purpose is an inherent part of our human experience, and it continues to hold relevance in a deterministic framework.

Understanding determinism can even serve to enrich our perspective on personal meaning. For instance, recognizing that we are part of a larger, interconnected web of causes and effects can cultivate a sense of unity and interconnectedness. We begin to see ourselves not as isolated beings, but as integral parts of a vast, complex, and beautifully intricate universe.

Moreover, the deterministic view can reinforce the importance of embracing our unique journeys, celebrating our achievements, learning from our mistakes, and growing from our experiences. After all, each of us is a unique product of an unrepeatable sequence of events, which is a profound and awe-inspiring realization. It encourages us to appreciate our individual stories and to strive towards creating a meaningful narrative within our given framework.

For instance, you might derive meaning from nurturing relationships, pursuing knowledge, advocating for causes you believe in, engaging in creative pursuits, or contributing to your community. These sources of meaning remain valid and significant, irrespective of whether your actions are determined or not. The process of finding and creating meaning, therefore, becomes a crucial strategy for coping with determinism.

Practicing Acceptance and Compassion

Another effective coping strategy is practicing acceptance and compassion. Acceptance here refers to the acknowledgment of determinism and the limitations it may impose, not a resignation or capitulation. It is about facing reality as it is, without denial or avoidance. Acceptance can alleviate the discomfort associated with the cognitive dissonance of holding onto the idea of free will while recognizing the evidence for determinism.

However, acceptance alone is not enough. It needs to be coupled with compassion – compassion for ourselves and others. The realization that we're all products of our genetic makeup, upbringing, environments, and a multitude of other factors beyond our control can engender a profound sense of compassion. Recognizing that people's actions and choices are heavily influenced by these factors can make us more understanding and forgiving of their faults and mistakes, just as we should be of our own.

This shift in perspective can have a transformative effect on our interpersonal relationships and our societal outlook. For instance, it can make us more empathetic towards individuals who come from difficult backgrounds, enhancing our understanding of social justice issues. Similarly, recognizing our own determined nature can foster self-compassion, helping us treat ourselves with kindness and understanding when we falter or fail.

Practicing acceptance and compassion can be challenging, but they offer a path towards greater emotional resilience and healthier relationships, thus serving as powerful coping mechanisms within a deterministic framework.

Reframing Success and Failure

In a deterministic world, our traditional notions of success and failure require reevaluation. If our actions are the result of a multitude of factors beyond our control, then the credit or blame we assign to ourselves for our successes and failures needs to be reconsidered.

Reframing how we view success and failure involves acknowledging the complex interplay of factors that contribute to our achievements and shortcomings. It means recognizing that our accomplishments are not just the result of our individual efforts but are also heavily influenced by circumstances that we didn't choose, such as our genetic predispositions, upbringing, socioeconomic conditions, etc.

Similarly, our failures are not solely our own but are often the result of external factors beyond our control. This realization can liberate us from the shackles of self-blame and regret that often accompany failures. It doesn't mean that we should dismiss our mistakes or absolve ourselves of responsibility. Instead, it encourages us to adopt a more nuanced understanding of our actions and their consequences, learning from our experiences without succumbing to debilitating self-criticism or shame.

For instance, if you didn't do well in an interview, instead of berating yourself for your perceived inadequacies, you could recognize that your performance was influenced by a host of factors – your state of mind on that day, the interviewer's disposition, the questions asked, etc. While you can strive to improve your interview skills, it's equally important to remember that not every outcome is within your control.

Reframing success and failure can lead to a healthier self-concept and a more balanced perspective on life, serving as an important coping strategy within a deterministic world.

Cultivating Flexibility and Open-Mindedness

Adapting to the deterministic perspective also involves cultivating flexibility and open-mindedness. As we've discussed in the earlier chapters, many of our societal norms and personal beliefs are built around the concept of free will. Letting go of these ingrained notions requires a flexible mindset that is open to new ideas and different perspectives.

It's about being willing to question our assumptions and reconsider our values in light of new understanding. It's about being open to the idea that our identity is not fixed but is shaped by a multitude of deterministic factors. It's about recognizing that our beliefs and attitudes, too, are not set in stone but can change and evolve over time.

Cultivating such a mindset can be challenging, given our natural resistance to change and our tendency to cling to familiar ideas and beliefs. However, it's an essential part of adapting to the deterministic perspective and can serve as an effective coping mechanism.

Flexibility and open-mindedness not only help us internalize the deterministic perspective but also enhance our capacity to deal with life's challenges more effectively. They enable us to adapt to new situations, learn from our experiences, and grow as individuals. They foster a sense of curiosity and a willingness to explore, allowing us to gain deeper insights into ourselves and the world around us.

In a deterministic world, flexibility and open-mindedness can serve as powerful tools for personal growth and self-improvement, enabling us to navigate life's ups and downs with greater ease and resilience.

Finding Meaning and Purpose

Finally, even in a deterministic world, it's possible—and indeed essential—to find meaning and purpose. As we've discussed in the previous chapter, meaning and purpose don't have to come from the belief in free will. They can be derived from our passions, values, relationships, and contributions to society, among other things.

Finding meaning and purpose involves identifying what's important to us, what brings us joy and fulfillment, and what aligns with our values. It's about setting goals that are personally meaningful and working towards them, not because we're free to choose any path but because these are the paths that resonate with our experiences, circumstances, and predispositions.

Finding meaning and purpose also involves contributing to something larger than ourselves. This can take many forms, from helping others to advancing knowledge in a particular field, to working towards social or environmental causes. Such contributions not only give our lives a sense of purpose but also reinforce our interconnectedness, reminding us that we're all part of a larger whole.

In a deterministic world, finding meaning and purpose can provide us with a sense of direction and a reason to strive, serving as an important coping strategy.

Navigating a deterministic world without free will can be daunting, but with the right coping strategies, it's not only possible but can also lead to a more nuanced understanding of ourselves and a more compassionate view of others. Whether it's through cognitive reframing, practicing acceptance and compassion, reframing success and failure, cultivating flexibility and open-mindedness, or finding meaning and purpose, we can learn to thrive within the deterministic framework.

18.2 SELF-AWARENESS AND MINDFULNESS: TOOLS FOR EMPOWERMENT

The journey through determinism has been challenging, even overwhelming at times. It can indeed feel like we're thrown into an ocean without a lifesaver. But as we continue to tread through the rough waters of understanding and accepting determinism, we realize that we have within ourselves the tools needed to stay afloat and even sail smoothly. Two of these tools are self-awareness and mindfulness, which we will explore in depth in this section.

Self-awareness can be likened to a mirror. It is the act of looking at ourselves, not just physically but also mentally and emotionally. It involves an understanding of our thoughts, feelings, motivations, and reactions. To be self-aware is to see and understand our place in the world, to know our strengths and weaknesses, and to acknowledge our needs and desires.

On the other hand, mindfulness is like a flashlight in the dark. It allows us to focus on the present moment, illuminating our experiences without judgment or reaction. It is being fully aware of what we are doing, feeling, or thinking at the moment without trying to modify it in any way. It involves acceptance of the present moment, acknowledging it without striving to change it.

Self-awareness and mindfulness are intertwined. One feeds into the other, creating a positive loop that promotes personal growth and acceptance. In a deterministic framework, these tools are invaluable.

Self-awareness allows us to comprehend our desires, actions, and reactions within a deterministic framework. We can analyze our responses, understand their origins, and thus manage them better. It can be a revelation to understand that our anger or sadness is not a reaction to the event itself but to the way we perceive it. It can be empowering to realize that our happiness is not necessarily a result of external events but of our internal perception and response to those events.

Mindfulness, on the other hand, brings us into the present, the only moment we truly have control over. It allows us to fully experience the here and now without clouding it with past experiences or future anxieties. It enables us to accept the present moment as it is, without judgment or a desire to change it. This acceptance is crucial in a deterministic framework where future events are not within our control.

By focusing on the present moment and accepting it as it is, we reduce stress and anxiety, promote mental clarity, and create a peaceful mind. This peaceful mind is more capable of understanding and accepting the deterministic nature of the world.

When we understand determinism and accept it, we become empowered. We are no longer at the mercy of the unpredictable future. Instead, we take control of the only moment we have – the present moment

Now, the question is, how do we cultivate self-awareness and mindfulness? It begins with intentional practice.

Practicing mindfulness could start with simple meditation exercises. You can begin by sitting in a quiet place and focusing on your breath. As thoughts come and go, observe them without judgment and return your focus to your breath. Over time, this simple practice can significantly improve your ability to stay present.

On the other hand, self-awareness can be cultivated through reflective practices like journaling or therapy. Writing down your thoughts and feelings can be a powerful way to understand yourself better. Similarly, talking to a therapist can provide valuable insights into your motivations and reactions.

Incorporating these practices into your daily life can lead to a significant shift in your understanding and acceptance of determinism. But remember, it's a journey and not a destination. So, be patient with yourself as you embark on this path.

Let's consider a few examples to illustrate the power of self-awareness and mindfulness.

Example 1: James is a successful entrepreneur, but despite his achievements, he struggles with feelings of insecurity and dissatisfaction. He constantly worries about the future of his business and fears that his success may not last. This chronic worry takes a toll on his mental health and his relationships. He can't fully enjoy his success because he's always anticipating potential disasters.

Through self-awareness, James can recognize these thought patterns and their impact on his life. He can acknowledge that these fears stem from his desire for control – control over the future, control over his business's success, and control over people's perception of him. Understanding these motivations allows him to approach his worries from a different perspective, realizing that he can't control everything.

Incorporating mindfulness into his daily routine, James learns to stay present. Instead of worrying about future uncertainties, he focuses on his current accomplishments and the joy they bring. He begins to find satisfaction in the present moment and realizes that he can't control the future, but he can control his response to the present. Gradually, his fears and insecurities lessen, and he begins to experience genuine happiness and contentment.

Example 2: Maria is a young woman who often feels overwhelmed by her emotions. When she's upset or angry, she reacts impulsively, leading to conflicts in her relationships and regrets later on. She feels like she's at the mercy of her emotions and often wishes she could react differently.

Self-awareness helps Maria understand her emotional patterns. She realizes that her reactions are often disproportionate to the events causing them, indicating that they might be triggered by deeper issues. For example, she discovers that her anger is often a response to feeling disrespected or unimportant, feelings that stem from her childhood experiences. This understanding allows her to differentiate between the trigger event and her emotional response, providing a buffer that reduces her impulsivity.

With mindfulness, Maria learns to stay present with her emotions, observing them without judgment. When she feels anger rising, she doesn't immediately react. Instead, she takes a moment to acknowledge her feelings and the thoughts accompanying them. This momentary pause gives her the opportunity to choose her response, preventing impulsive reactions and regrettable outcomes.

These examples illustrate how self-awareness and mindfulness, when practiced consistently, can lead to significant changes in our thoughts, emotions, and behaviors. They show that even in a deterministic world, we can find empowerment and control, not over external events, but over our internal world.

In conclusion, self-awareness and mindfulness offer valuable tools for navigating life within a deterministic framework. They help us understand ourselves better, remain present, and react to life's challenges in healthier ways. As we continue to practice self-awareness and mindfulness, we find that while we may not control the future, we can control our response to the present. And that can make all the difference.

Example 3: Consider Sarah, a high school teacher, who feels like she's stuck in a cycle of stress and burnout. The demands of her job, managing students, paperwork, and administrative duties, often leave her feeling drained and overwhelmed. Despite her passion for teaching, she begins to question whether she's in the right profession, as her stress levels seem unsustainable.

Sarah decides to incorporate self-awareness practices into her routine. She starts by observing her thoughts and emotions throughout the day, noticing patterns and triggers. She realizes that her stress spikes when she feels she's falling behind or not meeting her own high standards. This recognition is the first step in understanding her stress cycle.

Along with self-awareness, Sarah begins to practice mindfulness. During her lunch break, instead of working through her meal, she takes a few minutes to sit quietly, focusing on her breath and allowing her mind to rest. She also begins to apply mindfulness in her classroom, taking a moment to center herself before addressing her students, and encouraging her students to do the same.

Over time, Sarah notices a shift. The demands of her job haven't changed, but her reaction to them has. She becomes less reactive, more patient with herself and her students. By understanding her triggers and learning to stay present, she's able to navigate her stress and prevent burnout. She feels more engaged and satisfied with her work, reaffirming her love for teaching.

Example 4: Meet Tom, a father who feels disconnected from his family. His job demands long hours, and when he's home, he's often preoccupied with work-related concerns. He wishes he could be more present with his wife and children, but he feels caught in the cycle of work and worry.

Through self-awareness, Tom recognizes this disconnect and the toll it's taking on his family life. He sees that his preoccupation with work stems from his fear of failing as a provider. With this understanding, he can begin to address these fears and seek balance.

Incorporating mindfulness, Tom starts to intentionally carve out time for his family, making sure that during these periods, he's fully present. This means putting away his phone, not checking work emails, and focusing on his interactions with his family. Over time, these mindful moments build stronger connections and foster a sense of togetherness, enhancing his overall family life.

Each of these examples illustrates the transformative power of self-awareness and mindfulness. They highlight how these practices can empower individuals to navigate their emotional landscapes, foster meaningful connections, and cultivate fulfillment, even within a deterministic framework. When practiced diligently, self-awareness and mindfulness become guiding lights, helping individuals traverse the undulating terrain of life's joys and challenges. And so, we find, even without traditional free will, we have the power to influence our well-being, our relationships, and our life's journey.

Through these practices of self-awareness and mindfulness, we can observe and understand our patterns of thoughts and emotions and learn to respond instead of react. We may not have complete control over our circumstances or our initial reactions to them, but with these tools, we can influence our subsequent responses and our overall well-being.

This shift from a reactive state to a responsive one can have profound implications. It gives us a sense of agency within the constraints of determinism. It allows us to navigate life's challenges with grace and resilience. It helps us foster healthier relationships and find fulfillment in our everyday experiences. The key lies in cultivating this awareness and practicing mindfulness diligently and consistently.

As you explore these practices, remember that it's not about attaining perfection or eliminating all negative experiences. Life will continue to unfold with its inherent ups and downs. There will be moments of joy and moments of pain. Mindfulness and self-awareness are not about eradicating these experiences but learning to navigate them skillfully.

Remember, too, that these practices are deeply personal. What works for one person may not work for another. The goal is to explore and find what resonates with you, what helps you cultivate awareness, presence, and compassion for yourself and others. It's about finding your unique way of navigating life, even within the deterministic framework.

And so, we find that while our lives may be guided by deterministic principles, we are not devoid of influence or purpose. We can still find meaning, fulfillment, and joy. We can cultivate healthy relationships, pursue personal growth, and contribute to our communities. We can navigate the complexities of life with wisdom and compassion.

In the next section, we will explore further how to embrace uncertainty, a fundamental aspect of life, and find strength in acceptance.

So far, we have touched upon two significant tools that can help us navigate life in a deterministic framework: self-awareness and mindfulness. These practices guide us towards a better understanding of our thoughts, emotions, and actions, thereby equipping us with the ability to respond rather than react to situations. However, it is also important to remember that self-awareness and mindfulness are not about eliminating negative experiences or aiming for perfection. Life, with its ups and downs, continues to unfold, and the essence of these practices lies in navigating these experiences skillfully.

On a more extensive scale, they foster the creation of healthier relationships, assist in finding fulfillment in our everyday experiences, and encourage personal growth and contribution to our communities. They are a testament to the fact that even in a deterministic world, we can exert influence, find purpose, and experience joy. The next part of this journey involves developing the ability to embrace uncertainty.

Uncertainty is an inevitable part of life. Even in a deterministic universe where the future can theoretically be predicted based on the present, it is practically impossible for us to know or control everything that will happen to us. We live in a constant state of not knowing – not knowing what will happen next, not knowing why certain things happened in the past, and not knowing the best path to take in the present.

How do we navigate life with this inherent uncertainty? How do we find strength in acceptance? This is what we will explore in the next section.

18.3 EMBRACING UNCERTAINTY: FINDING STRENGTH IN ACCEPTANCE

In life, uncertainty is the only certainty. This paradoxical statement carries profound wisdom. Despite our best efforts to create order and predictability, life often unfolds in unexpected ways, leaving us to navigate the unknown. For many, this uncertainty can be unsettling, causing stress, anxiety, and fear. But what if we could reframe our perspective on uncertainty? What if, instead of resisting it, we learned to embrace it? And what if, in a deterministic universe, embracing uncertainty could become a source of strength and empowerment? That's what this section aims to explore.

Before we dive into strategies for embracing uncertainty, it's important to understand what it is and why it's such a significant part of our lives. In its simplest form, uncertainty refers to the state of being uncertain, of not knowing what will happen in the future. It's a fundamental aspect of human life. Despite our cognitive abilities to predict and plan, the future remains largely unknown to us.

But why do we fear uncertainty? It's primarily because humans are creatures of habit and comfort. We crave stability and predictability. Uncertainty threatens this comfort. It reminds us of our vulnerability and shakes our sense of control. But there's a paradox here. As we've explored throughout this book, from a deterministic perspective, everything in the universe, including our lives, follows precise laws of cause and effect. So, theoretically, if we knew all the variables, we could predict the future with complete accuracy.

Yet, we don't live our lives in a lab. We don't have access to all the variables. We live in a world full of complexity and chaos, where predicting even the simplest event can become incredibly difficult. The theoretical predictability promised by determinism clashes with the practical unpredictability of our lived experiences. This conflict, this tension between determinism and uncertainty, forms a crucial backdrop to our exploration.

So, how do we respond to uncertainty in a deterministic world? One way is through acceptance. Acceptance, in this context, doesn't mean passive resignation. It doesn't mean giving up or disengaging from life. Instead, it's about acknowledging the reality of our situation and working with it, not against it. Acceptance is about saying, "Yes, life is unpredictable, and that's okay. Yes, I don't have control over everything, and that's okay. Yes, I live in a deterministic universe, and that's okay." It's about releasing resistance and opening ourselves up to life as it is, not as we wish it to be.

When we practice acceptance, when we learn to embrace uncertainty, something transformative happens. We begin to find strength in the very thing we once feared. How? First, accepting uncertainty fosters personal growth. It pushes us out of our comfort zones, challenging us to adapt and grow. Second, it builds resilience. As we navigate life's unpredictability, we become more resilient, more capable of handling change and adversity. And finally, it promotes flexibility. Embracing uncertainty requires us to be flexible, to go with the flow of life rather than resist it.

Here, the concept of 'antifragility' comes into play. Coined by Nassim Nicholas Taleb, antifragility describes systems that actually improve when exposed to shocks, volatility, and randomness. In embracing uncertainty, we can aim to become antifragile, to not just withstand chaos but thrive in it.

Having understood the importance of embracing uncertainty, let's now explore some practical strategies for doing so.

Practice Mindfulness: Mindfulness is the art of being fully present in the moment, without judgment. It's about observing our thoughts, feelings, and sensations as they arise, without trying to change or resist them. This practice can help us become more comfortable with uncertainty by teaching us to stay present, even when we're uncomfortable or unsure.

Maintain a Growth Mindset: Cultivating a growth mindset involves viewing challenges as opportunities for learning and growth, rather than threats. When faced with uncertainty, instead of panicking or feeling overwhelmed, we can ask ourselves, "What can I learn from this? How can I grow?"

Develop Flexibility: Flexibility is the ability to adapt to changing circumstances. It involves being open to new experiences and willing to let go of old ways of thinking and doing. We can cultivate flexibility by regularly pushing ourselves out of our comfort zones and embracing change.

Foster Resilience: Resilience is our ability to bounce back from adversity. It involves developing coping strategies, seeking support when needed, and taking care of our mental and physical health. Resilience can be built through practices like regular exercise, meditation, and maintaining strong social connections.

Embrace Antifragility: As mentioned earlier, antifragility involves improving through exposure to volatility and randomness. We can embrace this concept by seeking out challenging experiences, taking calculated risks, and learning from our mistakes.

As we learn to embrace uncertainty, we find that it becomes a source of strength. Uncertainty pushes us to grow, to adapt, and to become more resilient. It teaches us to be present, to be flexible, and to see opportunities where others see threats. In a deterministic universe, where much of life is out of our control, embracing uncertainty can be empowering. It can provide us with a sense of peace, a sense of freedom, and ultimately, a sense of purpose.

In a world without free will, embracing uncertainty is not just a strategy; it's a necessity. It's a way to navigate the unpredictable waters of life and find meaning, purpose, and joy along the way. It's a way to take the deterministic framework that we've explored throughout this book and use it to empower ourselves, to become the authors of our own stories.

Cultivating Patience

In an era characterized by speed and instant gratification, cultivating patience may seem like a quaint, outdated notion. However, patience is more than just a virtue – it is a skill that can be developed and harnessed to help us better embrace uncertainty.

Patience involves being able to tolerate delays, difficulties, or discomfort without becoming unduly agitated or upset. It means accepting that some things cannot – and should not – be rushed. It also means recognizing that life unfolds at its own pace, regardless of our desires or demands.

When we practice patience, we allow life to unfold naturally. We give ourselves the freedom to experience and enjoy the present moment, without constantly worrying about what's next. We give ourselves the space to grow, learn, and adapt to new circumstances. We give ourselves the permission to be human, with all the messiness and unpredictability that entails. Here are some practical ways to cultivate patience in a deterministic world:

Meditation: Regular meditation can help us become more patient by training our minds to focus on the present moment and let go of our desire to control or predict the future.

Gratitude Practice: Cultivating gratitude can help us become more patient by shifting our focus from what we lack or desire to what we already have.

Reframing: Reframing involves changing the way we view or interpret a situation. Instead of seeing delays or obstacles as nuisances, we can view them as opportunities for growth and learning.

Mindfulness: Mindfulness involves being fully present and engaged in whatever we are doing. When we practice mindfulness, we become less impatient because we are not constantly thinking about the future or dwelling on the past.

Self-compassion: When we are kind and understanding toward ourselves, we become more patient with ourselves and others. Self-compassion can be cultivated through practices such as loving-kindness meditation and self-compassion exercises.

Embracing Imperfection

Often, our struggle with uncertainty arises from our deep-seated desire for perfection. We want our lives to be perfect, our decisions to be perfect, and our futures to be perfect. But life, by its very nature, is imperfect. It's full of surprises, missteps, and unexpected turns. And that's not necessarily a bad thing.

Imperfections can be beautiful. They make us unique, they give character to our lives, and they often lead to unexpected joys and discoveries. They also teach us to be humble, resilient, and adaptable. So instead of resisting imperfections, we can choose to embrace them.

Embracing imperfection involves adopting a mindset of growth and acceptance. It means recognizing that mistakes and failures are not the end of the world, but opportunities for learning and growth. It means accepting that we cannot control everything, and that's okay. It means being willing to let go of unrealistic expectations and ideals, and embracing life as it is, warts and all. Here are some practical strategies for embracing imperfection:

Acceptance and Commitment Therapy (ACT): ACT is a form of cognitive behavioral therapy that encourages people to embrace their thoughts and feelings rather than fighting or feeling guilty for them.

Self-Compassion: Practicing self-compassion means being gentle with ourselves when we make mistakes or face difficult situations. It means acknowledging our humanity and accepting that we are not perfect.

Growth Mindset: Cultivating a growth mindset means viewing challenges and failures not as evidence of unintelligence or deficiency, but as opportunities for learning and personal development.

Mindfulness: Mindfulness practice can help us accept our imperfections without judgment or resistance. It allows us to observe our thoughts, feelings, and experiences without labeling them as "good" or "bad."

Remember, accepting and embracing imperfection is not about settling for less than we deserve or abandoning our aspirations and standards. It's about finding peace and contentment in the present moment, and realizing that perfection is not a prerequisite for happiness and fulfillment.

Building Resilience in the Face of Uncertainty

The power of resilience cannot be overstated. It's our ability to bounce back from setbacks, adapt to change, and keep going in the face of adversity. Building resilience does not eliminate stress or erase life's difficulties, but it gives us the strength to tackle problems head-on, overcome adversity, and move on with our lives.

Resilience is not something we are born with, but a skill that we can cultivate. Here are some strategies to enhance your resilience in the face of uncertainty:

Stress Management: Learn healthy ways to cope with stress, such as meditation, exercise, or seeking social support. Stress can cloud our judgment and make it harder to deal with uncertainty, so managing it effectively can improve our resilience.

Mindset Shift: Challenge and change your thought patterns that reinforce uncertainty. For instance, instead of thinking, "I can't handle this," try thinking, "I will get through this."

Self-Care: Regularly engage in activities that help you relax and recharge. Self-care activities, like reading a book, taking a bath, or going for a walk, can help you maintain balance in your life.

Problem-Solving: Develop your problem-solving skills. When faced with a challenge, try to view it as an opportunity to grow and learn. Think about possible solutions, make a plan, and take action.

Positive Relationships: Build strong, positive relationships with supportive and trustworthy people who can offer help and advice when you're dealing with uncertainty.

Acceptance: Accept that uncertainty is a part of life and try to focus on things you can control.

By cultivating these skills, we not only enhance our ability to cope with uncertainty, but we also equip ourselves with the tools to navigate life's inevitable ups and downs with grace and poise.

Developing an Adaptive Mindset

In an uncertain world where free will might not be as it seems, having an adaptive mindset can be the key to thriving amidst the chaos. By being open to change and remaining flexible, we can adjust to new circumstances and continue moving forward despite the ambiguity that surrounds us. An adaptive mindset involves not resisting change, but rather embracing it as a natural part of life.

Start by reframing uncertainty. Instead of seeing it as something threatening, view it as an opportunity for growth. Uncertainty means that there are numerous possibilities available, and while we might not know what the future holds, we can be sure that it's brimming with potential.

Furthermore, remind yourself that it's okay not to have all the answers. In a deterministic universe, unpredictability doesn't necessarily mean that we're out of control, but rather that there's so much more to discover and understand.

It's also crucial to focus on what you can control. While we can't always control what happens to us, we can control our reactions and attitudes. By focusing on areas where you can make a difference, you'll feel more empowered and less overwhelmed by the circumstances.

Lastly, stay curious and keep learning. Uncertainty can often feel uncomfortable because it highlights what we don't know. Instead of letting this unsettle you, let it inspire you to learn more and broaden your horizons. Being a lifelong learner can help you adapt to new situations and make the most of the opportunities that uncertainty brings.

In embracing uncertainty, we find the strength to face whatever comes our way. It's not about eliminating doubt or fear, but rather about learning to live with it and using it as a tool to forge a meaningful and fulfilling life in a deterministic universe.

Cultivating Resilience

Resilience is the capacity to recover quickly from difficulties and adapt well in the face of adversity. It's a trait that is invaluable in a world that can often feel unpredictable and out of our control. Resilience does not mean not feeling the impact of life's hardships, but rather, it means being able to bounce back and grow from these challenges.

Begin by developing a strong support network. Being surrounded by supportive people provides a safety net that can help us navigate through difficult times. Having others to lean on provides not only emotional assistance but also different perspectives that can help us understand and manage our circumstances better.

Developing emotional intelligence can also strengthen resilience. This involves recognizing and managing our own emotions and understanding the emotions of others. By being more aware of our emotional responses, we can better regulate them and respond to adversity in healthier ways.

Maintaining a positive outlook is another crucial component of resilience. This doesn't mean ignoring life's challenges or pretending that everything is fine when it's not. Instead, it means keeping a hopeful outlook and focusing on what's going well even when things are tough.

Furthermore, take care of your physical health. Regular exercise, a balanced diet, and adequate sleep can enhance your mood, provide you with more energy, and boost your resilience. When our physical health is in check, we're better equipped to deal with emotional and psychological stressors.

Lastly, remember that resilience is not something that is developed overnight. It's a lifelong journey that requires patience, effort, and dedication. With each challenge that we overcome, we become a little more resilient, better prepared to face whatever life throws our way.

Embracing uncertainty might not always be easy, but it's an essential part of navigating a deterministic universe. By equipping ourselves with the tools and mindsets necessary to handle life's unpredictability, we can find strength and meaning amidst the chaos, paving the way for a fulfilling life without free will.

Embracing Uncertainty in Relationships

Often, our struggles with uncertainty extend to our relationships. We might worry about the future of a romantic partnership, the health of a loved one, or the stability of a friendship. It can be distressing to acknowledge that these things are largely beyond our control, yet it's an inevitable part of human relationships. Here, too, embracing uncertainty can lead to more meaningful connections.

Consider the uncertainties in your own relationships. They might involve unreciprocated feelings, unsaid words, or unresolved conflicts. Rather than letting these uncertainties create anxiety, see them as opportunities for growth and understanding. Engage in open conversations, express your feelings honestly, and listen empathetically to the other person's point of view. This process might be challenging and even uncomfortable, but it can deepen your relationships and make them more fulfilling.

Of course, not all uncertainties in relationships can or should be resolved. There will always be aspects of our loved ones' lives and experiences that we can't fully understand or control. Accepting this reality can allow for more authentic connections, as we let go of the need to control the other person and instead appreciate them as they are.

Remember, embracing uncertainty doesn't mean neglecting to work towards positive change or settle conflicts in our relationships. It simply means accepting that some things will always be beyond our control, and that's okay. Relationships, just like life itself, are not meant to be perfectly ordered and predictable. They are complex, dynamic, and beautifully uncertain.

Embracing Uncertainty: The Path to Personal Growth

At its core, embracing uncertainty is a powerful catalyst for personal growth. It's an invitation to question our deeply held beliefs, explore new perspectives, and engage more fully with the world around us. While uncertainty can be challenging, it is also an opportunity for profound learning and self-discovery.

Embracing uncertainty encourages us to take risks. When we acknowledge that the outcome of our actions isn't guaranteed, we can muster the courage to step out of our comfort zones and try new things. This could mean starting a new job, moving to a new city, or simply trying a new hobby. Regardless of the scale, these actions can open up new opportunities and experiences, leading to growth and fulfillment.

Finally, embracing uncertainty can foster resilience. Uncertainty is a fundamental part of life, and learning to navigate it effectively can make us more adaptable and better equipped to handle life's challenges. By viewing uncertainty as an opportunity rather than a threat, we can build resilience and develop a more optimistic outlook on life.

To conclude, embracing uncertainty is not about surrendering to chaos or living in constant fear of the unknown. Rather, it's about finding strength in acceptance, expanding our horizons, and learning to thrive amidst life's inherent unpredictability. This is the essence of a life lived without the illusion of free will, a life that is truly free and meaningful.

18.4 Practical Wisdom: Tips for Living Meaningfully

Throughout the course of this book, we have voyaged through vast realms of philosophy, psychology, and existentialism. We have scrutinized and scrutinized over the mind-bending puzzle of free will, determinism, and the complex intertwining of both. Yet, as much as the theory engages us, what truly comes to matter in the end is the practice: the pragmatic wisdom that emerges from these concepts and how we use them to charter our everyday lives with purpose and meaning. Thus, let us embark on this final section, a distillation of the entire journey's wisdom into pragmatic insights for living a meaningful life.

Perspective: The Gateway to Understanding

Our perspective is the lens through which we interpret our world. Every event, every interaction, every moment of joy or despair, is colored by the angle we view it from. The realization of our lives unfolding within the deterministic laws of the universe could usher in a profound shift in this perspective.

Instead of viewing ourselves as solitary entities, battling the world, this understanding unearths the vision of ourselves as an integral part of a universal symphony. Every action we take, every word we utter, contributes to the grand orchestra of existence. This realization can alleviate feelings of isolation and conflict, helping us adopt a more harmonious and inclusive perspective of life.

Practically speaking, cultivating this perspective requires conscious effort. It could be through daily meditation practices where we remind ourselves of our interconnectedness with the universe. Or it could be as simple as a contemplative walk in nature, where we allow ourselves to absorb the symphony of life unfolding around us.

These practices help us regularly touch base with our part in the universal flow, reinforcing our understanding of determinism, and imbuing us with a sense of belonging and peace.

Purpose and Meaning in the Quotidian

The question of purpose and meaning in a deterministic universe is a vital one. If our actions are not the product of free will, how do we derive meaning from them? The answer, perhaps surprisingly, is much closer to home than we might expect.

Determinism doesn't diminish the beauty of a sunset, the shared laughter between friends, or the contentment of a job well done. Instead, it provides a profound backdrop to these moments, casting them in a new light of understanding and acceptance.

The quest for purpose and meaning, therefore, is not a journey into the abstract but a venture into the very heart of our everyday lives. Every interaction, every accomplishment, every setback, contains within it seeds of purpose and meaning waiting to be discovered.

A 'Gratitude Journal' can be an effective tool for this purpose. Regularly jotting down things we are thankful for or moments that brought us joy can tune our minds towards the positive, helping us appreciate life's simple pleasures. Over time, we begin to see that the grand pursuit of purpose and meaning is not an outward journey but an inward realization.

The Art of Nurturing Relationships

Determinism brings a unique flavor to our relationships. It reinforces the understanding that every individual is a product of their circumstances and experiences, just as we are. This realization can instill a sense of patience and empathy in our interactions, helping us build deeper and more meaningful connections.

Active listening is a practical way to nurture relationships in a deterministic world. It involves fully focusing on the other person, withholding judgment, and giving them the space to express themselves. This deliberate attention not only shows respect but also allows us to understand their viewpoint from a deterministic perspective, further deepening our connection.

Resilience: The Anchor in the Storm

Life is a mixed bag of joys and challenges. In a deterministic universe, the understanding that we are not entirely in control of these fluctuations can provide a sturdy anchor during tough times.

Resilience, the ability to bounce back from adversity, is therefore an essential quality to cultivate. Simple practices such as maintaining a positive attitude, seeking support from loved ones, or pursuing hobbies that bring joy, can bolster our resilience. Additionally, reminding ourselves that challenging circumstances are often the most potent teachers can provide a sense of solace and purpose during difficult times.

Embracing the Present: Living in the Now

The deterministic viewpoint ushers in a new understanding of time. The past cannot be changed because it was governed by circumstances that led up to it. The future is yet to unfold, shaped by the accumulation of the past and the present. Thus, the only time we truly have is the present.

Embracing this realization liberates us from the shackles of past regrets and future anxieties. It allows us to fully immerse ourselves in the present moment, reaping its joy and learning from its challenges.

Meditation, particularly mindfulness, is a highly effective practice for embracing the present. By training our minds to focus on the present moment - the feel of our breath, the sensations in our bodies, the sounds around us - we learn to ground ourselves in the 'now'. Over time, this practice enables us to live more fully and peacefully, even amidst life's inevitable ups and downs.

Compassion: The Softening Touch

The understanding that each one of us is a product of a complex interplay of circumstances can infuse our hearts with a deep sense of compassion. We become more patient with ourselves and others, recognizing that our thoughts, emotions, and actions are influenced by factors beyond our immediate control.

Practically, we can cultivate compassion by regularly putting ourselves in others' shoes. When we witness behaviors that upset us or don't align with our values, we can pause and try to understand the circumstances that might have led to those actions.

We can also practice self-compassion by being kind to ourselves when we stumble or face setbacks. Instead of berating ourselves, we can acknowledge our human frailty, learn from our mistakes, and move forward with increased wisdom and grace.

Personal Growth: The Never-Ending Journey

In a deterministic world, personal growth becomes a continuous exploration of our potentials shaped by the interplay of circumstances and experiences. Every challenge or success we encounter can be viewed as an opportunity for growth.

We can foster personal growth by cultivating an open mindset that embraces learning and change. This might involve seeking new experiences, developing new skills, and remaining open to constructive feedback. The focus is on constant learning and evolution, propelling us to realize our potentials and contribute meaningfully to the world.

Harmony with Nature: Finding Peace in the Greater Scheme

While we may not have control over the deterministic workings of the universe, we can find peace in aligning ourselves with the natural rhythm of life. This entails respecting and cherishing the natural world, embracing its cycles and wisdom, and acknowledging our role as part of a greater, interconnected system.

Practically, we can cultivate harmony with nature through activities like spending time outdoors, practicing mindful eating, adopting sustainable living practices, and nurturing a sense of awe and wonder at the marvels of the natural world. Such practices help ground us, remind us of our interconnectedness, and enhance our emotional well-being.

Service: The Joy of Giving

In recognizing the deterministic nature of life, we can appreciate the role that society and other individuals have played in shaping our lives. This understanding naturally inspires a sense of gratitude and a desire to give back to the world in our unique ways.

Service can take many forms - volunteering for a cause we believe in, offering emotional support to someone in need, sharing our skills and resources for the betterment of society, or simply performing small acts of kindness in our daily lives. The act of giving not only contributes to societal well-being but also enhances our own sense of purpose and happiness.

Creative Expression: Unleashing the Inner Self

Despite living in a deterministic universe, we all possess a unique amalgamation of experiences, talents, and perspectives. Creative expression is a powerful means of exploring and sharing these unique facets of ourselves.

Whether it's through art, music, writing, dance, cooking, or any other form of creativity, we can express our emotions, ideas, and experiences in ways that resonate with others. Engaging in creative activities can also be therapeutic, helping us to process our feelings and experiences and infusing our lives with joy and fulfillment.

Community Building: Fostering Bonds of Connection

We are, by nature, social beings. The people around us – family, friends, community – greatly shape our experiences and our understanding of the world. As we realize that our actions are driven by deterministic factors, the value of fostering healthy and supportive relationships becomes even more apparent.

In practical terms, this can mean taking the time to nurture relationships with loved ones, getting involved in local community activities, or reaching out to those in need of support. It can also mean creating a culture of empathy, respect, and open communication within our social circles. By doing so, we can contribute to the wellbeing of others and, at the same time, enrich our own lives.

Lifelong Learning: Embracing the Journey of Growth

Understanding determinism can foster a profound sense of curiosity about life and the workings of the universe. It invites us to continuously explore, learn, and grow – to understand more deeply, to ask more thoughtfully, and to live more fully.

Lifelong learning can take many forms – reading, attending lectures or workshops, engaging in thoughtful conversations, or pursuing new experiences and skills. By remaining open and curious, we can broaden our horizons, deepen our understanding, and enrich our life experiences.

Meditation: Cultivating Inner Peace

Even as we navigate the deterministic realities of life, we can cultivate a sense of peace and stability within ourselves. One powerful tool for this is meditation – a practice that helps us to cultivate mindfulness, enhance self-awareness, and foster inner tranquility.

Whether it's through formal meditation practices like mindfulness or loving-kindness meditation, or simply through moments of quiet reflection in our daily lives, we can learn to navigate our experiences with greater equanimity. Over time, these practices can help us to cultivate a deep sense of inner peace, even amid the uncertainties and challenges of life.

Exploring the Arts: A Pathway to Understanding and Expression

Arts, in their various forms—be it painting, music, dance, literature, drama, or any other—offer a profound way to engage with our experiences and emotions. They can provide a medium to delve into our inner world, explore our thoughts and feelings, and express ourselves in ways that transcend the limits of language. In a deterministic framework, art can serve as a profound reminder of the depth of human experience.

Engaging with the arts need not mean becoming a master artist. It could be as simple as painting a picture, learning to play an instrument, writing a poem, or even just appreciating the beauty of a piece of art or music. This engagement can foster self-understanding, enhance emotional resilience, and offer a means to connect with others on a deeply human level.

Cultivating Gratitude: An Antidote to Despair

In a world without free will, it can be easy to fall into a trap of cynicism or despair. However, one powerful antidote to such feelings is the cultivation of gratitude. Despite the deterministic nature of our lives, there is much to be grateful for—the beauty of nature, the kindness of others, the simple pleasures of life.

Cultivating gratitude can be as simple as taking a moment each day to reflect on the things we appreciate. This practice can foster a sense of contentment, enhance our wellbeing, and provide a source of strength even in difficult times. Moreover, it can help us to recognize and appreciate the interconnectedness of our lives with the world around us.

Physical Activity: A Pillar of Wellbeing

Physical activity is a cornerstone of physical health, and it also plays a crucial role in our mental and emotional wellbeing. Regular exercise can enhance mood, reduce stress, improve sleep, and boost self-esteem. Furthermore, it can foster a sense of self-efficacy and resilience—qualities that can be especially valuable in navigating a life without free will.

Regular physical activity can take many forms—be it a brisk walk in the park, a yoga session, a game of soccer with friends, or a dance class. The key is to find activities that you enjoy and that suit your lifestyle. By incorporating regular physical activity into our lives, we can foster holistic wellbeing and enhance our capacity to navigate life's challenges.

Altruism: Finding Meaning in Service

Another key dimension of living meaningfully in a deterministic world is the cultivation of altruism—selfless concern for the wellbeing of others. By contributing to the wellbeing of others, we can find a sense of purpose and fulfillment that transcends our own individual existence.

Altruism can take many forms—from volunteering in our local community, to offering emotional support to a friend, to making lifestyle choices that contribute to the sustainability of our planet. These actions can foster a sense of interconnectedness, enhance our sense of purpose, and enrich our life experiences.

Developing Patience: The Virtue of Time

In a deterministic framework, developing patience can be a powerful tool to weather the storms of life. Understanding that our circumstances, reactions, and even our feelings are a result of a network of causes and effects can provide us with a more tolerant and patient perspective towards life. Recognizing that even the harshest of situations are temporary can imbue us with the patience needed to endure and navigate these times.

Developing patience can be a mindful practice in itself, where we deliberately slow down our pace, taking time to breathe, reflect, and choose our responses. This does not mean resignation, but rather developing an understanding and accepting approach to life's ups and downs.

Fostering Resilience: Embracing Challenges

Even in a deterministic world, cultivating resilience enables us to bounce back from adversities and maintain balance in our lives amid difficulties. Resilience is not about avoiding stress or living a problem-free life; instead, it's about developing a mental and emotional fortitude to cope with, adapt to, and recover from stress, adversities, and life's changing circumstances.

Building resilience can involve several components such as maintaining a positive view of oneself, accepting that change is a part of life, and learning to manage strong feelings and impulses. It also includes taking decisive actions rather than detaching completely from problems and stress, seeking opportunities for self-discovery and growth, and nurturing a positive outlook.

Finding Joy in the Mundane: Cultivating Mindfulness

Mindfulness, the practice of paying attention to the present moment non-judgmentally, can be a powerful tool in finding joy and satisfaction in everyday activities, even in a life without free will. It can transform mundane tasks like washing the dishes, cooking a meal, or taking a walk into a source of joy, wonder, and contentment.

When we bring a mindful attitude to these activities, we can discover new aspects and experiences even in the most routine tasks. This can bring a sense of novelty and excitement to our lives, enhancing our overall satisfaction and contentment.

Maintaining Balance: The Key to Holistic Wellbeing

Maintaining balance in various aspects of life—physical, emotional, social, spiritual, and intellectual—is essential for holistic wellbeing in a deterministic world. Ensuring balance does not mean every aspect must receive equal attention; rather, it's about ensuring that no single area consistently overpowers the others.

Maintaining balance can involve setting boundaries, managing time efficiently, fostering positive relationships, and caring for physical health. Regular self-reflection can help identify any areas that might need more attention or any areas that might be receiving too much attention, thereby disrupting the balance.

Investing in Personal Growth: Seeking Evolution

Understanding the concept of determinism can allow us to approach personal growth from a unique angle. Instead of stressing about the changes we want to make, we can focus on setting the right causes in motion that will eventually lead to the desired effects.

Investing in personal growth can involve reading widely to broaden our understanding of the world, taking up new hobbies, enrolling in courses for skill development, and consistently reflecting on our beliefs and actions. This focus on self-improvement not only enhances our capabilities and expands our knowledge but also contributes to our self-esteem and sense of accomplishment.

Cultivating Empathy: Understanding Others

In a deterministic perspective, cultivating empathy can be particularly enlightening. Recognizing that others, like us, are also a product of numerous factors beyond their control can deepen our understanding and compassion for them. Empathy is not about condoning harmful actions or attitudes; rather, it's about realizing the complex web of factors that have shaped an individual.

Cultivating empathy can involve active listening, putting ourselves in others' shoes, and suspending judgment. This not only improves our relationships but also enhances our emotional intelligence and contributes to a more understanding and compassionate society.

Embracing Imperfection: Letting Go of Perfectionism

Understanding determinism can also help us let go of perfectionism. Recognizing that our abilities, skills, and outcomes are determined by an extensive network of causes and effects can liberate us from the constant pursuit of perfection and the resulting stress and dissatisfaction.

Embracing imperfection can involve adopting a growth mindset, where we view mistakes & failures as opportunities for learning and growth rather than indications of inadequacy. It can also involve practicing self compassion, where we treat ourselves with kindness and understanding when we fall short of our own or others' expectations.

Practicing Gratitude: Acknowledging the Good

In a deterministic universe, practicing gratitude can enhance our well being and satisfaction. Gratitude is not about ignoring the challenges or injustices of life; instead, it's about consciously acknowledging the positive aspects, no matter how small or ordinary they may seem.

Practicing gratitude can involve maintaining a gratitude journal, expressing appreciation to others, and cultivating a mindful awareness of the everyday blessings in our lives.

Numerous studies have shown that gratitude can enhance our mood, improve our relationships, and increase our overall life satisfaction.

Engaging in Physical Activity: Nurturing the Body

Regular physical activity is crucial for maintaining our physical health and mental wellbeing. Exercise triggers the release of endorphins, also known as 'feel-good hormones,' which can enhance our mood and serve as a natural antidote to stress, anxiety, and depression.

Engaging in physical activity can involve structured exercises like jogging, cycling, or gym workouts, as well as informal activities like dancing, gardening, or walking the dog. Regular exercise can boost our energy, improve our sleep, enhance our self-esteem, and even increase our life span.

Pursuing Passion: Igniting Inner Joy

Finally, pursuing our passions can provide a profound sense of fulfillment and joy, even in a deterministic world. Our passions represent our authentic selves, free from societal expectations and pressures.

Pursuing passion can involve turning a hobby into a career, volunteering for a cause close to our hearts, or simply dedicating time each week to an activity that brings us joy. This can ignite our inner spark and infuse our lives with excitement, satisfaction, and a sense of purpose.

Each of these practical tips for living meaningfully offers a pathway for navigating life without free will—a way to engage deeply with our experiences, to cultivate inner resources of strength and resilience, and to find fulfillment in our interconnections with the world around us.

Concluding Part V

The journey through the understanding of free will and determinism has been long, arduous, and filled with surprising insights. From tracing the origins of free will in evolutionary processes and exploring its neurobiological basis, we've wrestled with the moral and legal implications of a deterministic world. We've studied philosophical debates about free will and finally tried to navigate the conundrum of leading a life seemingly devoid of genuine free choice.

It's vital to remember that although the findings lean towards a deterministic world, it does not translate into a life without meaning, purpose, or responsibility. Instead, it calls for a shift in our understanding of these concepts, thereby creating a fresh perspective on life.

Determinism might seem like a bleak perspective, stripping us of the power of choice and implying a predictable pattern to life. However, it also underscores how interconnected our lives are - to our genes, our environment, and the society we inhabit. Understanding this spider web of connections and influences can lead us to be more empathetic towards each other and more insightful about our own behavior.

Rather than viewing our lives as constrained by external factors, we could see ourselves as actors in a grand narrative of life, shaped by myriad influences, yet continuously striving for self-determination. This understanding opens up avenues for personal growth and self-improvement, while also reminding us of our shared human experience.

Understanding our cognitive biases, recognizing the external constraints that shape our decisions, and understanding the biological influences on our behavior can empower us to make more informed and thoughtful choices. Moreover, it can encourage greater self-awareness and mindfulness, allowing us to lead a life that, while being influenced by deterministic factors, is still rich, purposeful, and fulfilling.

We should also remember that science, by its nature, continues to evolve and what we understand now might be superseded by new theories and discoveries in the future. Free will and determinism continue to be areas of active research, and we may yet uncover new dimensions that reshape our understanding.

The message is one of hope and resilience. Even in a deterministic framework, we can create meaningful lives, deep connections, and make an impact on the world. This understanding of our place in the universe, framed by the boundaries of determinism, yet inexhaustibly creative and vibrant, is the ultimate revelation of our journey. The quest for free will has led us to find freedom in understanding, acceptance, and, above all, boundless human potential.

Thus, while we may be navigating a life without absolute free choices, we are also navigating a life full of discovery, growth, and a deep sense of interconnectedness. This, in essence, captures the true spirit of human existence, and perhaps, is the real testament to our 'free will.'

EPILOGUE

As we close the final chapter on our exploration of free will, it's crucial to pause, reflect, and distill the essential insights we've gained through this extensive journey. From our primal origins to our sophisticated cognitive machinery, we have probed the depths of our conscious and unconscious minds. We've navigated the complex domains of neurobiology, morality, law, philosophy, and the challenges of life itself, wrestling with the paradox of choice in a deterministic universe.

In the beginning, we posed a fundamental question: Are we truly free agents, or are we bound by the unrelenting chains of determinism? Through the course of our journey, it became evident that our lives are a complex tapestry of interconnected influences – genetic, environmental, societal, and even chemical. Yet, even amid these constraints, we found pockets of freedom – a sense of autonomy that stems not from an abstract concept of free will but from a nuanced understanding of ourselves and our circumstances.

While the notion of free will as an absolute, independent force may have been challenged, our exploration has not diminished our humanity. Instead, it has added depth, richness, and an understanding of the strength of our adaptability. We've come to understand that within the deterministic architecture of our existence, there is room for growth, change, and the pursuit of purpose.

Confronting determinism has brought forth an expanded view of freedom - a freedom that lies in self-awareness, mindfulness, and acceptance. This freedom allows us to understand ourselves better, empathize with others more deeply, and navigate life more thoughtfully. By shedding light on our inherent biases and the invisible forces that drive our decisions, we can approach life's choices with greater wisdom and clarity.

The deterministic view of life does not imply fatalism or diminished responsibility. Instead, it reframes our notion of accountability, urging us to be more compassionate and less judgmental, both towards ourselves and others. It reminds us that while our choices may be influenced, they are still ours, and they significantly contribute to the shape of our lives and the world we live in.

The journey through this book is not a tale of the loss of free will but a story of rediscovery. It's a testament to our capacity to seek meaning and purpose in a complex, deterministic world, and to the resilience inherent in the human spirit. The understanding that we are both influenced by and influencers of the world serves as a powerful reminder of our interconnectedness and collective potential.

The interplay of determinism and freedom, as we've discovered, is not a limiting factor but an open door, leading us towards a deeper understanding of ourselves and our place in the world. It invites us to a life of conscious decision-making, empathy, resilience, and above all, the profound realization that even within constraints, we can find freedom, purpose, and meaning.

As we turn the last page, let's carry forward the enlightenment and insights gathered, knowing that our journey doesn't end here. With each step and each choice we make, we continue to navigate this fascinating dance between free will and determinism, shaping our lives and the world around us. This, in essence, is the human experience – rich, complex, and endlessly intriguing.

GLOSSARY

1.　**Affordance Theory:** A concept in ecological psychology that refers to the possibilities for action that objects or environments provide to an organism. In the context of free will, this theory suggests how our environment influences the range of actions available to us.

2.　**Agency:** Refers to the capacity of individuals to act independently and make their own free choices. In the context of free will, it refers to the ability to make choices that are genuinely one's own.

3.　**Algorithmic Determinism:** The idea that processes, decision making and future outcomes are determined by algorithms or computational procedures.

4.　**Behavioral Neuroscience:** A subfield of psychology that examines the neural basis of behavior, using animal models to understand the brain mechanisms that control behavior.

5.　**Cognitive Dissonance:** A psychological theory that describes the mental discomfort experienced when holding contradictory beliefs, values, or attitudes. Relevant to discussions on free will, particularly in understanding how individuals reconcile their belief in autonomy with evidence of determinism.

6.   **Compatibilism:** The belief that free will and determinism can coexist. Compatibilists argue that determinism is compatible with human freedom and moral responsibility.

7.   **Consequentialism:** An ethical approach suggesting that the morality of an action should be judged solely based on its consequences. This view is critical when discussing moral and ethical implications in the context of free will.

8.   **Consciousness:** In the context of this book, it refers to an individual's awareness of their unique thoughts, memories, feelings, sensations, and environments. Consciousness plays a significant role in the discussions on free will and determinism.

9.   **Determinism:** The philosophical belief that all events, including moral choices, are determined completely by previously existing causes. Determinism is often contrasted with free will.

10. **Dopaminergic Pathways:** Neural pathways in the brain that transmit the neurotransmitter dopamine from one region of the brain to another.

11. **Epigenetics:** The study of how behaviors and environment can cause changes that affect the way genes work. It highlights the interplay between genetics and environmental factors in shaping human behavior, challenging simplistic notions of genetic determinism.

12. **Emergent Properties:** New properties that emerge with each step up the hierarchy of life, owing to the arrangement and interactions of parts as complexity increases.

13. **Existentialism:** A philosophical theory that emphasizes the existence of the individual as a free and responsible agent determining their own development through acts of will.

14. **Free Will:** The ability to choose, think, and act voluntarily. For many philosophers, to believe in free will is to believe that human beings can be the authors of their own actions and to reject the idea that human actions are determined by external conditions or fate.

15. **Functional MRI (fMRI):** A neuroimaging technique used to measure and visualize brain activity by detecting changes associated with blood flow.

16. **Genetic Determinism:** The belief that genes, along with environmental conditions, determine morphological and behavioral phenotypes.

17. **Genotype:** The genetic constitution of an individual organism, which in turn influences the individual's observable traits or "phenotype."

18. **Heuristics:** Cognitive shortcuts or rules of thumb that simplify decision making. Pertinent to the discourse on free will and determinism as they demonstrate how not all decisions are the result of deliberate, conscious choice.

19. **Hard Determinism:** The philosophical view that all events, including moral choices, are determined completely by previously existing causes.

20. **Hormones:** Chemical messengers that travel throughout the body coordinating complex processes like growth, metabolism, and fertility. In the context of this book, they are discussed as influencers of decision-making.

21. **Intentionality:** In philosophy and psychology, the quality of mental states (e.g., beliefs, desires, hopes) that are directed at, or about, objects and states of affairs in the world. This concept is key in understanding the nature of conscious decision-making and free will.

22. **Incompatibilism:** The view that a deterministic universe is completely at odds with the notion that persons have a free will.

23. **Just-World Hypothesis:** The belief that people get what they deserve and deserve what they get, which was first theorized by Melvin J. Lerner in 1980.

24. **Libertarianism (Metaphysical):** A philosophical position in the debate of free will which posits that determinism is false and that we do indeed have free will, generally emphasizing the importance of moral responsibility.

25. **Moral Responsibility:** The status of morally deserving praise, blame, reward, or punishment for an act or omission, in accordance with one's moral obligations.

26. **Natural Selection:** The process whereby organisms better adapted to their environment tend to survive and produce more offspring.

27. **Neuroplasticity:** The brain's ability to reorganize itself by forming new neural connections throughout life. This concept is essential in discussions of free will and agency, suggesting that our brains can adapt and change in response to experiences.

28. **Neuroethics:** The ethics of neuroscience, and the neuroscience of ethics. It stands at the crossroads of neuroscience, ethics, philosophy, law and multiple related

fields, focusing on the right and wrong, the good and bad, of the brain and mind.

29. **Neurotransmitters:** Endogenous chemicals that enable neurotransmission. They transmit signals across a chemical synapse, such as a neuromuscular junction, from one neuron (nerve cell) to another target neuron, muscle cell, or gland cell.

30. **Ontology:** A branch of metaphysics concerned with the nature of being and existence. In discussions about free will, ontology addresses fundamental questions about whether free will can exist within the frameworks of reality we understand.

31. **Operant Conditioning:** A type of learning where behavior is controlled by consequences.

32. **Phenomenology:** A philosophical movement that describes the formal structure of the objects of awareness and of awareness itself in abstraction from any claims about the existence of the objects of awareness.

33. **Pragmatism:** A philosophical tradition that emphasizes the practical application of ideas by acting on them to actually test them in human experiences. Relevant to the discourse on free will in its emphasis on the practical implications of philosophical concepts.

34. **Phenotype:** The set of observable characteristics of an individual resulting from the interaction of its genotype with the environment.

35. **Qualia:** The internal, subjective component of perception and experience. In debates on consciousness and free will, qualia are significant in understanding what it's like to have an experience and how this relates to the notion of agency.

36. **Quantum Indeterminacy:** A fundamental concept in quantum mechanics maintaining that the properties of particles are not determined until they are measured.

37. **Quantum Physics:** The study of matter and energy at its most fundamental level. A central tenet of quantum physics is that energy comes in indivisible packets called quanta.

38. **Rational Choice Theory:** An economic principle that assumes that individuals always make prudent and logical decisions that provide them with the highest amount of personal utility.

39. **Reductionism:** The philosophical position that a complex system is nothing but the sum of its parts, and that an account of it can be reduced to accounts of individual constituents. This is pertinent in the free will debate, especially in discussions on whether human behavior can be entirely explained by physical processes.

40. **Self-Actualization:** A term introduced by the organismic theorist Abraham Maslow. The concept was brought to prominence in Maslow's hierarchy of needs theory as the final level of psychological development that can be achieved when all basic and mental needs are fulfilled and the "actualization" of the full personal potential takes place.

41. **Self-Determination Theory (SDT):** A macro theory of human motivation and personality that concerns people's inherent growth tendencies and innate psychological needs.

42. **Teleology:** The philosophical study of design and purpose. A teleological school of thought is one that holds all things to be designed for or directed toward a final

result, that there is an inherent purpose or final cause for all that exists.

43. **Unconscious Bias:** Unconscious biases are social stereotypes about certain groups of people that individuals form outside their own conscious awareness.

44. **Utilitarianism:** A theory in normative ethics holding that the best moral action is the one that maximizes utility, usually defined as that which produces the greatest well-being of the greatest number of people.

45. **Volition:** The cognitive process by which an individual decides on and commits to a particular course of action. It's often used interchangeably with "free will".

46. **Xenopsychology:** A hypothetical field of study of the psychology of extraterrestrial beings, i.e., how such beings might think, perceive, or act differently from humans due to their differing biological and environmental context.

47. **Zeitgeist:** Refers to the general intellectual, moral, and cultural climate of an era. The term is of German origin and literally translates to "spirit of the time". It's often used to encapsulate the ideas and beliefs that shape a particular era.

REFERENCES & READINGS

1. **Augustine, Saint.** *On the Essence of Free Will.*
2. **Baumeister, R. F.**, & **Vohs, K. D.** (2007). *Encyclopedia of Social Psychology.* Sage Publications.
3. **Benzer, S.** & **Konopka, R.** Study on *Drosophila melanogaster.*
4. **Crick, F.** (1994). *The Astonishing Hypothesis: The Scientific Search for the Soul.* Simon & Schuster.
5. **Dennett, D. C.** (1984). *Elbow Room: The Varieties of Free Will Worth Wanting.* MIT Press.
6. **Frankfurt, H. G.** (1971). Freedom of the will and the concept of a person. *Journal of Philosophy, 68(1),* 5-20.
7. **Frankl, V.** *Man's Search for Meaning.*
8. **Gage, P.** (No date). Case study in neurology.
9. **Kane, R.** (1996). *The Significance of Free Will.* Oxford University Press.
10. **Kierkegaard, S.** Exploration of existentialism and personal responsibility.
11. **Libet, B.**, **Gleason, C. A.**, **Wright, E. W.**, & **Pearl, D. K.** (1983). Time of conscious intention to act in relation to onset of cerebral activity (readiness-potential). *Brain, 106(3),* 623-642.
12. **Nagel, T.** (1986). *The View from Nowhere.* Oxford University Press.
13. **Nietzsche, F.** Advocated life affirmation and will to power.

14. **Nozick, R.** (1981). *Philosophical Explanations.* Harvard University Press.
15. **Rawls, J.** (1971). *A Theory of Justice.* Harvard University Press.
16. **Sapolsky, R.** Discussed the biological underpinnings of human behavior.
17. **Sartre, J.-P.** Explored bad faith and personal agency under deterministic frameworks.
18. **Searle, J. R.** (2001). *Rationality in Action.* MIT Press.
19. **Strawson, G.** (1986). *Freedom and Belief.* Oxford University Press.
20. **Velleman, J. D.** (2000). *The Possibility of Practical Reason.* Oxford University Press.
21. **Wegner, D. M.** (2002). *The Illusion of Conscious Will.* MIT Press.
22. **Kanwisher, N.** Explored neural mechanisms involved in visual recognition and perception.
23. **Darwin, C.** *On the Origin of Species.* Explores the theory of natural selection and its implications on the development of species.
24. **Watson, J. D.**, & **Crick, F. H. C.** (1953). Molecular structure of nucleic acids: A structure for deoxyribose nucleic acid. *Nature, 171,* 737-738.

Dear Reader,

I extend my heartfelt gratitude for reading "Probing Freewill." This book, a journey through the maze of human autonomy, has been both a challenge and a triumph for me. Sharing my philosophical reflections and personal insights with you is a profound privilege, and I sincerely hope this exploration has offered you new perspectives, deeper understanding, and perhaps a touch of inspiration.

As an author, your feedback is invaluable. It not only helps refine my future works but also aids others in discovering this book. Reviews play an important role in spreading the word and promoting a broad conversation on the themes discussed.

If you could take a moment to share your thoughts in a review, it would mean the world to me. Knowing that you've engaged with my work encourages me to continue this intellectual and existential journey.

Here's why your review matters:

- **It Guide Others:** Your insights can help potential readers find this book and benefit from its discussions.

- **It Supports the Author**: Reviews are vital for authors, especially those tackling complex and often personal subjects. Your feedback can help me reach a wider audience.

- **I'll Read Every Review**: I read every review with great interest. Constructive criticism helps me grow, while positive notes inspire me to keep exploring and writing.

Thank you for joining me on this philosophical voyage. Your support is deeply appreciated.

Warm regards,

Waleed Mahmud

www.ingramcontent.com/pod-product-compliance
Lightning Source LLC
Chambersburg PA
CBHW051458150726
47997CB00001B/20